Literary Ghosts from the Victorians to Modernism

Routledge Studies in Twentieth-Century Literature

Literary Ghosts from the Victorians to Modernism

The Haunting Interval

Luke Thurston

Routledge
Taylor & Francis Group

NEW YORK   LONDON

First published 2012
by Routledge
711 Third Avenue, New York, NY 10017

Simultaneously published in the UK
by Routledge
2 Park Square, Milton Park, Abingdon, Oxon OX14 4RN

*Routledge is an imprint of the Taylor & Francis Group,
an informa business*

Library of Congress Cataloging-in-Publication Data
Thurston, Luke.
   Literary ghosts from the Victorians to Modernism : the haunting interval /
Luke Thurston.
      p. cm. — (Routledge studies in twentieth-century literature ; 27)
   Includes bibliographical references and index.
  1. English literature—20th century—History and criticism—Theory, etc.
2. English literature—19th century—History and criticism—Theory, etc.
3. Modernism (Literature)—Great Britain.   4. Ghosts in
literature.   I. Title.
   PR478.M6T48 2012
   823'.087330908—dc23
   2011052172

ISBN13: 978-0-415-50966-4 (hbk)
ISBN13: 978-1-138-01621-7 (pbk)

Typeset in Sabon
by IBT Global.

For Paula, George and Henry

Contents

Preface

Many friends and colleagues have helped me in writing this book by lending an ear to my ghostly mutterings over the years—my special thanks go to Matt Jarvis, Stewart Mottram, Damian Walford Davies, Lyn Pykett and Peter Barry, whose vote of confidence in the project came at just the right time. I must also thank Robert Ireland and my brother Toby Thurston for helping me with my bit o' Latin and Greek; Jon Shears and Jen Sattaur for their constructive comments; and Pam Thurschwell for her positive response. I am grateful to many students on my *Haunting Texts* module at Aberystwyth University for their enthusiastic and often wildly creative reactions to my ideas. I thank Emma Joyes for a useful tip, Liz Levine, Julie Ganz and Eleanor Chan for all their patient editorial help, and Routledge's readers for some extremely useful comments.

Above all I must thank my beloved Paula for her tireless support, and of course my very own spectre-deflectors, George and Henry. The book is dedicated with love to all three of you.

Acknowledgements

Quotations from the work of May Sinclair and Elizabeth Bowen are reproduced with permission of Curtis Brown Group Ltd, London, on behalf of the Estates of May Sinclair (© May Sinclair, 1923) and Elizabeth Bowen (© Elizabeth Bowen, 1980). I am grateful to the Department of English and Creative Writing at Aberystwyth University for financial assistance with obtaining these copyright permissions.

We stand upon the brink of a precipice. We peer into the abyss—we grow sick and dizzy. Our first impulse is to shrink from the danger. Unaccountably we remain. By slow degrees our sickness and dizziness and horror become merged in a cloud of unnamable feeling.

—Edgar Allan Poe, "The Imp of the Perverse"

Death is the sanction of everything that the storyteller can tell.

—Walter Benjamin

Prologue
Beyond My Notation

Writing in 1890 to Violet Paget (better known to us by her pen-name Vernon Lee) to thank her for sending him her volume of ghost stories *Hauntings*, Henry James was careful to pepper his thanks with some delicate reservations about the dubious fictional genre Lee had chosen to work in:

> The supernatural story, the subject wrought in fantasy, is not the *class* of fiction I myself most cherish (prejudiced as you may have perceived me in favour of a close connotation, or close observation, of the real—or whatever one may call it—the familiar, the inevitable).[1]

Eight years later, after the popular success of *The Turn of the Screw* had brought him not only fan letters but a number of anxious enquiries from readers worried about the state of the governess's mind, James repeatedly re-affirmed his prejudice against the supernatural, doing his best to ward off all interpretations based on the more lurid possibilities of a "subject wrought in fantasy." In a letter to H. G. Wells, James speaks wearily of his desire to find "a refuge from the vulgarity" of the literary marketplace, adding with a hint of embarrassment that with *The Turn of the Screw*—"the young woman, the spooks, the style, the everything"—he may have unwisely entangled himself too closely with the popular mentality served by that marketplace; after all, he drily concludes of his famous best-seller, "the thing is essentially a pot-boiler and a *jeu d'esprit*."[2]

The ghost story, then, is glossed by James in these remarks as a fictional genre "wrought in fantasy," removed from the "close observation" of reality, indeed recklessly careless of all the established canons of plausibility and stylistic restraint. Of course, the disparaging tone of this Jamesian criticism of supernatural fiction as vulgar stylistic excess was nothing new—indeed, it owed much to the kind of response which had been generated almost a century earlier by Gothic writing (thus reviewers of Mary Shelley's *Frankenstein* had consistently been appalled by its fantastic "extravagance and over-writing").[3] But by the time of the *fin de siècle* resurgence of the literary gothic in the form of the ghost story—and James himself was sharply conscious of this change—a distinctly anti-gothic aversion to stylistic extravagance had become almost a defining mark of the revived genre itself, a sign indeed of its *neo*-gothic and thus ironically disenchanted, 'modern' style. Hence, when Edith Nesbit began her 1893 ghost story "Man-Size in Marble," the narrator could protest that "Although every word of this story is as true as despair, I do not expect people to believe it."[4] Readers were no longer to be pictured as the wide-eyed dupes of gothic fantasy, but now as sceptical modern rationalists; so that the lurid fictionality of the gothic, with all of its conventional scenarios and fantastic tropes, could be redeployed and framed in opposition to *this* story, which could in turn be presented as no longer a mere literary contrivance but a piece of documentary truth—and thus as something all the more chilling.

The late Victorian ghost story could therefore neatly combine in a single gesture a conventional repertoire of gothic stylistic devices—and "Man-Size in Marble" of course has its due quota of gloomy churches, full moons, uncanny portals and so on—with an arch, self-consciously 'modern' irony vis a vis those very literary devices. And it is this split reference—on one side to the most extravagant literary rhetoric; on the other to the bare truth of 'life itself' as an ironic repudiation of all mere 'style'—that Henry James reproduces with exemplary neo-gothic panache in *The Turn of the Screw*. Suddenly confronted by the figure of a man staring down at her from the mock-gothic battlements of Bly—a figure, the text slyly informs us, "as definite as a picture in a frame"—the governess rushes in her imagination to the Gothic tradition as a set of fictive scenarios that might conceivably mirror the 'real' one she appears to be involved in: "Was there a "secret" at Bly—a mystery of Udolpho or an insane, an unmentionable relative kept in unsuspected confinement?"[5] Of course, although the reader is playfully invited to ponder these familiar gothic scenarios as provisional ways to interpret the governess's predicament, their metafictional dimension—the fact that they come into the narrative already knowingly marked as literary fabulations, almost as signs of the 'literary' itself—means that they are never taken seriously by the reader, genuinely accepted as appropriate explanations of the 'fact', depicted by James with such minute photographic realism, of the man up there on the tower.

The "secret" of *The Turn of the Screw*, as several generations of critics have by now testified, lies in the magic of the "withheld glimpse," as James puts it in one of his prefaces: the power of the text, that is, to suggest a range of scenarios that *might* make sense of its fragmentary narrative, without ever allowing any one scenario to do so in a decisive or fully coherent manner.[6] Crucial to this spellbinding effect is the first-person narration used by James: in other words, in the absence of a framing authorial metanarrative to mediate and interpret the governess's experience, the reader is left trapped 'with her,' as it were, caught up in the hermeneutic toils of her text—and deprived, like her, of any final revelatory moment that would put an end to the restless shifting and sifting of narrative signifiers. Another way of seeing this "secret" of the text and of its endless screw-turning is as an effect of metafictional citationality: that is, the empirical substance of the governess's reality is progressively rendered doubtful, divided from its proper self-identity, by being marked as a mere quotation from the literary-mnemic archive (and in particular the section labelled 'Gothic romance'). Thus, instead of asking "Was there a secret at Bly," she asks "Was there a 'secret' at Bly:" the very possibility of finding a solution to the epistemological puzzle, in other words, is already fully marked as citational, mediated by the archive of generic literary convention, thus as a 'knowing' literary conceit rather than an 'innocent' diegetic reality.

The argument of this book will not include yet another effort to solve the secret—or rather "solve the 'secret'"—of *The Turn of the Screw*. This is not, or not only, due to the citational gridlock that gravely threatens the viability of any such effort today; but rather because the peculiar magic of that Jamesian text is bound up with its endless deferral of a moment which happens, for our current purposes, to be of central interest: that is, the moment of the ghostly encounter, of the apparition 'itself.' For if, as we have noted, there is a characteristic divergence in the *fin de siècle* ghost story between the citational use of the traditional paraphernalia of Gothic style and an implicit ironic critique of that style in the name of truth, of 'life itself,' that divergence does not always imply the endless *jeu d'esprit* or interpretive maze that keeps the Jamesian screw turning (and the critics reinterpreting). Indeed, the texts that will concern us here (mostly, though not all, identifiable as ghost stories) centre on what Dickens makes visible in *Our Mutual Friend* as "a token of life"—a strange sensory irruption or suspension of diegetic reality itself, the uncanny manifestation of something vital that is incompatible with the logic of the signifier.[7]

That the ghost story should involve a problem to do with the textual manifestation of *life* is perhaps, at first sight, unexpected. We will argue that one of the defining scenarios inherited by the ghost story from the Gothic tradition offers us a way of thinking about this convergence of the living and the undead: namely, the curious relation between host and guest (with each of those terms an etymological cousin of 'ghost'). It is hard indeed to find a ghost story that does not feature, at the diegetic level, the arrival of a guest or a strange act of hospitality; and as we shall see the genre often features (in the work of M. R. James, say, or that of May Sinclair) a deliberate exploitation of the equivocal seme *hostis* in the artful deployment of words like "hostile" or "hospitable."

The ghost story can thus, we will argue, be seen as both a *host* story and a *guest* story; and this will open a way for us to approach the topic of the genre's fascination with the problem of inscribing or calculating the uncanny singularity of life. What the narrative encounter of host and guest effectively amounts to, as we will see, is a version—a 'meaningful' diegetic version—of a more traumatic encounter between the signifying space of narratable reality and an absolute otherness marked there as 'a life' but skewed away from, ontologically inconsistent with, the very structure of discursive signification. It is in this figure of life as indiscernible, irreducible to the logic of the signifier that we will seek what essentially constitutes the ghost as a singular 'guest' in the semiotic system of narrative; and we will link this figure, in its asemic vitality, to an 'anamorphic' reorientation of the reading eye that attempts—by attending above all to the agency of stray or unaccountable graphic or acoustic elements in the text—to disfigure the habitual space of legibility presented in and as what we will term the 'host-narrative.'

Our argument will move from a philosophical engagement with a scene in a Dickensian novel, through aspects of the *fin de siècle* and early twentieth-century ghost story, to a glimpse of the ghostly afterlife of that genre in the modernist writings of May Sinclair, Virginia Woolf, James Joyce and Elizabeth Bowen. Throughout, we will be dealing with literary hospitality in more than one sense: from the diegetic level, with the simple arrival of a guest at a hotel, to the level of meta-textuality, examining the agency of 'hostile' textual figures within a 'hospitable' narrative. We will also be dealing with traumatic encounters, from Dickensian accidents to the ghostly epiphanies of Henry James, Sinclair, Woolf, Joyce and Bowen; encounters that reveal the ghost to be not, as Stephen Dedalus once sought to define it, "one who has faded into impalpability through death" but instead an incalculable event: a point of unbearable vital intensity.[8]

A NOTE ON GHOSTS AND 'THEORY'

At a single moment in one of his greatest ghost stories, "The Jolly Corner," Henry James leaves us a striking testimony to the spectral apparition of life itself in his narrative. As the protagonist Spencer Brydon imagines himself coming face to face with his phantasmal adversary he experiences an ecstatic realization of its "ineffable identity," determined, the narrator suddenly exclaims "by an influence beyond my notation!"[9] This, the sole intervention by the narrator in James's story, emerges in effect as the antithesis of the metafictional gothic asides in *The Turn of the Screw*— whereas they lead our reading into the endless citational maze of literary re-interpretation, it forces that interpretation to confront the unspeakable singularity of the apparition.

This book is an attempt to explore a series of singular literary events or "ineffable" identities, of the kind posited by the Jamesian narrator (in a seeming paradox) as non-inscribable, thus ontologically positioned beyond the diacritical register of the signifier. How then can we claim to be developing a *theoretical* argument through an engagement with these "ineffable" or indiscernible figures? Surely theory, if it is to be of any use at all in literary criticism, should aim to lighten the darkness and make the dumb speak, and so should bring the Jamesian ghost firmly back into the domain of "notation," of coherent critical discourse. Indeed, a glance at the list of thinkers invoked in our argument, most working in the overlapping fields of psychoanalytic and post-structuralist interpretation, might for some readers immediately confirm the suspicion that the book is an attempt to use Theory to decipher and thus 'explain away,' like some semiotic ghost-buster, the haunting literary presences it considers.

In fact, however, my argument will be that the very reverse is true. All of the theoreticians involved in the chapters in this volume, for all their heterogeneity, share a fundamental commitment to conceptualizing an ontological register 'beyond the signifier,' impossible to decode or analyse exclusively in terms of a consistent semiotic system. It is thus that ghosts in literature can be seen not as insignificant but precisely as *vital* because they are "beyond my notation," inherently at odds with the meaningful structure of discursive narration. The unspeakable or indiscernible is no longer, for the theoreticians in question here, merely a symptom of some ideological or pathological distortion, but rather it opens onto the question of a fundamental ontology. If, as Gilles Deleuze sees it, the Dickensian text plays host to a "spark of life," this is registered by the philosopher as a point of vitality *in excess of* a discursive structure, something precisely inconsistent with the sphere of narrative signification (and this excessive spark of life will turn out, I will argue, to be the ghost 'itself,' shorn of its conventional, reader-friendly gothic trappings). Likewise, the Lacan whose work is relevant to my engagement with ghosts here is less a semi-otician of the unconscious than a thinker in search of different ways to render the real in art or in theory—ways to envisage, that is, something of the irresolvable discrepancy between the symbolic order and its intractable kernel of *jouissance.*

As was shown by Jean-François Lyotard's early challenge to Lacanian structuralism in *Discours, figure* (1971), and as Slavoj Žižek's more recent work has tirelessly emphasized, it was anamorphosis, that old painterly trick, that was to prove one of the most effective and enduring of Lacan's theoretical discoveries in his exploration of the topological limits of inter-pretive structure. Throughout our argument, the figure of anamorphosis, as the dramatic cleavage of the topology of signification into incommensu-rable fields or perspectives, will return as a key way to think the indiscern-ible singularity of the ghost, its essential incompatibility with the semiotic regime of discourse.

Lacan's late work is marked by a fundamental shift from a focus on linguistic structure to the pursuit of quasi-mathematical formalization, a transition from structuralist theory to the so-called "matheme." This movement 'beyond the signifier' is obviously of great relevance to my cur-rent argument, where the approach to the literary ghost will aim not to decode—not even, in one sense, to *interpret*—that figure, but instead will link it to attempts (mostly by philosophers and psychoanalysts) to think through and beyond the limits of discursive structure. The most important and challenging of these recent attempts to think a fundamental ontology through a mathematical framework has been that of Alain Badiou. Badiou's major work *Being and Event* came into English in 2005, and I discovered it shortly afterwards, just as I was beginning work on the current project. I had already formulated the core ideas of my argument, in which the literary ghost is to be conceived of as an intrusive, illegible 'guest' element at odds with a 'host' structure of discursive legibility, when I encountered Badiou's provocative formulations on truth as an event of singular, unprecedented disruptive force in the field of knowledge. If my incipient concept of the ghost thus already uncannily resembled the truth-event, the fact that Badiou had especially privileged modernism (Mallarmé, Hölderlin, Pessoa, Celan, Beckett) as the exemplary literary site of such an event, made things still better (or worse). For in my argument the ghost story can be given its full aesthetic significance only when seen as a gap or 'haunting interval' between Victorian literature and the modernist moment: what emerges there as the literary ghost—especially on the very cusp of that interval, in the work of Henry James, say, or May Sinclair—is essentially sited in the future anterior (the key temporal mode of Badiou's thinking): that is, it is an event awaiting ontological determination, a suspension of being that could reveal, in Badiou's resonant phrase, "the incandescent non-being of an existence."[10]

The ghost as truth-event; therefore as indiscernible at the point of its emergence and so always only interpretable through *Nachträglichkeit*, the 'afterwardsness' or future anteriority of Freudian signification.[11] This notion, it struck me, certainly has many echoes in literary tradition, where the advent of the ghost is often associated with the disruptive return of buried secrets or repressed truth (think only of the opening of *Hamlet*). But what was crucial, as my argument took shape, was not to see this as offering some kind of new universal key to the meaning of the literary ghost, since it should constitute nothing less than the *suspension* of discursive meaning as such. What I therefore aim to show in the following chapters, working through close readings of the texts, is how what takes place as an uncanny disturbance of the known or legible world is given—by each text in turn, but also across texts in an uncanny or telepathic tradition of some kind—a specific inscription, its own figure as a momentary transgressive breach of the plausible or acceptable discursive representation of being.

The ghost, I will argue, emerges as a special kind of 'event' that is situated on the edge of the void, to use Badiou's language: that is, as the rupture of consistent presentation, of the plausible discursive 'order of things'—thus as an uncanny effect of the inconsistency of Being itself. Being is a multiplicity which a semiotic system cannot represent, argues Badiou, since it cannot do without the concept of 'one,' of ontological unity, and thus (unlike set theory) cannot deal with the inconsistent multiplicity of Being, which is "founded, like the world" as Joyce puts it "on the void."[12]

The scare quotes around 'event' are therefore no superficial theoretical mannerism: they indicate the radical breach or suspension of diegetic

reality involved—and it is this disobedience of the laws of rational narrative that can make the literary ghost a truly disturbing event. As I will try
to show through detailed readings of the following texts, the theory of the
ghost as a figure on the edge of the void allows us to see it as an anamorphic eclipse of ordinary discourse, a fundamentally strange momentary
encounter with something—a trace of ontological inconsistency: thus of
'life itself'—insistently warded off or disavowed by the everyday signifier
and the self it supports. The ghost is thus properly unspeakable, anamorphically skewed away from the familiar fictional discursive mesh of narrative reality: and it is this non-discursivity that will emerge as the primary
source (if not the 'primal scene') of the incessant power and undying fascination of the ghost story.

If we pause to consider for a moment the golden age of the ghost story—
from the late nineteenth century, let's say, until the First World War (the very
period, that is, usually thought of as marking the origin of modernism)—it
is no coincidence that the same period saw a dazzling proliferation of 'spiritualist' metanarratives, from Madame Blavatsky's cult to the mesmerism
dabbled in by Poe and Dickens or the séances and Ouija boards of Yeats
and H. D. The interest of so many writers and intellectuals in these para-
psychological or mystical movements, as ably documented by Helen Sword
in *Ghostwriting Modernism* (2002), testifies not to some general outbreak
of weak-mindedness or even to the fleeting historical plausibility of those
pseudo-explanatory movements, but to an insistent demand, on the part of
human subjects, for decisive hermeneutic closure on certain fundamental
ontological questions that were becoming ever-more insistent in the course
of an accelerating, disruptive modernity. What these discourses of mystical
otherness claimed to provide was a quasi-religious or pseudo-medical solution to the fundamental enigma of the ghostly encounter: in effect a way of
cancelling out its anamorphic indiscernibility by returning it to the formal
site of a coherent, consistent narrative, however ludicrous the 'mystical'
content may have been (and such texts usually harbour a dispiritingly 'realist' ontology of otherworldly entities).

If, as I believe, the ghost story at its most powerful bears the mark
of something which the human subject longs to have 'theorized away,' a
theoretically informed critical engagement with the genre needs to tread
especially carefully. Isn't psychoanalysis, to take one of the main theoretical references of my argument, simply an heir to those mystical pseudo-
sciences discussed in Sword's book, like them determined to put the ghost
to bed by providing a doctrinal solution, and like them drawing its esoteric wisdom from ancient myth, now no longer the myth of Horus or the
Sphinx but that of Oedipus? The best answer to this allegation is given
in the title of an exemplary article by Jean Laplanche: "Psychoanalysis as
anti-hermeneutics."[13] The human subject, writes Laplanche there, is domi-
nated by an "incorrigible yearning for synthesis, despite all the efforts of
analysis."[14] In other words, it is precisely as an active *resistance* to the

demand for hermeneutic satisfaction, for a synthetic metanarrative to salve the ontological wound of the ghostly encounter, that the Freudian discovery avoids relapsing into a mere diagnostic apparatus or knowledge. In this sense, the theory used in the following argument will be, as far as is humanly possible, resolutely anti-hermeneutic. The only way to deal with ghosts is to follow Freud's advice to clinicians: the path to interpretation begins with the refusal of knowledge.

Part I
Literary Hospitality

1 The Spark of Life

DELEUZE'S DYING BREATH

At first glance, the philosophy of Gilles Deleuze might seem an improb-
able starting-point for an investigation of ghosts and literature. "At the
centre of Deleuze's work," writes Simon Critchley "is a concept of life
that is not simply organic. [. . .] This life is felt affectively through the
experience of affirmative creation, an intensity that produces the feeling
of joy."[1] And surely the title of Deleuze's best-known work, *Anti-Oedi-
pus*, encapsulates his polemical opposition to the dominant spectrology
of Freudian thinking, its insistence on the ghostly return of the past, on
a death-drive underlying all human culture? Indeed, one of Deleuze's
aphoristic definitions of art gives an ironic twist to the psychoanalytic
cliché of the artist in thrall to the past, possessed by a psychical revenant: "Art is defined . . . as an impersonal process in which the work
is composed somewhat like a cairn, with stones carried in by different
voyagers and beings-in-becoming rather than ghosts [*devenants plutôt
que revenants*]. . . ."[2]
So what has this philosopher of life, with his refusal to prioritise
revenance over 'becoming,' got to say about ghosts? An answer comes,
appropriately enough, in the last text published by Deleuze before his
death in 1995, a short piece entitled *Immanence: Une vie. . . .* It is not
that this final text marks a radical shift in Deleuze's philosophical orientation, as he takes up the very figures of mortality and revenance he
appeared to repudiate in his earlier work; but rather that it re-opens,
with exemplary clarity, the whole question of ghosts by linking it to a
fundamental ontology.
For Giorgio Agamben, *Immanence: Une vie* . . . stands as a genuine
testament, Deleuze's "supreme gesture," to be read as the ultimate statement on the key question of the philosopher's work: how to approach
"immanence," how to begin thinking a non-transcendent ontology.[3] But
what is most striking about this final philosophical gesture, this last
Deleuzean effort to locate a figure of the self-manifestation of being or
"absolute immanence," is that it takes as its principal reference not, as

one might expect, a text from ancient philosophy or esoteric poetry, but one from English literature: a Victorian novel, in fact—Dickens's *Our Mutual Friend* (1865). Why should that novel—the last published by Dickens during his lifetime, so arguably another "supreme gesture"— strike Deleuze's eye at such a significant moment? The answer is that for Deleuze the Dickensian novel (or rather, and this will be crucial, a particular *scene* within it) plays host to an exemplary ontological event:

> No one told better than Dickens what a life is, taking account of the indefinite article as an index of the transcendental. At the last minute, a scoundrel, a bad subject despised by all, is saved as he is dying, and at once all the people taking care of him show a kind of attention, respect, and love for the dying man's smallest signs of life. Everyone tries to save him, to the point that in the deepest moment of his coma, the villainous man feels that something sweet is reaching him. But the more he comes back to life, the more his saviours become cold, and he rediscovers his coarseness, his meanness. Between his life and his death there is a moment that is nothing other than that of *a* life playing with death. The life of the individual gives way to an impersonal yet singular life, a life that gives rise to a pure event, freed from the accidents of internal and external life, that is, of the subjectivity and objectivity of what happens. "Homo tantum," for whom everyone feels and who attains a kind of beatitude.[4]

The last Dickensian novel, as seen in the dying breath of Deleuzean thought, thus hosts the "pure event" or self-manifestation of a life, a life momentarily set apart from the detailed network of signification embedding it in the narrative history of a specific character—that is, one "Rogue" Riderhood, a well-known scoundrel in *Our Mutual Friend*. But if we turn to the Dickensian text, we find that this suspension of meaningful subjectivity that allows the "spark of life," as Dickens calls it, to appear—and the effect of that suspension and apparition on the ordinary subjectivities of the bystanders—is already presented quite 'philosophically' by the novelist. The narrative voice, for all its sheen of Dickensian irony, poses questions that ultimately bear on the enigmatic topography of the human psyche:

> If you are not gone for good, Mr Riderhood, it would be something to know where you are hiding at present. This flabby lump of mortality that we work so hard at with such patient perseverance yields no sign of you. If you are gone for good, Rogue, it is very solemn, and if you are coming back, it is hardly less so. Nay, in the suspense and mystery of the latter question, involving that of where you may be now, there is a solemnity even added to that of death, making us who

are in attendance alike afraid to look on you and to look off you, and making those below start at the least sound of a creaking plank in the floor. [. . .]

See! A token of life! An indubitable token of life! The spark may smoulder and go out, or it may glow and expand, but see! The four rough fellows seeing, shed tears. Neither Riderhood in this world, nor Riderhood in the other, could draw tears from them; but a striking human soul between the two can do it easily.

He is struggling to come back. Now he is almost here, now he is far away again. . . . And yet—like us all, when we swoon—like us all, every day of our life, when we wake—he is instinctively unwilling to be restored to the consciousness of this existence, and would be left dormant, if he could. (*OMF* 504)

The key word here is "if": the "suspense and mystery" of the vital, and very philosophical, question—where is life, what is life?—opens a virtual or spectral space where reality itself becomes hypothetical, experimental, speculative. For a brief spectral interval during which the consensual signifying laws of "reality" are suspended, the witnesses are cut off from their familiar hostility toward this shabby rogue in his mundane existence and held transfixed, in a state of trembling fascination. What fascinates them, indeed, is inseparable from the eclipse of the proper functioning of signs, the opening of a space where they might, who knows, actually *see* what language cannot name: the absolute "thing," the limit or precise location of consciousness, identity or life.

But we need to look more carefully at what may be specifically *ghostly* about this resuscitation scene extracted by Deleuze from *Our Mutual Friend*. Agamben's remarks—to add another twist to the textual knot—offer a good way in:

Deleuze's reference is to the episode in *Our Mutual Friend* in which Riderhood nearly drowns. It suffices to skim these pages to realize what could have so forcefully attracted Deleuze's attention. First of all, Dickens clearly distinguishes Riderhood the individual and the "spark of life within him" from the scoundrel in which he lives. . . .[5]

"It suffices to skim these pages:" with his apparently inconsequential phrasing, Agamben takes us to the heart of the question of thinking the ghost. For what is crucial is that Deleuze does not *read* the Dickensian text, has no time to engage with its intricate narrative complexity, but instead *sees*, has his attention grabbed by, the "spark of life" that manifests itself there. Note how in discussing the novel Deleuze shifts into the present tense of anecdote or parable ("At the last minute, a scoundrel, a bad subject despised by all, is saved . . ."), as if deliberately to suppress its status as writing in favour of some other, implicitly non-textual way of telling or counting.

In one sense, of course, this merely repeats a rhetoric frequently used by the Dickensian text itself, where the narrative voice often switches to the dramatic present; as it does here—"See! A token of life!" (*OMF* 504)—to bring the scene of Riderhood's resuscitation to life, as it were. The various onlookers surrounding the patient (as we will see, the language of the hospital is unavoidable here) are confronted, we are told, by an "abeyance," in the juridical term relished by Agamben: an abeyance of life, but also of the laws of signification, so that the temporary inability of the witnesses to *read* "Riderhood," whose punning name evokes a dense signifying fabric of villainy and duplicity, is strictly commensurate with their momentary identification with the "bare life" left behind. In the signifier's abeyance, what emerges is an intense concern or fascination that is essentially *specular* (and speculative: the key word, again, being "if"). So that what the philosopher draws attention to, the distinction between what Dickens calls "the outer husk and shell of Riderhood" (*OMF* 503) and the pure event of a life hosted within, is something the novel's characters already "know" at some implicit or unconscious level; and what holds their gaze in fascinated concern over the patient is also the thing that fixes Deleuze's philosophical eye on the resuscitation scene set apart from the text: the "indubitable token" or point of the signifier's abeyance. The Dickensian text plays on the Latin root of 'doubt,' *dubium* or 'two:' what falls outside the discursive regime of reality marks a point *beyond doubt*, the singular apparition of a life as undivided by the signifier—and thus outside the consensual legibility of the novel.

The reduplication of scenes or *mise en abyme* here can be schematised, with a view to our question of ghostly manifestation, in terms of the interrelation of host and guest:

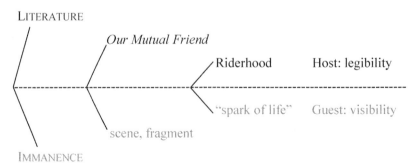

Figure 1.1

This schema is anamorphic, in that only the momentary "abeyance" of the legislative, textual host allows the pure "spark" or manifestation of a life; or, we might say, the spectral advent of the ghostly guest. In Holbein's famous portrait *The Ambassadors*, the intricate text of the main image, with its cryptic allusions to Reformation politics and esoteric lore, contrasts with the strange, entirely "unrealistic" skewed blot disfiguring the picture's foreground.

Thus only an estranging twist of perspective—exactly paralleled by Deleuze's decision not to *read* the narrative of *Our Mutual Friend* but instead to extract a scene from it—allows the emergence of the thing "normally" kept at bay, held in abeyance, by the consensual-discursive signifier. Just as Riderhood's familiar narrative "meaning" as scoundrel has to be held in eclipse for the transcendental immanence of "a life" to appear momentarily at the apertures of the body (it is always at the eyes, ears and the breathing orifices, mouth and nose, that this apparition takes place), so the philosopher has to overlook the semantic intricacies of the text to discern—for a fleeting moment, from a strange angle—the immanent apparition it hosts.

Thus, once the "short-lived delusion" (*OMF* 506) of the hospital interlude is over, we return to "real life" and the quasi-verisimilitude of Dickens's "host" narrative, with Riderhood re-assuming his signifying shroud of well-known duplicitous scoundrel. At this point, those who just a moment before had been intensely involved with his life, their eyes riveted on every twitch of eyelid or nostril, become cold again, as Deleuze notes: the "host" discourse of intersubjective reality, with its plausibly equivocal signifiers, leaves no room for the enthralling singularity of "a life . . ." (the Deleuzean ellipsis indicating semiotic non-closure, a self-manifestation of being irreducible to the differential play of signification).

We are therefore justified in seeing the resuscitation scene picked out by Deleuze as an anamorphic stain on the overall design of *Our Mutual Friend*—it is a phantasmatic interlude or psychical 'guest' in the hospitable narrative and in the lives of Dickens's characters, a momentary phantasm from which they immediately awaken and which they soon forget once the narrative laws governing their everyday world have resumed.

 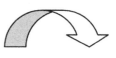 

Figure 1.2

It is here that we can turn to a remark by Walter Benjamin on the special 'aura' given to an utterance by the proximity of death. Benjamin is discussing the work of Nikolai Leskov and the disappearing art of storytelling, and he links the latter to how in modern times "the thought of death has declined in omnipresence and vividness."[6] Since today (he is writing in the mid-1930s) "people live in rooms that have never been touched by death," continues Benjamin, modern culture risks foreclosing on an essential dimension of storytelling—its power to transmit what is irreducible to mere narrative signifiers: the singularity, the event, of life itself. For, writes Benjamin,

> . . . not only a man's knowledge or wisdom, but above all his real life— and this is the stuff that stories are made of—first assumes transmissible form at the moment of his death. Just as a sequence of images is set in motion inside a man as his life comes to an end . . . suddenly in his expressions and looks the unforgettable emerges and imparts to everything that concerned him that authority which even the poorest wretch in dying possesses for the living around him. This authority is at the very source of the story.[7]

Thus even Rogue Riderhood, one of the poorest of Dickens's many poor wretches, accrues a fascinating aura, becomes an unforgettable presence instead of just another urban non-entity, during the uncanny suspension of his life. In making contact with death, in other words, the Dickensian rogue briefly conveys to onlookers the sanctity of life as such—as Deleuze concurs, seeing him as "'Homo tantum,' for whom everyone feels and who attains a kind of beatitude."[8] But what Benjamin adds, crucially, is that this strange anamorphic shift from insignificance to transcendent authority is the source of the story's power to hold our attention, to keep us in fascinated suspense. It is here that we can begin to see what the anamorphic-immanent interval picked out by Deleuze from Dickens's novel has to tell us about ghosts, and indeed about the undying fascination of the ghost story. But to learn more about this vital "source of the story," we will have to ignore Agamben's advice for a moment, and instead of merely skimming the pages of *Our Mutual Friend* look rather more closely at the Dickensian text, in particular at the character of Rogue Riderhood.

A MOST DISGRACEFUL SHADOW OF A MAN

Let us start, though, with a remark by one of the first major critics of Dickens's work, G. K. Chesterton. Writing in 1906, Chesterton observed that

> Dickens [. . .] had a sort of literary hospitality; he too often treated his characters as if they were his guests. From a host is always expected, and

always ought to be expected as long as human civilisation is healthy, a strictly physical benevolence, if you will, a kind of coarse benevolence. Food and fire and such things should always be the symbols of the man entertaining men; because they are things which all men beyond question have in common.[9]

Although Chesterton clearly intended this idea of Dickens as literary host to be a jovial rebuke, the humour masks a crucial insight. As we saw in the episode of Riderhood's resuscitation, what allows the apparition of "a life" as transcendent epiphany or beatitude is precisely an uncanny *interval* in what we termed Dickensian "hospitality:" the suspension, that is, of the signifying laws that ordinarily make narrative reality legible, make it a consensual matter "which all men beyond question have in common"—laws according to which Riderhood can only be read as an outsider (read, that is, through the idea of *hostility*). Dickensian hospitality, in this sense, is not, as perhaps Chesterton thought it, merely a matter of the writer's occasionally implausible benevolence toward his characters; instead it becomes a properly *ethical* question, that of the subject's relation to the absolute other. It is clear that Dickens deliberately chooses to place the least amiable and least worthy guest, the most hostile other, at the centre of the "hospital" scene, to show how the eclipse of narrative hospitality there, the abeyance of any reassuringly legible or consensual "meaning," opens onto the very being of the other, the immanence of a life in its pure form.

If we now turn to the place of this "rogue" character in the narrative of *Our Mutual Friend* itself, we will be able to see how the question of hospitality, of the ethical relation to the other, connects with the figure of the ghost. In the first Book of the novel, two young gentlemen, Mortimer Lightwood and Eugene Wrayburn, old school friends whose jobs as barristers don't seem to involve much actual work and yet who are wealthy enough to have rented "a bachelor cottage near Hampton, on the brink of the Thames" (*OMF* 191)—and waterside locations are extremely significant in this novel—have just finished dining in Lightwood's well-furnished office. Dickens sets the scene with his best mock-Gothic panache:

> It had grown darker as they talked, and the wind was sawing and the sawdust was whirling outside the paler windows. The underlying churchyard was already settling into deep dim shade, and the shade was creeping up to the housetops among which they sat. 'As if,' said Eugene, 'as if the churchyard ghosts were rising.'
>
> He had walked to the window with his cigar in his mouth, to exalt its flavour by comparing the fireside with the outside, when he stopped midway on his return to the arm-chair, and said:
>
> 'Apparently one of the ghosts has lost its way, and dropped in to be directed. Look at this phantom!'

Lightwood, whose back was towards the door, turned his head, and there, in the darkness of the entry, stood a something in the likeness of a man: to whom he addressed the not irrelevant inquiry, 'Who the devil are you?'

'I ask your pardons, Governors,' replied the ghost, in a hoarse double-barrelled whisper, 'but might either on you be Lawyer Lightwood?'

'What do you mean by not knocking at the door?' demanded Mortimer.

'I ask your pardons, Governors,' replied the ghost, as before, 'but probable you was not aware your door stood open.'   (*OMF* 194–195)

This scene of strange hospitality provides a thumbnail sketch of the ghostly or guestly encounter that will recur throughout Victorian literature and beyond. The "phantom" turns out soon enough to be merely "an ill-looking visitor with a squinting leer" (195) called, of course, Rogue Rider-hood; but the fact that he is introduced by Wrayburn to the scene as a ghost is of the utmost significance. In the first place, the apparition of a member of the dangerous criminal underclass of Victorian London in a setting of upper-class privilege must be read through a mass of literary and political contexts. The effete complacency of Wrayburn's moment of reverie by the window contrasting the domestic comfort of the plush interior with the harsh urban world outside is punctured by the sudden intrusion of "a something in the likeness of a man:" an element, that is, outside the properly human domain, that domain being implicitly circumscribed, for a moment, by the wealthy Victorian interior. It is thus the doorway, the point where that privileged definition of "humanity" opens onto a hostile Gothic space beyond it, that serves to frame the ghostly apparition; and Riderhood's disregard of the gentlemanly protocol governing that interval or transition—that turning-point or trope—signals his transgressive function in the novel, his ghostly evasion of the ordinary laws of accountability or legibility. It is impossible, that is, ever quite to *locate* Riderhood: as we have already glimpsed in the resuscitation scene, he cannot be placed securely either "in this world or the next." The Rogue is both guest and ghost, both a real visitor and a mere simulacrum of the human, an uncanny double (or "devil," as Lightwood's hostile question implies).

It is clear that the introduction of Riderhood as "this phantom" situates him as an anamorphic 'guest,' according to our schema (Figure 1.1). He thus corresponds to a gap in the 'host' domain—doubly figured as open door and disgraceful breach of gentlemanly decorum—that results in the momentary abeyance of the signifier; so that for a brief spell he is "unspeakable," a visible phenomenon with no place in reality, a hallucination outside the legitimate bounds of the narrative world: part ludicrous spook, part terrifying spectre. Indeed, this anamorphic quality of Riderhood is re-iterated throughout Dickens's text in little descriptive touches that twist the image of the character away from a 'straight' or realistic perspective (his head, with its "squinting leer" [195] is "set askew" [199], he walks "aslant" [204] and so on).

It is here that the queer reading of Dickens, largely initiated by Eve Kosofsky Sedgwick, is especially relevant.[10] The first appearance of Riderhood as the transgressive guest of the two gentlemen, a visible stain on their decorous domestic world and a momentary threat to its 'straight' legibility—such a scenario is an uncanny version of the risky encounter between the upper-class Victorian and his (often working-class) male object of desire. The infamous "fall" of Oscar Wilde in 1895 will offer an especially traumatic version of this scene of queer hospitality, with a show of transparent legibility compromised by a secret, hypothetical or half-imaginary "stain" or grimace of transgressive enjoyment. We will return to the queer implications of the ghostly apparition later in our argument, notably in our reading of Henry James (for whom the rise and fall of Wilde was so significant).

If Rogue Riderhood, then, is an anamorphic guest in the host narrative of *Our Mutual Friend*, how else does the Dickensian text inscribe that peculiar status? As we have seen, the twisting or skewing (we might even say the queering) of the character's presentation in the narrative figures its oblique relation to the novel's implicit centre of privileged interiority, propriety and legibility. At the diegetic level, this obliquity can also be seen in Riderhood's subjective resistance to the apparatus of identification imposed by his wealthy hosts—with "Who the devil are you?" rephrased as the official questions of name, address, occupation—and in particular his response to the last of these 'interpellating' demands: his self-definition, that is, as "Waterside character" (197). The sly ambiguity of that response only half-conceals Riderhood's real occupation: as a "river-finder" or "dredger," someone who makes money by salvaging corpses drowned in the Thames, stealing any valuables on them and then claiming the "inquest money" upon delivery of the body to a magistrate.[11] But of course "waterside character" may also, at a symbolic level, describe an essentially transitional or liminal being or signifier: someone located on the edge of the void, a discursive element wavering on the borders of legibility.

What is most important here, though, is the *voice* of the "phantom:" it is this above all that encapsulates its ghostly dimension. When Riderhood first speaks, still caught in the liminal ontological space of the encounter, the not-necessarily countable, what emerges is a "hoarse double-barrelled whisper:" emphatically not, that is, the transparent vessel of meaning spoken in the Victorian salon by the likes of Wrayburn and Lightwood (whose voices are never marked, remarked on, by the narrator). This "rogue" voice is thick, weighted, as if visibly clogged by excess matter, its discursive contents obscured by formal impropriety; and yet it remains only a "whisper," a spectral remnant or simulacrum of an authentic, authoritative voice. The ghost-voice is therefore truly "double-barrelled," both too much voice and not enough: like its spectral speaker, it is only half-present in the world of representation, its advent impeded by some singular, unreadable materiality.

There is something unspeakable, then, about the ghost-voice; and it is this that points us back to the philosophical significance of *Our Mutual Friend* as host for an 'anamorphic' Riderhood. "The voice says nothing," writes Agamben; "instead, it shows itself . . . It therefore cannot become the subject of discourse. Philosophy can only lead thought to the limit of the voice; it cannot say the voice."[12] Like the anamorphic stain disfiguring the pictorial text of Holbein's *The Ambassadors*, the voice in this sense does not inhabit a legible or narratable space-time: it "shows itself" non-metaphorically, an ontology that does not partake in the diacritical network of signifiers that makes possible the interpretability of the human subject. Again, if we look carefully enough at the text of *Our Mutual Friend*, we can glimpse for a moment this figure of voice as non-metaphorical ontological manifestation. Before Riderhood has even been identified as someone with a name, he demands to be "took down. . . in pen and ink" (196). "First," demands Lightwood,

> . . .let us know what your business is about.'
> 'It's about,' said the man, taking a step forward, dropping his hoarse voice, and shading it with his hand, 'it's about from five to ten thousand pound reward. That's what it's about. . . .'   (OMF 196)

When a voice is 'dropped' in a prose narrative, we do not usually understand this non-figuratively, as if the voice risked landing on someone's toes. But with the next phrase, "shading it with his hand," the Dickensian text makes something appear that is neither literal (like the step taken forward) nor simply metaphorical: what Riderhood shades with his hand—for a fleeting moment of *trompe l'oeil* that suspends the gap between the literal and the figurative—is a spectral manifestation of voice itself: *psyche*, breath or life before it has entered the consistent domain of discursive human reality.

When Riderhood first intrudes on the world of wealth and privilege, then, it is as a true outsider, "a something in the likeness of a man" (195); not simply a metaphorical ghost but a *real* one. And it is voice or breath as inhuman *thing* that constitutes this ghostly real, with the human body only "shading" or playing host to it; just as the "outer husk and shell" (503) will later host the pure "spark" or immanence of a life ("It is the soul itself which the voice calls forth from the other," remarks one of Jean-Luc Nancy's philosophical personae).[13]

Now, the same distinction between human host and vocal-psychical thing reappears later in *Our Mutual Friend* in yet another encounter between the wealthy protagonists of the "host" narrative and a subhuman guest from the Victorian underworld: a degraded, broken version of the wily Rogue Riderhood. But here a significant point of intertextuality allows us to open a new perspective on the ghostly dimension of the scene. In the novel's Third Book, Lightwood and Wrayburn are again comfortably ensconced by the fire (note their "fireside" names[14]), now preoccupied by the problem of locating the stray Lizzie Hexam. An "undecided knock" at the door brings Wrayburn to his feet; and then

> [Lightwood] had barely had time to recall the unprecedented gleam of determination with which he had spoken of finding this girl, and which had faded out of him with the breath of the spoken words, when Eugene came back, ushering in a most disgraceful shadow of a man, shaking from head to foot, and clothed in shabby grease and smear.
>
> (*OMF* 600)

Like Riderhood, this guest is only a "shadow of a man," and as "disgraceful" ontological stain it is not even entitled to a proper human name (Wrayburn decides to call him "Mr Dolls" on a purely metonymic basis, since the man is the "bad child"—in fact the dissolute, infantile father—of Jenny Wren, dressmaker for dolls). But this time the encounter with the underworld ghost is associated in particular with "the breath of the spoken words:" with voice or vibrating psyche. Once the disgraceful guest has departed, and Wrayburn has hired him as a "scout" to report on the whereabouts of Lizzie, Lightwood reproaches his friend for dealing with such a "shameful scout" (*OMF* 604). But Wrayburn's response is illuminating:

> . . . sit down, and I'll tell you something that you really will find amusing. Take a cigar. Look at this of mine. I light it—draw one puff—breathe the smoke out—there it goes—it's Dolls!—it's gone—and being gone you are a man again.
>
> (*OMF* 604)

The cigar, of course, regardless of any future Freudian significance, is an emblem of Victorian patriarchal privilege: a sign of gentlemanly affluence and of a special leisured breathing or measured temporality (recall the cigar savoured by Wrayburn at the window before the first ghostly apparition of Riderhood). Here cigar smoke is deployed as a playful metaphor for the ephemeral apparition and disappearance of the shameful ontological aberration: just as Riderhood, by shading his voice with his hand, allowed the unspeakable *form* of the voice to show itself, so Wrayburn's puffs of rhetorical smoke materialise the shadowy presence of the intruder and mime its ghostly temporality, its implausible manifestation and fading.

But the last phrase from the quotation, with its echo of Shakespeare's *Macbeth*, is the key. "Hence, horrible shadow," Macbeth tells the ghost of Banquo, his murdered rival, "Unreal mockery hence. Why so, being gone, /I am a man again."[15] The Shakespearean apparition has two features directly relevant to the Dickensian scene: first, the ghost is an "unreal mockery," a ludicrous breach of proper reality and its consistent narrative representation (thus both Riderhood and Dolls are presented, with full Dickensian black comedy, as "unrealistic," not "straight" or properly human). And secondly, the appearance of the uncanny spectre has the effect of jeopardising the ordinary onlooker's presence-to-self, separating him from his own familiar, plausible identity (as man or as human: we will come back to this uncertainty). So that when Wrayburn jokes, with a touch of Podsnappery, that Mr Dolls does not really exist, has no more substantial reality than a puff of cigar smoke, he is reconfirming his privileged masculinity both through the homosocial ritual of shared cigar smoking and, at an intertextual level, by partaking in Macbeth's return to self after the ghostly interval.

What is actually being shared, though, in this declaration: "being gone you are a man again"? By having his text host an anamorphic fragment of Shakespearean tragedy, and thus metonymically linking it back to literature's most searching inquiry into the definition and limits of the human, Dickens can hardly be thought to be endorsing his character's flippant attempt to dispel the "horrible shadow" whose appearance has disturbed the familiar contours of reality that guarantee the security and Podsnappish comfort of the wealthy. Rather, in its haunting echo of *Macbeth* the Dickensian text lets us glimpse something too unsettling to be assuaged by a little homosocial bonding over a cigar: how the ghostly interval opens up fundamental questions about being human.

CAUGHT ASLANT ON THE TURN

What, then, is a ghost? Our Dickensian and Deleuzean texts have allowed us to see how a manifestation of *psyche*—breath, soul or voice—comes between a self and its presence-to-self, intervenes in the domain of equivocal legibility where an ontological consistency opens a space of narrative hospitality in which I am recognised by, and dialectically recognise myself in, the Other. We saw how, in the Dickensian "hospital" scene isolated by Deleuze, the signifier withdrew, went into abeyance, around Riderhood's vacillating life-in-death, at a moment seen by the philosopher as the pure event or immanence of a life. The effect of that signifying abeyance on those who witnessed it was to alienate them from their own familiar identities, to plunge them for a moment into an uncanny interlude exempt from the ordinary laws of their narrative world: an interlude in which they acted strangely, self-unrecognizably (showing reverence for the beatitude of a psyche or life belonging to someone they knew, at the level of everyday narrative sense, to be essentially hostile). In the parenthesis of ordinary narrative hospitality, what appears is therefore something *hostile to the Other*, an event characterised by non-recognition of the fictional space that produces and determines intersubjective rationality. And what is crucial is that this nonsensical interval outside the socially constitutive gaze of the Other entails a direct, bodily *identification with the other*, a becoming-one-with the singular apparition of "a life."

Another essential characteristic of what appears in the ontological parenthesis or interval is its epiphenomenal status, its occurrence as a mere "spark" or fleeting glimpse: it corresponds, that is, to the aesthetic space-time of the *fragment*. Like the poetic fragment, the ghost is never more than a "spasm of thought," to quote Nancy: it can never be seen 'straight' or consistently represented, made present again, in a narrative discourse.[16] Now, the poetic fragment was the key figure in the turn to literary texts repeatedly performed by philosophy from the Romantic period onwards, as the philosophical narrative struggled to respond to the Kantian demolition of the old metaphysical certainties. An exemplary Romantic formulation of this philosophical predicament is given by Friedrich von Schlegel, for whom the universe of human experience is

> . . . an infinitude which cannot be reduced to rational order, a chaos, a complex of contradiction and incongruity, for our limited intellects cannot fathom the order of the absolute. We may at times catch a glimpse of this order, but once we try to realize it for ourselves or express it to others we are involved in contradiction and paradox.[17]

On this view, our cognitive habits, the ways we narrate the world and ourselves as consistent entities, are just not compatible with the fundamental truth of ontology; or, to use Platonic terms, the space of *mathemata*, of the expressible or epistemologically consistent, necessarily excludes *to pragma auto*, the thing itself, conceived of as an irreducible immanence or singularity.[18] The fragmentary glimpse of "the absolute" here corresponds to the immanent self-manifestation of being that Deleuze discerns as Riderhood awakens in the Dickensian "hospital:" the ghost may appear there for an ephemeral instant, a breath or puff of smoke, but as soon as the "cold" order of rational discourse is set in motion again, the consistent host-narrative returns and what was a momentous apparition becomes mere incongruous shards of signification, bits of litter no longer enlivened by the spirit. And this, of course, is why literature (above all in the form of the poetic fragment) proves so vital to the philosopher, since what literature can do—and starts doing much more frequently from the Romantic period onward—is to *show* what cannot be properly "said" or fully narrated, to return to Agamben's remark quoted earlier on the voice as non-discursive manifestation.

At this point, we can see how the literary fragment takes its place as an anamorphic guest in the host domain of philosophy, according to our first schema, which we can now rewrite as follows:

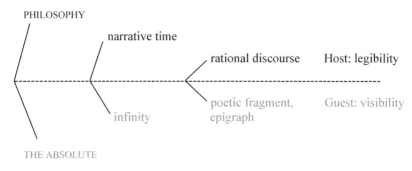

Figure 1.3

What cannot be said in the rational discursive order of philosophical statement can nevertheless, on this view, "show itself" (the reflexivity of the expression is essential) in the non-cognitive domain of the aesthetic, with the signifying ontology of the conscious ego momentarily overridden, swept aside by the impersonal force, the libidinal drive, of mystical or 'poetic' inspiration.

But we might immediately object that this Romantic account risks idealizing the aesthetic, imagining the poetic fragment as some metaphysical dream of direct contact with the absolute, unfettered by the inconvenient temporality of rational discourse (and we might, along similar lines, recall how Deleuze seemed to overlook completely the specific textuality of *Our Mutual Friend* in his final paean to immanence). Isn't all experience, however epiphenomenal or inspired, ultimately a textual product, determined by effects of the signifier? And how can a literary text present a point of pure visibility *set apart from* a field of discursive legibility?

We need to formulate an initial response to these questions by examining some more technical aspects of the ghostly interval in literature. Here is Lacan in his 1955 seminar, four decades before Deleuze's terminal engagement with Rogue Riderhood, on a story by Dickens's contemporary Edgar Allan Poe:

> Edgar Poe always juxtaposed the themes of life and of death, in a way not lacking in significance. As an echo of [the] liquefaction of Oedipus, I would choose *The Facts in the Case of M. Valdemar.*
>
> It's about an experiment in the sustentation of the subject in speech, by means of what was then called magnetism, a form of theorisation of hypnosis—someone *in articulo mortis* is hypnotised to see what will happen. A man at the end of his life is chosen, he has only some few breaths left, and in every other way he's dying. [. . .]
>
> In fact, the subject passes from life into death, and remains for some months in a state of sufficient aggregation to be still in fair

condition—a corpse on a bed, which, from time to time, speaks, saying *I am dead.*

This state of affairs is maintained . . . until the passes contrary to those that put him to sleep are started in order to wake him up, when several screams from the poor wretch are heard—*For God's sake!—quick!—quick!—put me to sleep—or, quick!—waken me!—quick!—I SAY TO YOU THAT I AM DEAD!*

He's already been saying he's dead for six months, but when he is awakened, M. Valdemar is no more than a disgusting liquefaction, something for which no language has a name, the naked apparition, pure, simple, brutal, of this figure which it is impossible to gaze at face on . . . the complete collapse of this species of swelling that is life—the bubble bursts and dissolves down into inanimate putrid liquid.[19]

Like Rogue Riderhood, Monsieur Valdemar enters the *val de mort,* the spectral ontological interval between life and death; but unlike the Dickensian character he never gets back to the cold narrative consistency of everyday life; he is therefore melted, liquefied by contact with something foreclosed from "legitimate" reality: the "absolute," we might say, following Schlegel, or "absolute immanence" to use Deleuzean terms. The result is Poe's weird black comedy, centring on what Lacan describes as "a thing empty of any plausible appearance" (232): a manifestation or "naked apparition" of life without any support from an ontologically consistent host narrative. Whereas the Dickensian narrative resumes, after the ghostly interval of the "hospital" resuscitation, as if waking from a disturbing dream, Poe's story can only suffer stylistic meltdown, as it were, with the narrative itself collapsing into the unspeakable while the "facts in the case" initially set out with such apparent precision are revealed to have been no more than *trompe l'oeil.*

Roland Barthes produced a celebrated structuralist analysis of the Poe story in question, which can help us pinpoint the textual strategy of "apparition" here, of making something visible through and as an abeyance of signification. Having first identified the sentence "I SAY TO YOU THAT I AM DEAD" as an "enantioseme" or self-contradictory lexeme, Barthes tries to push his analysis beyond structuralist semiotics:

And yet, we have to go further still: it is not simply a matter of a simple negation, in the psychoanalytic sense, 'I am dead' meaning in that case 'I am not dead,' but rather an affirmation-negation: 'I am dead and not dead;' this is the paroxysm of transgression, the invention of an unheard-of category: the 'true-false,' the 'yes-no,' the 'death-life' is thought of as a whole which is indivisible, uncombinable, non-dialectic, for the antithesis implies no third term; it is not a two-faced entity, but a term which is one and new.[20]

This radically non-dialectical point or "indivisible remainder" (as Žižek will rename it in 1996) is fundamentally at odds with the linguistic act that paradoxically allows it to become manifest. Valdemar's statement, that is, specifically foregrounds its own status as discrete speech act ("I say to you that. . ."), a message necessarily caught up in and determined by the Other, the rational structure of intersubjective communication; while simultaneously proposing as the content of that message precisely what escapes that "rational order," to recall Schlegel's formulation: an absolute, transcendental knowledge, the knowledge of life and death. If the latter can only show itself in momentary epiphanies—and can only be seized in an elliptic "spasm of thought" or poetic fragment—in Poe's text it would seem to be mockingly "represented" as something fully "sayable." Except that Poe precisely *refuses* to present Valdemar's utterance as an ordinary speech-act, instead marking its fundamental ontological strangeness, its otherness to the domain of the signifier, at the level of narrative form. What the form of the narrative, with the pseudo-archival verisimilitude of the "facts in the case" thus plays host to is a vocal apparition that ruptures the discursive consistency of intersubjective identity. This makes the voice from the *val de mort* or ghostly interval both a *hapax* or unique apparition—"it is quite impossible that any human being could have been prepared" for it, as Poe warns us—and a kind of sensory traumatisation of the signifier: the voice, says the narrator, "impressed me (I fear, indeed, that it will be impossible to make myself comprehended) as gelatinous or glutinous matters impress the sense of touch."[21]

When Lacan talks of something appearing in Poe's text "empty of any plausible appearance," or when Barthes identifies there a "paroxysm of transgression" irreducible to rational formulation, both thinkers are touching on what we could thus formulate through our distinction between legible host and visible or sensory guest. Poe's story, seen in this light, is based on the derisory aim of making legible, spelling out in broad daylight, a radical ontology that can only be glimpsed or sensed—not simply "read"—as an anamorphic interval in the "host" discourse of narrative legibility. The result, of course, is a deliberately contrived stylistic catastrophe, the implosion of the tale's surface verisimilitude and the emergence, as Lacan puts it, of something "impossible to gaze at face on." "Valdemar," indeed, makes clear the fundamentally anti-realist orientation of Poe's writing; as moreover do the technical recommendations set out in "The Philosophy of Composition" (1846), where Poe proposes that the literary work should be a pure fragment of enjoyment to be consumed in a single sitting, its "unity of effect" not jeopardized by a complicated, extended narrative entanglement with any putative real world.

In terms of literary technique, then, it may seem self-evident that what is foreclosed from the signifying domain can only be made manifest in a text at the formal level, that of its literal *materiality*. In the case of the "tale of terror" both conceptualised and written by Poe, this would correspond to the essentially fragmentary dimension of the text: the abrupt, enigmatic openings and the deliberate lack of 'proper' narrative endings. The ending of "Valdemar" is a good instance: "Upon the bed, before that whole company, there lay a nearly liquid mass of loathsome—of detestable putrescence."[22] The abject thing presented is the opposite, we might say, of a narrative element, an anti-lexeme: it cannot be articulated or made to signify, but remains a startling, enigmatic stain on the page. That is to say—and we will see how important this is in ghost stories—Poe's ending breaks with the constitutive semantic teleology of narrative: it is irresolvable, an undying interval or endless vibration.

Another crucial aspect of literary apparition can best be examined if we turn to another neo-Gothic text; one published a generation before the mature writings of Dickens and Poe, namely Charles Maturin's novel *Melmoth the Wanderer* (1820). What we have already glimpsed, a thing extimate to narrative, "impossible to gaze at face on" and only visible at the anamorphic interstices of signification—Riderhood's shading of his voice, Wrayburn's ghostly cigar smoke, Valdemar's endless liquefaction—this implausible apparition can already be seen emerging in *Melmoth*; but here it is framed as a question of the ontological limits of diegetic representation, a problem of narrative "exhaustion."

We are given the clearest presentation of this at a crucial break in Maturin's novel, between its First and Second Volumes: an interruption of the narrative marked as a vital necessity for the character telling the story (and implicitly for the reader attempting to follow it too). "At this part of the narrative," we read at the close of Volume One, "the Spaniard became so much agitated, though apparently more from emotion than fatigue, that Melmoth intreated him to suspend it for some days, and the exhausted narrator willingly complied" (*MW* 130). Then we are faced with a blank page; the narrative is suspended due to narrative exhaustion: but the pause for breath is more to do with the psyche than with the merely physical, derives "more from emotion than fatigue." At the start of the next Chapter and a new Volume—the double inscription of a new beginning—the theme of narrative interruption by voice or psyche is again taken up. I quote the text in full:

VOLUME II

CHAPTER VI

τηλε μειργουσι ψυχαι, ειδωλα καμοντων
Homer

WHEN, after some days interval, the Spaniard attempted to describe his feelings on the receipt of his brother's letter, the sudden resuscitation of heart, and hope, and existence, that followed its perusal, he trembled,—and uttered some inarticulate sounds,—wept;—and his agitation appeared to

Melmoth, with *his uncontinental feelings*, so violent, that he entreated him to spare the description of his feelings, and proceed with his narrative.

'You are right,' said the Spaniard, drying his tears, 'joy is a convulsion, but grief is a habit, and to describe what we never can communicate, is as absurd as to talk of colours to the blind.'

(*MW* 131; emphasis in the original)

This last reflection by the Spaniard offers us a set of ready-made theoretical tools to gloss the linked problems of narrative interruption and of affect or psyche, what the text calls, in a phrase inexplicably italicized, "*uncontinental feelings.*" Indeed, with the opposing terms joy and grief linked in turn to "convulsion" and "habit," we are already uncannily close to psychoanalytic thinking, with its distinction between intractable *jouissance* or trauma and the ontological clearing made possible by the symbolic order. A "convulsion," that is, designates precisely what *interrupts* narrative discourse—not due to any empirical contingency but due to something inherently incommunicable or "uncontinental:" something wholly incompatible with the intersubjective structure of discursive knowledge. In this sense, Maturin's "convulsion" is another name for Schlegel's "order of the absolute," an ontological manifestation that occurs in fleeting epiphanies but which cannot be subsequently realized or expressed, re-presented for the Other, without becoming paradoxical nonsense. "Habit," conversely, is a name for narration itself, the proliferating layers of storytelling which in *Melmoth the Wanderer* will describe a variety of "habits"—both monastic uniforms of sham humility and perverse sado-masochistic rituals—as the term is quickly turned into an ironic, self-reflexive pun.

And this pun, we might say, is precisely the point: for it gives a glimpse of how Maturin's text in effect *resists* the binary opposition set up within its own narrative, just as Poe's "Valdemar" resisted the 'realistic' distinction between living substance and dead letter. If the word "habit," designating the non-convulsive, the symbolic or rational, dimension of *Melmoth* is itself revealed to be "uncontinental," semantically unstable or duplicitous, the text opens up a playful or diabolical rendering-doubtful of sense that amounts to an interruption of discursive logic or narrative time. At the very point, that is, where it names narrative as habitual order, predictable temporality, *Melmoth* inscribes a pun that exempts itself, through a momentary signifying surplus, from that same order. A similar economy of uncanny wordplay will be used by Dickens in *Our Mutual Friend*: "Riderhood" connoting both clothing and "Little Red Riding Hood," habitual familiarity and menaced fairytale innocence.

Melmoth, then, situates what it represents as the difference between the communicable and the absolute, realistic discursive habit and inarticulate convulsion, at a significant suspension of its own narrative: the transition from its first to its second Volume. This act of narrative self-interruption or resuscitation makes the point effectively enough: since what is at stake is not of the order of communicable knowledge, it can only be an *apparitional* ontology, made manifest in and as the suspension of narrative "habit," in the breathing space, the psychical interval between segments of text. But what makes Maturin's novel especially relevant to our argument is that, like Wrayburn's Shakespearean cigar smoke in *Our Mutual Friend*, it folds into its momentary suspension of narrative an anamorphic intertextual fragment that allows us to *read* the apparition. In *Melmoth* the intertextual "guest" is clothed in a classical form: that of the epigraph.

So what does Maturin's epigraph "say"? We can only read it, of course, if we know Greek—and if we know enough Greek we may also be able to spot a mistake in the line (and thus go a step farther than Maturin's modern editor, who merely labels it "misquoted"[23]). The line is from Book 23 of Homer's *Iliad*, which in its correct version reads τῆλέ με εἴργουσι ψυχαὶ εἴδωλα καμόντων. Douglas Grant, the Oxford University Press editor of *Melmoth*, gives as translation "Far off the spirits banish me, phantoms of men outworn" without referring to a specific translator (Robert Fitzgerald's version is "Shades that are images of used-up men motion me away"[24]).

Who is speaking, though, on the line from the Homeric text? The fragment comes towards the end of the *Iliad*, when the hero Achilleus is asleep after an exhausting day's combat during which he has killed the Trojan general Hektor, thus both turning the war decisively in favour of the Achaians and avenging the death of his lover Patroklos, whom Hektor had earlier killed. At line 65, the ghost or breathing spirit (ψυχὴ) of Patroklos appears ὑπὲρ κεφαλῆς, "above the head" of Achilleus to reproach him for neglecting the funeral rites required to allow a ghost to pass across the river Styx and fully enter the realm of the dead; without such rites, Patroklos cannot die 'properly,' must remain one of the living dead trapped in the uncanny borderland between life and death.

The narrative interruption performed and cryptically glossed by Maturin's Homeric epigraph, then, also makes visible a crucial ontological ambiguity. For the voice of Patroklos emanates from a space "between two deaths" (that theoretical vortex of literary, philosophical and psychoanalytic interpretation): the paradoxical site of life-in-death, of "life deprived of support in the symbolic order," as Žižek puts it.[25] Only the καμόντες, that is, only subjects fully mortified or "used up" by the signifier—properly supported by the rational, non-absolute order of the symbol—can be read as distinct signifiers or "images," εἴδωλα, sited in a legible space beyond the wavering anamorphic distortion of the spectral. But the encounter between Patroklos and Achilleus takes place *on the near side* of the river Styx, as it were: in other words it is still stained by the pathological substance of life and thus deprived of effective symbolic agency. The first effect of this is a drastic ontological uncertainty: it is not clear whether Patroklos still exists, can still speak as a distinct "I," or whether his voice is instead no more than a haunting memory, a post-ontological stain. Just as the absolute thing in Schlegel's post-Kantian epistemology can only appear in a fleeting epiphany, can never be taken into the domain of coherent narrative representation by a rational subject, so the pathological-psychical stuff of an unmortified memory overwhelms the rational ontology made possible by discourse, traverses and obliterates the borders that define subjects as distinct entities.

What therefore comes to *Melmoth* from afar, τῆλέ, from the *Iliad*—a Greek guest to an Irish host—is the voice of a ghost. But as such that voice is already ontologically unstable or diffracted: as we saw in our reading of *Our Mutual Friend*, the advent of a ghost-voice immediately unsettles any coherent narrative topography of texts or subjects. In tracing the intertextual link from Dickens's text to *Macbeth*, where "being gone you are a man again" marked an encounter between a human subject and the spectral double that jeopardized that subject's ontological self-consistency, we could discern the essentially "double-barrelled" dimension of the ghost-voice: like Riderhood's spectral whisper, it seems both to emanate from a real speaker and to manifest an impersonal vibration irreducible to the "rational order" that makes the speaker's reality consistent, representable, liveable.

Now, this "double-barrelled" dimension of the spectral voice is already visible, at least on one reading, in the *Iliad*; so that the line quoted in *Melmoth*'s epigraph might entail the advent not merely of the ghostly Patroklos but of the dubious two-in-one couple of ghost-voice and dreamer, Achilleus and ontological phantasm. It is the ghostly immanence of a life, as we saw in the resuscitation of Riderhood, that unravels the narrative consistency of individual subjects: Maturin's Spaniard, confronted by a letter with his own "sudden resuscitation," for a moment loses his grip on the signifier and can only utter "inarticulate sounds," as if dispossessed of his own voice, made to utter a ghost-voice. And at the textual level, *Melmoth* makes strikingly visible this ghostly collapse of subjective consistency through a combination of syntactical ambiguity and enigmatic emphasis. The narrating Spaniard, we recall, was overwhelmed with emotion " . . . and his agitation appeared to Melmoth, with *his uncontinental feelings*, so violent, that he entreated him to spare the description of his feelings" (*MW* 131; emphasis in the original). But precisely *whose* are these italicised "uncontinental feelings"? The repeated pronouns deliberately blur the distinct identities of the two characters, while the italicized phrase serves almost as a metafictional gloss on this moment of textual incontinence or indeterminacy, this interruption of the text and its characters by the convulsive, the affective—in other words, by an unmortified psychical reality.

What interrupts the "habit" of narrative discourse, then, like Maturin's Homeric epigraph, is ψυχή: "psyche," often translated as soul, ghost or spirit. But the original Greek meaning of that word—"breath"—gives the full sense of its status as constitutive breach of discourse; psyche, that is, designates a breathing, living substance that both permeates and perforates being-in-language, the vital immanence that preconditions the ontological opening of the subject and yet resists, remains untranslatable by, the symbolic enclosure of discourse. The apparition of Patroklos is just such a non-narratable manifestation of psyche: what breathes ὑπὲρ κεφαλῆς, next to the head, of the sleeping Achilleus is the pure immanence of life, vocal substance minus ontological consistency or "deprived of support in the symbolic order," to recall Žižek on the apparition between-two-deaths. What is important to understand about psyche in this sense is that it is paradoxically *more alive* than the conscious speaking subject, in that the latter is still wrapped in the narrative "habits" (or Dickensian "red riding-hood") from which the ghostly breathing-spirit has disinvested—those habits forming a signifying shroud over the subject's being, reducing it to a mere punctual after-effect of the mortifying agency of the letter.

When psyche appears, then, it does so as an ontological breach of narrative hospitality, as an aperture in legitimate discourse: and it is this that makes its manifestation so dangerous, so "unspeakable." This is the "convulsion" opposed to the legible structures of representation by Maturin's Spaniard, and simultaneously encrypted by *Melmoth* in its formal and intertextual dimensions, as break and resuscitation, in the ghostly Greek epigraph.

Indeed the epigraph itself, as literary convention, can be seen as a kind of 'guest,' an enigmatic apparition at the doorway or aperture of a host-text. As epigraph, that is, it seems both part of the text and yet at odds with it: lodged in the 'extimate' interval between the title of a work and its 'first' line, the epigraphic fragment is an ambiguous supplement that both completes a text and remains outside it (it is often written aslant, in italics, as if to figure this difference). We might therefore give the epigraph the peculiar status of *textual graphic*: a shard of signification appearing "on the edge of," not fully caught up in, the discursive network of the host-text. An epigraph is often written in a foreign language (as here in *Melmoth*); and moreover its precise relation to the ensuing narrative remains largely enigmatic (a commentary? a metanarrative? an imprimatur?). The epigraph should therefore be accorded a primarily *visual* status: it is not an ordinary textual element to be interpreted via the narrative grid of signifiers, but instead a kind of textual spectre, shorn of any 'original' context and thus deprived of its discursive orientation. As such, the epigraph is essentially 'aimless' or endless: just like "a life . . . " in Deleuze's thought, an epigraphic text can therefore never be subject to the signifying closure determining a discrete narrative statement but must break off hauntingly, elliptically: an intertextual ghost-voice.

The Homeric epigraph in *Melmoth the Wanderer* thus offers us a way to read the convulsive interruption of narrative communicability— staged by Dickens in Riderhood's resuscitation; by Poe in Valdemar's impossible utterance—as a ghostly intertext-interval. The uncanny voice of Patroklos intervenes in Maturin's text not merely as a revenant from a dead classical culture to a living novel, but as something horrifically *still alive*, the trace of an unmortified *jouissance* that is impersonal and endless, that like the repulsive ending of Poe's "Valdemar" or the ghost-voice "shaded" by Riderhood, manifests an incessant, incomprehensible vibration.

POSTSCRIPT: "*I AM GONE*"

The question of the edges of a text or the limits of its legibility provoked by the literary apparitions we have been examining returns intriguingly at the very end of *Our Mutual Friend* in a note added by Dickens to the final edition of the novel, dated September 2, 1865, and entitled "Postscript: in Lieu of Preface." The initial problem of locating this final textual supplement—an afterword in place of a foreword; an ending marked as displaced or substitute opening—points to a topological ambiguity that gives a last Möbius twist, as it were, to the ghostly problem we have been exploring in Dickens's novel: that of locating or identifying the errant, ephemeral "spark of life" (*OMF* 503). What this last Dickensian word, wavering on the uncertain textual edge of *Our Mutual Friend*, makes visible is something that may come as an uncanny surprise to the reader: that the novel itself, like its character Rogue Riderhood, almost succumbed to what Henry James will call "the insolence of an accident."[26] "On Friday the Ninth of June in the present year," writes Dickens,

> Mr and Mrs Boffin (in their manuscript dress of receiving Mr and Mrs Lammle at breakfast) were on the South Eastern Railway with me, in a terribly destructive accident. When I had done what I could to help others, I climbed back into my carriage—nearly turned over a viaduct, and caught aslant upon the turn—to extricate the worthy couple. They were much soiled, but otherwise unhurt.   (*OMF* 894)

In fact, as critic Jill Matus writes, Dickens himself had "narrowly escaped death when the train on which he was travelling from Folkestone to London jumped a gap in the line occasioned by some repair work on a viaduct near Staplehurst, Kent."[27] The "little turn-up with Death" (*OMF* 509) dramatized within the novel thus 'returned in the real,' to use the Lacanian gloss on uncanny repetition; and the very figure used by Dickens in his postscript-preface to capture the surreal shock of the event—the image of the carriage "caught aslant upon the turn"—provides us with a perfect trope for the anamorphic, apparitional dimension of the text: what can only be glimpsed "aslant" there, without being fully legible. The suspension of the railway carriage on the verge of nothingness—it "seemed impossibly balanced in the act of tilting" writes Dickens in a letter[28]—is an uncanny figure for the suspension of narrative discourse at the point of apparition or anamorphic intertextuality; and the accident itself, of course, is rhetorically placed beyond narrative: "No words can describe the scene," as Dickens put it in another letter.[29]

So how should we interpret this odd coincidence of text and event? It clearly shows that what opens in the ghostly interval—figured as the extimate space of ghost-voice, intertextual fragment or epigraph—is also a matter of traumatic collision, collision with what lies outside "habit," to use *Melmoth*'s language, outside the hospitable space of consistent narrative representation. If, as we have seen, such a traumatic or convulsive encounter had been ennobled, spiritualized by Romantic philosophy as an epiphanic glimpse of the "absolute," by contrast Dickens's "little turn-up with Death" (*OMF* 509) at the Staplehurst viaduct must have shown him that the inhuman machinery of modern life now offered a more mundane, though no less impersonal and terrifying, way to demolish the habitual narrative fabric of reality.

When Poe's Monsieur Valdemar finally speaks, his message—"I SAY TO YOU THAT I AM DEAD"—is impossible, too ludicrously macabre to be plausibly sustained by a fictional discourse: revealing the "case" that supposedly contained it to be no more than an illusion, a cheap conjuring trick. On 13 June 1865, four days after the Staplehurst crash, Dickens writes to Thomas Mitton describing a real encounter with something very like Valdemar's life-in-death utterance:

> Suddenly I came upon a staggering man covered with blood (I think he must have been flung clean out of his carriage) with such a frightful cut across the skull that I couldn't bear to look at him. I poured some water over his face, and gave him some to drink, and gave him some brandy, and laid him down on the grass, and he said "I am gone" and died afterwards.[30]

Could this genuinely "staggering" apparition (Dickens still can't help punning), this unbearably real spectre, impossible to look in the face and with the impossible temporality of its final utterance—could this thing still be hosted or safely conveyed by a legible Dickensian narrative? In the next chapter, we will see.

2 Zigzag

The Signalman

These dark pictures seem almost as if they were literally visions; things, that is, that Dickens saw but did not understand.

—G. K. Chesterton

Published in 1866, Dickens's *The Signalman* comes between two of the most significant moments of technological innovation that revolutionized communication in the nineteenth century. The telegraph, which features explicitly in Dickens's story, had been in use in public life and on British railways from the mid-1840s; although by contrast the telephone, a still more socially transformative invention, was not to enter everyday life until the 1880s, thus after Dickens's death. Roger Luckhurst argues that "the investigation of inter-phenomena," mapping the very space of communication and intersubjectivity, was provoked in part by these Victorian technologies, and that such "tele-effects" were recurrent objects of public fascination and scientific interest throughout the period.[1] And "inter-phenomena" are clearly at stake, in a variety of ways, in *The Signalman*, a text that will open a new, 'telegraphic' perspective on the ghostly manifestations we have been investigating.

However, before setting out to interpret *The Signalman* too swiftly or exclusively in terms of the historical impact of modern technology, we should first consider its relation to what we have already identified as characteristic of the ghostly or apparitional dimension of literary texts. For a start, if we consider the epigraph, which we envisaged as a cryptic 'guest'—a presence both alien and intimate—at the opening of the host-text of *Melmoth the Wanderer*, we can see it as a kind of textual "tele-effect" (and Maturin's Homeric fragment even seems to say as much with its first word: τῆλέ). The epigraph is thus a literary telegraph *avant la lettre*, an intertextual facsimile afloat in a strange virtual space above the line that supposedly initiates and defines textual meaning as such. With this in mind, let us turn to the opening of Dickens's *The Signalman*:

'Halloa! Below there!'
When he heard a voice thus calling him, he was standing at the door of his box, with a flag in his hand, furled round its short pole. One would have thought, considering the nature of the ground, that he could not have doubted from what quarter the voice came; but, instead

of looking up to where I stood on the top of the steep cutting nearly over his head, he turned himself about and looked down the Line.[2]

There is no epigraph here, one might at first think. But it is as if the "tele-effect" of the epigraph, the disorienting impact of an enigmatic message coming from another space, supervening on the textual "line" (this Dickensian text, as we shall see, is especially prone to puns)—as if such an effect had "fallen into" the diegetic space of the narrative itself, no longer in the conventional textual form of the epigraph: in its full "telegraphy," we might say. Except, of course, that what supervenes on the line here is not only a grapheme but a *voice*: it is thus a tele*phonic* effect, and one that even sounds like the conventional opening of a telephone conversation: hello!

"Before any appliance bearing the name 'telephone' in modern times," writes Jacques Derrida, "the telephonic *technē* is at work within the voice, multiplying the writing of voices without any instruments. . . ."[3] The telephonic speech-act "Halloa! Below there!" marks at once the instantiation and the multiplication of voice in the Dickensian text, breaching the borderlines of the text itself and those of its characters' psyches. Its very first appearance is an enigma, and as such is wholly uncharacteristic of Dickensian writing: whose words are these? Who is making this primordial telephone call, and who is supposed to answer it? The text deliberately makes the reader participate in the perplexity it oversees in this opening paragraph, with the initial utterance not located, its speaker not identified as "I," until the end of a complex sentence with several sub-clauses: a veritable zigzag path of circumlocution. It is as if the text is miming at its formal level some distortion or blockage of communication, checking the conversational hospitality that by 1866 readers had come to expect from Dickensian narratives (especially those published, like *The Signalman*, during the traditionally hospitable season of Christmas).[4] But if the telephonic first word of *The Signalman* both opens and momentarily suspends its narrative legibility, the remainder of the first paragraph opens up a whole new dimension of obscurity. The narrator observes how the signalman "looked down the Line:"

> There was something remarkable in his manner of doing so, though I could not have said for my life, what. But I know it was remarkable enough to attract my notice, even though his figure was foreshortened and shadowed, down in the deep trench, and mine was high above him, so steeped in the glow of an angry sunset that I had shaded my eyes with my hand before I saw him at all. (*SM* 17)

This shading or masking of the eyes with the hand is the first textual stroke or notch in an uncanny replicative pattern that, as we will see, will characterise the ghostly path or ontological trajectory of *The Signalman*. But the visual distortion presented in this first, vertical non-encounter between the two men already suggests a blurring or duplicity of identity, with "eyes" quietly but insistently punning on the personal pronoun. Thus, the signal-man's apparent confusion on hearing a voice from above is mirrored by the narrator's confused reflection in the face of what he sees: each man, it seems, cannot interpret the enigmatic message of the other, manifested in a "remarkable" but opaque apparition of voice or gaze. Something illegible thus appears in this opening scene of *The Signalman*, something fundamentally at odds with the narrative dimension as such; and that "something"—twice marked as "remarkable" by the narrator—is a *sensory* thing, an "air," a way of seeing, looking or speaking. If we attend again to the opening telephoneme, and its near repetition—"Halloa! Below!"—we can see that this illegible element is in fact a gesture, an act defined by reference to a specific moment and location: what linguists call a "deictic." Here it is worth quoting a remark by Geoffrey Bennington, though its theoretical significance will only become apparent later in our argument:

> Deictics are indubitably part of language, and yet they do not strictly speaking signify: rather they open the 'flat' negativity of the language-system onto the 'deep' negativity of the sensory-field.[5]

In this sense, the "deep trench" of the railway cutting, metonymically linked to the foreshortening or anamorphic distortion of the human image, will figure *another ontology*: a figural dimension of being that is radically at odds with the semiotic space of narrative representation and semantic consistency.

But let us follow the trajectory of the Dickensian text a little further. Having managed to attract the signalman's attention, the narrator now asks him "Is there any path by which I can come down and speak to you?" (174) The implication is clearly that the "deep trench" defining the deictic speech act as displaced (somewhere "up here") in effect *precludes meaningful speech*; and that what is required to open a genuine signifying exchange is a "path" to another, more horizontal or homogenous space. In this desire for a way back to a space of ordinary conversational discourse—of traditional Dickensian hospitality, we might add—the narrator is already responding to the fundamental question raised by this text about the ontological consistency of narrative events, their very narratability; and his response, as we shall see, will be diametrically opposed to that of signalman himself (although in other senses, as we have seen, the two are presented as uncanny doubles). Indeed, it is as if in *The Signalman* Dickens in some sense sets out to explore two contrasting ways of trying to track the thing, the disaster, that happens: the way of speech and the way of writing, we might say, although both of these terms require further clarification. Let us return to the Dickensian text after the narrator's first request for a path back from non-communication to speech:

> He looked up at me without replying, and I looked down at him without pressing him too soon with a repetition of my idle question. Just

then, there came a vague vibration in the earth and air, quickly changing into a violent pulsation, and an oncoming rush that caused me to
start back, as though it had force to draw me down. When such vapour
as rose to my height from this rapid train, had passed me and was
skimming away over the landscape, I looked down again and saw him
re-furling the flag he had shown while the train went by.   (*SM* 174)

The first thing to note about the disruptive interval of modern technology here is how Dickens presents it via the letter as textual graphic: that is,
in the words "vague vibration," "violent," "vapour" the repeated letter "v"
constitutes a figure, a visual pun, for cutting or valley, for inter*val* (and this
graphic use of the letter by Dickens recalls the work of Poe, where Monsieur Valdemar's name both puns *val de mort* and shows its own initial "V"
as figural *val*). The text becomes for a fleeting moment, that is, a place of
shapes to see rather than merely a set of letters to read.

To help us understand what happens here to (and through) the Dickensian text we need to turn briefly to the early work of Jean-François Lyotard,
specifically his book *Discours, figure* (1971). There Lyotard distinguishes
between two incommensurable spaces of signification, that of the language
system (in its Saussurean definition as virtual site of pure semiotic difference)
and that of the body "in the world," conceived of in a phenomenological
sense (by Merleau-Ponty, for instance). Bennington clarifies this distinction
by relating it to literary texts, which are not *only* linguistic spaces, although
they may appear so:

> The space of the text is barely spatial: it is *flat,* and the signs are linked
> according to a simple principle of horizontal contiguity. Against this,
> the visual space of the world is complex, multi-dimensional and *deep,*
> oriented around the spatiality of my own body held within it.[6]

The discursive text is thus "barely" figural, to use Lyotard's terms: indeed as
linguistic event it should in principle be absolutely *non*-spatial, a pure virtual
effect of syntagmatic differences; although in fact—as shown in the famous
"thickness" of the letter unintentionally evoked when Saussure likens the sign
to a sheet of paper—the linguistic event always entails a material or figural
dimension, at least a little "depth." But if the text must therefore always be
spatial and figural it is still only "barely" so: just as it is almost ridiculous to
see the letter "v" as a "picture" of a railway cutting, so the serious reading
eye must in principle disregard or repress the sensory figures of discourse as it
moves to reassemble the semiotic units of the text. To do otherwise would be
to *look* at a text, like a young child, a mad person or someone who does not
know the language (recall how in *Melmoth* the figural status of the epigraph
was bound up with its being written in Greek): to approach discourse, that is,
as a sensory thing and not a semiotic matrix.

The moment of "vague vibration" in Dickens's story, then, opens onto
a graphic, sensory or infantile textual dimension which is forbidden by

the realist discursive narrative to its responsible, grown-up reader. There is already a sense here of the text staging and investigating the borderlines of its own textual interpretability, opening an interval or "deep trench" in its flat discursivity. Indeed, Lyotard's comments on the literary dimension can be seen as directly relevant to the problem of reading which is reflexively staged in *The Signalman*:

> Fiction, which is what makes figure out of text, consists entirely in a play on intervals; the figure is a deformation that imposes a different form onto the disposition of the linguistic unities. This form is not reducible to the constraints of structure.[7]

The very embodiment of semiotic codes in specific artworks, that is, deforms or opens an interval in the structural economy of the linguistic system that makes them interpretable. And this has everything to do with the illegible singularity of voice or body: "Visible and mobile," writes Maurice Merleau-Ponty, "my body is a thing among things; it is caught in the fabric of the world, and its cohesion is that of a thing."[8] The opening paragraph of *The Signalman*, with its "foreshortened and shadowed" human figure, seems indeed to plunge the narrative subject into the "fabric of the world," giving it a dimension of embodied depth irreducible to the "horizontal" plane of meaningful discourse. But what is crucial in the Dickensian text is what happens *between* the narrator's two requests for a path back to a level space of intersubjective dialogue—that is, the "vague vibration in the earth and the air" (174), where the fabric of the world is torn, violated and where for a fragile hallucinatory moment language *becomes like a body*: becomes, that is, "a thing among things," something sensory, visible and no longer legible. There is also, of course, a traumatic dimension implied by the "deep trench" in the Dickensian text that makes it more than simply a phenomenological critique of "flat" narrative discourse; although such a critique, I will argue, can be seen as bound up with its response to the ghostly traumatic interval itself.

How, then, does the narrator react to the "figural" disruption caused by the passing train? "Just then, there came a vague vibration in the earth and air, quickly changing into a violent pulsation, and on oncoming rush that caused me to start back, as though it had force to draw me down" (174). What is crucial is the man's surprise, his unpreparedness for this event—he has just been asking for a way back to a space of intersubjective dialogue, of the hospitable human contact supposedly available in the world of Dickensian fiction—and this impersonal "vibration" makes him *start*, in one of the story's key puns: makes his body respond to the force of the train with its own "pulsation," that is, but also takes his narrative back to *its* "start," to the telephonic strangeness and groundlessness of its opening. The narrator is seized by or plunged into a momentary "vertical" opening in the ground of interpretable reality, a phantasmatic void "down in the deep trench" at the indivisible deictic apex of the letter "v:" for a vertiginous or "precipitate" (175) moment, he is plunged into the traumatic cutting of "world" occupied by the signalman.

But the narrator persists in his search for a way back to the horizontal topology of novelistic dialogue:

> I repeated my inquiry. After a pause, during which he seemed to regard me with fixed attention, he motioned with his rolled-up flag towards a point on my level, some two or three hundred yards distance. I called down to him, "All right!" and made for that point. There, by dint of looking closely about me, I found a rough zig-zag descending path notched out, which I followed. (*SM* 174–175)

The signalman's response is thus not discursive but deictic; as such, it "does not strictly speaking signify," to recall Bennington's remark, but involves the bodily, sensory dimension—note the triple inscription of the gaze: "he *seemed* to *regard* me with fixed *attention*"—a dimension already remarked in the opening paragraph as enigmatic and therefore "remarkable" (174). Hence, during the spatiotemporal interval of the zig-zag path, the narrator duly recalls "a singular air of reluctance or compulsion with which he had pointed out the path" (175). The signalman's signal thus opens up not only epistemological but *ontological* uncertainty, its groundless "air" a sign either of reluctance or compulsion, hesitation or impetuosity, plus or minus: an undecidable oscillation or zigzag of antithetical senses.

The zigzag path that takes the narrator from "the natural world" (175) to the moment of face-to-face contact with the signalman is the story's key figure (in Lyotard's sense). To see this, we need to *look* at the textual trajectory in quite a strange way:

> When I came down low enough upon the zigzag descent, to see him again, I *saw that he was* standing between the rails on the way by which the train had lately passed [. . .] I resumed my downward way, and, stepping out upon the level of the railroad and drawing nearer to him, *saw that he was* a dark sallow man . . . His post *was* in as solitary and dismal a place as ever I *saw*. (*SM* 175; italics mine)

As the text zigzags away from the natural world, down into the phantasmatic non-world of the signalman, we see its language undergoing a peculiar semantic "cutting" of its own. Just as the figural interval of the passing train was marked *à la lettre* by the letter "v," so down in the cutting the chiasmic symmetry of "saw" and "was," repeated three times in the space of a mere fifteen lines, marks the uncanny *exposure* of words, the unmasking of signifiers as things seen. We can picture this zigzag path of occult designification as follows:

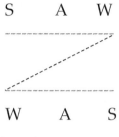

Figure 2.1

As a figure, the zigzag is not simply a visible phenomenon that interrupts or occludes the legibility of the narrative discourse: "saw that he was" remains no more than a straightforward lexical unit—provided, that is, we restrict our reading to the habitual register of realist discourse. It is only once we have seen how the text poses the question of the figure—as a sensory dimension at odds with the flat discursivity of realist narrative—that we can begin to discern the ghostly apparition (and this is probably on a second reading: like Dickens's narrator, we have to visit *The Signalman* twice).

It is this figural apparition, at odds with, aslant or athwart, the ostensibly verisimilar narrative, that constitutes the "abeyance" of the signifier we saw at the level of diegetic content in the resuscitation of Riderhood in *Our Mutual Friend*: there, however, the Dickensian narrator actively took control of that eclipse of signification by an apparition, playfully dramatising it as an "unrealistic" interlude in the novel's discourse, a momentary specular estrangement or suspension of an otherwise consistent narrative world. The radical, proto-modernist truth-event of *The Signalman* can be seen in the fact that it has no such novelistic narrative framing buffer: the "unrealistic" interlude it presents coincides entirely with the fragmentary text itself, which thus offers no way back to "the natural world" (175), to the flat representational horizon of a consistent narrative universe. In this sense, to use Badiou's language, *The Signalman* takes place "on the edge of the void," at the point where "the inconsistency of Being fractures the consistencies of presentation," as Andrew Gibson puts it.[9]

Once we have perceived the zigzag reversibility of "saw" and "was," at any rate, we can start to trace its occurrence as spectral figure throughout the text. From the very beginning, the uncanny reversal "I [saw/was] him" is writing itself; as can be seen if we look again at the first scene in the cutting, where

> . . . his figure was foreshortened and shadowed, down in the deep trench, and mine was high above him, so steeped in the glow of an angry sunset that I had shaded my eyes with my hand before I saw him at all. (*SM* 174)

Surely, if we pause for a moment over this description, something odd must strike us. It is after all not the signalman's but the *narrator*'s figure that is "steeped in the glow" of the sunset; so why should it be *him* and not the man below in the dark trench, who needs to shade his eyes against the bright sky? "I saw him" thus seems to topple over, as it were, into "I was him:" the narrator is somehow impossibly both eye and object, both up and down, zig and zag. When he finally gets to introduce himself to the signal-man face to face, he reports what he says as follows: "In me, he merely saw a man who had been shut up within narrow limits all his life. . ." (176). Again, "saw" reverses into "was:" for the words are an uncannily apt description of the man being addressed, whose "post," insistently figured in vertical images, is indeed "shut up within narrow limits" in a cutting "extremely deep and unusually precipitate" (175).

We can interpret this reversible figure of saw/was in terms of the guest/host relation we have been exploring as a central crux of the literary apparition. The narrator is supposedly positioned as "our" host, the implicit controlling centre of narrative legibility, but he is obviously—at the diegetic level—the guest of the signalman, an initially unwelcome intruder on his signifying space, both his "cutting" and his "box." Indeed, as the source of the story's opening voice, with its "telephonic" intrusion on the signal-man's "line," the narrator may perhaps appear to be the only "real" *ghost* to appear in this ghost story. And that, of course, is precisely how the sig-nalman first perceives him.

Let us look more closely at the uncanny mirror-scene of the encounter between the men down in the railway cutting. The narrator tells us of his response to the signalman's "curious look" in the direction of a red light by the tunnel:

> That light was part of his charge? Was it not?
> He answered in a low voice, "Don't you know it is?"
> The monstrous thought came into my mind as I perused the fixed eyes and the saturnine face, that this was a spirit, not a man. I have speculated since, whether there may have been infection in his mind.
> In my turn, I stepped back. But in making the action, I detected in his eyes some latent fear of me. This put the monstrous thought to flight.
> "You look at me," I said, forcing a smile, "as if you had a dread of me."
> "I was doubtful," he returned, "whether I had seen you before."
> (*SM* 176)

It is diabolically hard here, at every turn, to distinguish between the two spectators: the speculative "infection in his mind" is matched by the "monstrous thought" infecting "my mind" via the specular: each eye "was doubtful," saw double. Like the eponymous protagonist we meet in Poe's story "William Wilson" (1839), the narrator of *The Signalman* seems to encounter none other than *himself*, as the semantic coherence of his identity runs into an incomprehensible "confusion of hands and heads" (182), an impossible zigzag or oscillation of eyes, minds, bodies, spirits—in sum, a disastrous breach of the rational intersubjective space that supposedly forms the basis of an intelligible, consensual reality.

After this catastrophic head-to-head encounter, then, what hope is there of an ensuing narrative with any chance of amusing the reader, of offering the stylistic hospitality that had become Dickens's festive trademark? It is here that the signalman's "box" is crucial, for it provides a kind of supplementary fragment of "world" within the ontological "cutting" or phantasmatic vortex of the narrative setting. As the narrator labours to convince the signalman of his (the narrator's) plausible verisimilitude, an ephemeral intersubjective "opening" seems to occur between them: "His manner cleared, like my own" (176). This allows the signalman to show a vestige of "human" hospitality:

> He took me into his box, where there was a fire, a desk for an official book in which he had to make certain entries, a telegraphic instrument with its dial face and needles, and the little bell of which he had spoken.   (*SM* 177)

The box seems to be a kind of minimalist home, with its basic furniture and domestic hearth (although more prominence is given to the office equipment); and in it the signalman can therefore host a minimal kind of signifying exchange, implicitly but pointedly claiming, according to the narrator, to be a kind of essential, stripped-down human subject, "nothing but what I found him" (178). What is clear, however, is that the provisional hospitality offered here is precisely that: only provisional or supplementary, a mere way of passing the time; and as such is clearly felt by the signalman, much to the chatty narrator's distress, to be essentially trivial or meaningless, a discourse about nothing. This is most evident in his automaton-like subjection to the mechanical temporality of the telegraphic ghost-voice:

> He was several times interrupted by the little bell, and had to read off messages, and send replies. Once, he had to stand without the door, and display a flag as a train passed, and make some verbal communication to the driver. In the discharge of his duties I observed him to be remarkably exact and vigilant, breaking off his discourse at a syllable, and remaining silent until what he had to do was done.   (*SM* 178)

The signalman's duties are "flat," in the Lyotardian sense: they lack discursive "thickness," have no immediate phenomenological sense or embodied reference to perceived human reality; but instead they disrupt the intersubjective temporal milieu of that reality, making the subject suspend his speech, with surreal exactitude, in mid-syllable. In other words, while the box may at first appear to be a welcome shelter from the hostile gothic abyss outside, it turns out to be no more than a telephonic earpiece or ghostly receiver, a vibrating apparatus sensitive to transmissions from beyond the borderlines of human community, outside the space of hospitable signifying interaction.

Indeed, what defines the signalman's distance from the world, his dislocation from the rational space of intersubjective discourse, is given a distinct textual figure by Dickens: that of *silent apparition*. The crucial point of rupture in the provisionally "natural" host-guest exchange inside the box is the signalman's double interruption of his own discourse in response to the silent bell that signals the arrival of the ghost and leaves an "inexplicable air upon him" (178). And the narrator, keen to re-establish the ground rules of "Dickensian" narrative hospitality, returns to the question of this ghostly telepathic transmission on his second visit. The signalman has just described how the ghost "rings my little bell:"

> I caught at that. "Did it ring your bell yesterday evening when I was here, and you went to the door?"
> "Twice."
> "Why, see," said I, "how your imagination misleads you. My eyes were on the bell, and my ears were open to the bell, and if I am a living man, it did NOT ring at those times. No, nor at any other time, except when it was rung in the natural course of physical things by the station communicating with you."
> He shook his head. "I have never made a mistake as to that yet, sir. I have never confused the spectre's ring with the man's. The ghost's ring is a strange vibration in the bell that it derives from nothing else, and I have not asserted that the bell stirs to the eye. I don't wonder that you failed to hear it. But I heard it."
> "And did the spectre seem to be there, when you looked out?"
> "It *was* there." (*SM* 183)

Note how this last phrase replays the reversible figure of saw/was: the "realistic" explanation, that what the subject "saw" had no guarantee of real existence, is doubled by the "mad" singularity of the telepathic apparition, an ontological transmission with none of the signifier's debatable equivocity. Although the narrator's "if I am a living man" ironically undercuts his efforts to invoke "the natural course of physical things" (he has forgotten that here in the signalman's cutting everything is haunted, estranged from being merely itself by a spectral double), he is determined to salvage some minimal ground of intersubjective rationality, some possibility of "communicating with you" (183). But the signalman sets him right with almost scholarly precision: the spectral vibration "derives from nothing else:" it has no truck with the signifying Other, nothing to do with discursive communication; but rather "*I* heard it," with the italicised pronoun again doubling "eye." *Eye heard it* indeed encapsulates the telepathic certitude at the point where a hospitable world circumscribed by equivocal signification collapses: the spectral point of the ghostly interval.

The text itself, moreover, is marked by this exposure or unveiling of its signifying dimension, as we have already seen in the zig-zag figure of saw/was. Another instance of this figural or telepathic exposure of the signifier comes at a deictic or asemic crux in the narrator's first encounter with the signalman, just after the latter has doubted "whether I had seen you before:"

> "Where?"
> He pointed to the red light he had looked at.
> "There?" I said.
> Intently watchful of me, he replied (but without sound), Yes.   (*SM* 176)

The original Dickensian text of *All the Year Round* prints no quotation marks around the last word here (although of course modern editions often 'restore' the missing punctuation). The question is, if we're true to the text as Dickens deliberately printed it, *how* was the word spoken, not merely very softly but actually "without sound," without being spoken? Like the spectral vibration of the silent bell, only *eye heard it*: the apparition speaks a telepathic language of the eye, a showing or shading of the spectral voice (recall phantom-Riderhood "dropping his hoarse voice, and shading it with his hand," *OMF* 196).

At both the formal and the diegetic level, then, *The Signalman* speaks a language of the eye. When the narrator asks his host how on earth he passes his time down here in the desolate cutting, the reply is a revelation:

> Regarding those many long and lonely hours of which I seemed to make so much, he could only say that the routine of his life had shaped itself into that form, and he had grown used to it. He had taught himself a language down here—if only to know it by sight, and to have formed his own crude ideas of its pronunciation, could be called learning it. He had also worked at fractions and decimals, and tried a little algebra; but he was, and had been as a boy, a poor hand at figures.
>
> (*SM* 176–177)

The signalman has therefore learnt a language but only "to know it by sight:" a language, that is, wholly distinct from any linguistic community or real speech act, reduced to a visible surface or speculative utterance, hence deprived of any actual intersubjective meaning. Like the "strange vibration" in the ghostly bell, in fact, this language comes *ex nihilo*, "derives from nothing else," has no origin or ground: it can thus have no place in the social discourse of reality, no communicative point or end. And it is no accident that after this unreal, specular language the next link in the metonymic chain of the signalman's discourse should be *mathematics*: the ontological space of "figures," a space where things can be put together or divided, shown but not said.

What we need to pause over here is this sense of an "algebraic" or non-communicational space extimate to language. Why does the signalman spend his long and lonely hours doing sums and inventing a private language, spoken only according to "his own crude ideas"? When he is cornered into admitting, in his spectral "peculiar low voice" (179) that he is "troubled" (178) by something, the key is his resistance to saying more:

> "It is very difficult to impart, sir. It is very, very difficult to speak of. If ever you make me another visit, I will try to tell you." (*SM* 178)

Whatever has happened to the signalman has troubled not just one man's mind but the very space of discursive communication, the consensual basis of community or intersubjective identity. The result is that the signalman's cutting is defined by an ontology *hostile to the Other*: there is no room here for the metaphorical duplicities of speech, the roundabout ways of the signifier. The signalman therefore specifically forbids the narrator to "call out" when he reaches the end of the zigzag path back up to the realistic "natural" world: the language of the cutting can only be apparitional, a signal-language, only for the eye ("I'll show my white light, sir:" 179). And this hostility to the signifying Other is reiterated a moment later by the signalman's literalism, his defiant rejection of the narrator's tendency to dissolve letters into the semiotic fluidity of paraphrase. "Let me ask you a parting question," says the signalman:

> "What made you cry, "Halloa! Below there!" tonight?"
> "Heaven knows," said I, "I cried something to that effect—"
> "Not to that effect, sir. Those were the very words. I know them well."
> (*SM* 179)

Again, this interruption of paraphrase is an effect of *figure* impacting on *discours*, to use Lyotard's terms. As Bill Readings puts it, "An understanding of narrative as figure [means that] the scene of narration insistently returns to, and disrupts, any attempt to reduce the act of narration to a described content or effected communication."[10] Our narrator is clearly a staunch advocate of "described content:" large sections of his conversations with the signalman are "condensed" (177) summaries instead of direct speech. But the text unfailingly reminds us of the inadequacy of any such attempt to "see through" or dissolve away the singular instance of narration: "To such purpose I spoke to him; but I am far from sure of the terms I used, for, besides that I am not happy in opening any conversation, there was something in the man that daunted me" (176). This discursive vagueness about the detail of signification contrasts with the signalman's algebraic precision: "Those were the very words."

We should explore this contrast between a "discursive" narrator and a "figural" signalman a little further. First, we can note how the narrator seldom asks or declares anything *once*—his speech-act always tends to double or re-present itself: there are two "Halloas" at the opening, two initial questions ("I repeated my inquiry:" 174) and his key questions are double: "With what? What is your trouble?" (178), "But nothing followed? Nothing came of this?" (182), "O how did this happen, how did this happen?" (186). The signalman himself seems to have picked up on (and even perhaps found slightly annoying) this habitual double-talk of the narrator's: "I have made up my mind, sir," he declares on their second meeting, "that you shall not have to ask me twice what troubles me" (179). The narrator already has, of course, asked him that question twice; but what the signalman now proposes is to eliminate doubt, signifying doubleness or equivocity—to attempt, that is, to present an ontological figure that is hostile to the flat discursivity of speech, an unspeakably "deep trench" in representable reality.

Now, the signalman's account must of course inhabit discourse—like the narrator and everyone else, he is a subject unconsciously divided from full self-identity by the signifier; but his performance is punctuated, or rather *punctured*, by deictic signs irreducible to discourse, figures in excess of the narrative account: "I followed his action with my eyes" (180) says the narrator, himself adding an interpretation of the action, seeking to include it in the narratable dimension. The signalman thus *acts out* his narrative, adding an extra figure to the account, a figure that remains strange before a supplementary gloss is added to make it fit into the logic of the narrative. It is this performativity that disturbs the flat surface of representation, introducing points of *presentation*, figures non-veiled or dis-closed by signifying space-time (we could see the latter as marked by the replicative prefix: "re-"). There are indeed strange verbal traces of this non-verbal figurality—"I looked all round the red light with my own red light" (180), recalling the earlier "he stepped back one step" (175): the figure can only be figured, the asemic or indivisible point only named, nonsensically, as circular repetition. What is alien to signifying replication, in other words, the singular thing on the edge of the void, can only feature in the account as an empty supplement or pointless loop in time.

But the performativity of the singular in the signalman's discourse is also a matter of the body, and especially of bodily gesture. Throughout the conversation, the narrator is constantly being *touched* by the performance. The first of these touches seems, at first sight, figurative enough: "Resisting the slow touch of a frozen finger tracing out my spine, I showed him how that this figure must be a deception of his sense of sight. . ." (180). But the duplicitous proximity of "finger" and "figure" links the two halves of this sentence, so that the sensible hypothesis of the visible figure being a mere sensory delusion is uncannily doubled, dislocated by the invisible finger's sensory reality (or is it just a "deception of his sense"?). In the ensuing conversation, real and figurative touches are increasingly hard to tell apart: first "he slowly added these words, touching my arm;" then "a disagreeable shudder crept over me" (181). These rhetorical-actual touches build up to a kind of deictic climax, with the signalman "again laying his hand upon my arm" (181) and then, after the narrator's "But nothing followed? Nothing came of this?" "He touched me on the arm with his forefinger twice or thrice, giving a ghastly nod each time" (182). The ghastly nod is another ghostly or silent *yes*, a sign for *aye* in the language of the eye. But what we should not overlook is the *algebraic* significance of the performative speech-act: why do the ghostly finger and silent *aye* occur "twice or thrice"?

There is a distinct, insistent algebraic subtext to be read in *The Signalman*. The recurrence of the number two is the first thing to strike us: two opening "Halloas" are followed by two questions about the path; then later the signalman "twice broke off" (178) his speech and declares "you shall not have to ask me twice" (179); and finally, after his second visit, the narrator leaves "at two in the morning" (185). But it is not so much the number two as the doubtful addition of *one more*, a ghostly third that haunts the narrative, marking an underlying symptomatic or non-discursive significance. The signalman's first gesture with his flag is to point "some two *or three* hundred yards" away (175); he nods "twice *or thrice*" (181); then reports that the ghost has appeared twice and "is not to be doubted *this third time*" (184). This spectral third element indeed entails what the number two, the sign of replication or re-presentation, must always leave out: an indivisible remainder. What the endless series of pairs in the narrative cannot account for, that is, is *presentation itself*, the original ontological ground on which what is to be counted first appears, becomes manifest as such. This third element is therefore zero, "counts for nothing," but at the same time it is all-important, the underlying numerical condition of the whole account, whose very ontological consistency thus depends on it.

The flat narrative discourse of *The Signalman* is therefore doubled by a line of numbers that do not signify (only) on the plane of that discourse but (also) figure the ontological void of its very opening, its emergence as an 'algebraic' space where things can be counted or figured at all. It is this empty ground of representation that is marked self-reflexively by the text as its *literal* dimension, the site of "the very words" which the signalman invokes to counter the narrator's airy talk of having said "something to that effect" (179). Narrative discourse flattens out and covers up the deictic singularity of its original textual dimension, discounting as utterly implausible the traumatic sensory opening which is retro-foreclosed by its own discursivity.

It is because the signalman has *seen* that figural "nothing" excluded from the narratable account of things, indeed, that he appears as a haunted man, a spectral figure. Let us look again at the narrator's first clear picture of him:

He had his left hand at his chin, and that left elbow rested on his right
hand crossed over his breast. His attitude was one of such expectation
and watchfulness, that I stopped a moment, wondering at it.

(*SM* 175)

There is clearly something wrong with this "attitude," something unnat-
ural or unrealistic, as if it constituted more of a *sign* than an ordinary
bodily posture; indeed, we could see the alternate crossing of the signalman's limbs as yet another of the "figural" zigzag paths in the text. And the
man's demeanour becomes no less "remarkable" when the narrator gets up
close to him: "Before he stirred, I was near enough to him to have touched
him. Not even then removing his eyes from mine, he stepped back one
step and lifted his hand" (175). The signalman has unlearned, as it were,
the unconscious bodily protocol that ordinarily regulates intersubjective
reality, makes it liveable: the zigzag disposition of his limbs and gestures is
abnormal, surreal—indeed, more than that, it expresses a degree of *hostility* to the "normal" space of communication, an outright disbelief in the
pacifying neutrality of the big Other. The signalman's problem is that he
knows, as the Lacanian formula has it, that "the Other does not exist:"
what has become visible to him is something foreclosed from reality as it
is narrated and lived outside the cutting, and this revelation has exposed
that "reality" as a precarious, incomplete discursive fabrication. The conventional space of narrative representation therefore cannot provide a just
response to the "dreadful calamity" (184) of the apparition. What is nota-
ble here is how the Dickensian text shows us this disbelief in the Other not
only in the signalman's language but on the *surface* of his body, through
the "inexplicable air upon him" (178), the enigmatic, 'autistic' disposition
of gesture and gaze.

The silent apparition of *The Signalman*, then—occurring in, through
and ultimately *as* the text itself—is a fundamental breach of the space and
time of discourse, the site of narrative legibility and coherent identity. What
Lyotard sees as the "interval" between the flat plane of discourse and an
unaccountable figure—deictic or sensory "pulsation"—is also made manifest in this text as a disturbance of the space between subjects, an interruption of the topological horizon that allows the fiction of a consensual
or 'hospitable' reality to be maintained. When the signalman disconcerts
the narrator by "assuming that there could be no serious question of fact
between us" (184), the text is silently showing how the discursive plane of
intersubjectivity collapses into the uncanny "depth" occupied in turn by
narrator, signalman and ghost, where each imitates the zigzag gesture or
silent vibration, the shading or showing of eye and voice, always performed
or imitated first by the Other.

What is also clear, however, is that while the figural disruption of legibility staged in *The Signalman* has the effect of repeatedly confusing the site
of its characters and its narrative elements, there is nevertheless a crucial

difference inscribed in the text between two divergent ways of responding to the traumatic event endlessly taking place there. The narrator's path, as we have suggested at various points, is to try to salvage the discursive economy of traditional narrative hospitality, both with his rather Podsnappish "scientific" explanations and his efforts to obtain reliable, narratable material through "rational" cross-examination. By contrast, we might characterise the signalman's path as an experimental deviation from the 'readerly' habits of novelistic discourse, with his secret algebra and private language emerging as possible ways to figure out an ontological dimension he has glimpsed or sensed outside the "hospitable" space of narrative legibility. There can be little doubt that the Dickensian text itself has chosen to follow the latter of these two paths.

In other words, for the Dickens of *The Signalman*, whether or not we see him (as Jill Matus does) as still haunted by the traumatic spectrality of the Staplehurst railway disaster, what emerges in this story is something that can no longer inhabit the legible space of "Dickensian" narrative hospitality. The spectral apparition introduces things that should be properly and responsibly warded off or covered up by that space, things with their own uncanny algebra of sensation and apprehension. Above all, this sense of apparition as an ontological rupture of discursive identity makes *The Signalman* untimely: makes it not simply a response to modern trauma but a ghostly "tele-effect" anticipating the technical experiments of literary modernism: "I telegraphed both ways" (180).

POSTSCRIPT: THIN GHOSTS AND FAT BOYS

"The name of Charles Dickens," wrote J. A. Hammerton in 1910 without a hint of irony, has become "synonymous with that of Father Christmas."[11] The run-away success in 1843 of *A Christmas Carol* (that "enjoyable nightmare," as Chesterton calls it[12]), which Dickens subtitled "A Ghost Story of Christmas," had launched its author on a series of four more "Christmas books" during that decade, culminating in the spooky *The Haunted Man* (1848); and from 1850 onwards, as editor first of *Household Words* then of *All the Year Round*, Dickens made sure that the special Christmas number of each periodical always contained a "supernatural" element, with usually at least one ghost story by himself or another writer.

This coincidence of ghost stories and "festive cheer" may be in fact little more, then, than the result of Dickens's shrewd sense of how to create and maintain a reading public; but almost immediately critics sought to probe the deeper significance of what Chesterton calls "the kinship between gaiety and the grotesque" evident in these Yuletide Dickensian publications.[13] "Dickens's identification with Christmas," remarks Catherine Waters, "was noted by his reviewers" and soon became "a major source for [his] reputation as prophet of the hearth."[14] But if Dickens saw himself as a Victorian

Santa Claus, a benevolent guardian of the bourgeois home, nonetheless at least one of the gifts in his festive bag each year was distinctly unhomely, *unheimlich*—and none more so, as we have seen, than the uncanny tale he delivered from *Mugby Junction* in 1866.

Before we move on to explore in the next chapter how the self-invented Dickensian "tradition" of ghosts at Christmas was taken up and adapted by M. R. James, we need to pause a little further over the ambiguous negotiation of "gaiety and the grotesque" around the ghostly in Dickens. The first Christmas number of *Household Words* edited by Dickens in 1850—and intended as a veritable manifesto of "*Carol* philosophy," he told his friend Charles Forster[15]—included under the title "A Christmas Tree" an extended eulogy of all things festive, with children, toy theatres, music, dancing and so on; but also with a long meditation on ghost stories, a discourse indeed that threatens to become literally *interminable*:

> There is no end to the old houses, with resounding galleries, and dismal state-bedchambers, and haunted wings shut up for many years, through which we may ramble, with an agreeable creeping up our back, and encounter any number of ghosts, but (it is worthy of remark perhaps) reducible to a very few general types and classes; for ghosts have little originality, and "walk" in a beaten track. . . .[16]

It is arguably, indeed, the very non-originality of the ghost story, the endless citationality of its genre, that makes its nightmares enjoyable (to recall Chesterton's description of *A Christmas Carol*). Like Christmas itself, in fact, the ghost story is a feast of cliché, its capacity to disturb or innovate fatally hampered by the instant legibility of its stylistic conventions, its "beaten track" of readymade apparitions, non-mysterious signs and predictable revelations. And just as "there is no end" to these ghostly clichés, so Dickens's recital of them begins to suffer from the same non-closure, as a seemingly unstoppable flow of paragraphs ensues, each starting with "Or. . ." and adding yet another well-known uncanny scenario, before at last the discourse simply abandons any pretence at narrative coherence and fades into a hazy diorama of festive goodwill.

What becomes visible here is how a problem of textual *excess* in the generic background of the ghost story haunts, so to speak, the genre itself, threatening to undermine its very identity as serious literature. The trouble with the "accredited ghostly circumstances," as Dickens ironically dubs them in *The Haunted House* (his Christmas story for 1859), is indeed their sheer *abundance*; or rather the carnivalesque dimension bound up with that abundance, with the potentially endless proliferation of "ghostly circumstances," scenes, properties, traits, outfits, *stuff*. While all of these material features are implicitly coded as "excess," supplementary "circumstances" that merely "stand around" the ghostly thing itself, it would nevertheless be impossible, it is implied, to write an effective, "accredited" ghost story without them. And of course, as is already hinted by the Dickensian irony of "accredited ghostly circumstances," this excess materiality is *enjoyable*, like a self-indulgent festive treat. This means, in effect, that the ghost story as genre constantly threatens to digress from itself, as it were, to tip over into comedy as the sheer repetitive enjoyment of its narrative conventions smothers whatever uncanny apparition is supposed to lurk at its core. The appearance of the ghost in literature thus coincides, it seems, with an ungovernable rhetorical excess, an unstoppable carnival of verbiage that threatens the very possibility of generic coherence or even narrative closure.

The Haunted House of 1859 is perhaps Dickens's most flagrant exercise in festive ghostly pastiche, with the comic potential of the "beaten track" of literary convention in the ghost story quite deliberately exploited. Intriguingly, however, what will spell out the unspeakable dimension of the apparition in *The Signalman* can already be glimpsed in this earlier text—namely a ghostly language of the eye; but here that language is lit for garish comic effect. The narrator makes the conventional enquiry at the local inn about the legend of the haunted house:

> "This gentleman wants to know," said the landlord, "if anything's seen at the Poplars."
>
> "Ooded woman with a howl," said Ikey, in a state of great freshness.
>
> "Do you mean a cry?"
>
> "I mean a bird, Sir."
>
> "A hooded woman with an owl. Dear me! Did you ever see her?"
>
> "I seen the howl."[17]

Here the apparitional voice or visible utterance—"I seen the howl"—emerges through the stage comedy of the cockney accent; but it will return non-comically as the spectral call, heard only by the eye, of the signalman's bell. And if the 1866 story will mark the phantom vibration of a passing train with the visible-invisible letter V, Dickens is already alive in *The Haunted House* to the uncanny comedy of ghostly letters once freed from the constraints of discourse: "So, from the first, I was haunted by the letter B" reports the narrator of his stay in "Master B's chamber."[18] But of course in this earlier text the letter does not figure an unspeakable "cutting" in and of narratability, as it will in *The Signalman*; on the contrary, here the letter B serves only as a matrix of enjoyable textual *excess*, a device for generating an endless comic proliferation of additional signifiers (". . .like a Bounding Billiard Ball"). We could even take the contrasting letters themselves—the thin pointed V and the bulbous B—as graphic emblems of, on one side, the narrowing-down of representation to an unspeakable spectral point, and on the other its curvaceous expansion into an irrepressible bubble or babble of dialogic variation.

It seems, then, that the ghost story has to tread carefully if it is not to stray from the narrow path of the truly ghostly. What is non-original about the literary ghost—all of its traditional textual paraphernalia—entails the constant possibility of a formal collapse into parody: that is, into the *wrong kind of enjoyment* for the genre. Indeed, the enjoyment we have seen marked in *The Haunted House* by the bulging letter B constitutes something truly Bakhtinian; involving addition, digression, dilation, laughter, excess, mingling bodies—involving, in other words, two of the best-known antidotes to anything ghostly: comedy and sex.

Now, the opposition of B and V, of the carnivalesque-comic body and the silent-uncanny apparition, is clearly in one sense a matter of different literary genres. "Our modern attraction to short stories," writes Chesterton in his 1906 study of Dickens,

> is not an accident of form; it is the sign of a real sense of fleetingness and fragility; it means that existence is only an impression, and, perhaps, only an illusion.[19]

The natural habitat of the ghost would seem in this light to be the short story, the domain of the glimpse, of the fleeting impression. We might think of Poe's insistence on the need to make the "tale of terror" short enough to be devoured in a single sitting, but see it now as a writerly privileging of textual *restraint*: as Poe sensed, in other words, only a strategic *lack* of narrative signifiers, not their excessive proliferation, will allow the literary spectre to show itself.

But we need to understand this generic distinction not simply in terms of textual quantity. The novel itself, conceived in terms of our "B for Bakhtin" characterization of it, is implicitly committed to a construction of the world as an essentially *social* milieu, where the empirical or sensory is not left stranded at the level of isolated sensory impression but caught up in, supported by, a structure of consensual co-existence and rational discursivity. In this sense, the ineluctable "hospitality" of the Dickensian novel has an implicitly moral and political orientation, privileging the crowded (and usually urban) site of interacting subjects and intercommunicating texts, as against the supposed purity of an isolated lyrical consciousness. And this hospitality of the novel would seem, by the same token, to make it essentially *in*hospitable toward the ghost, that unhomely intruder; for the pleasures of hospitality can be seen as the quintessentially Dickensian pleasures: of communication and consumption, of being (with) the other and eating (with) the other.

Orwell famously rebuked Dickens for what we might nowadays term his excessive Bakhtinian proclivities, his tendency to turn every literary performance into something of a festive pantomime:

> As a novelist his natural fertility greatly hampers him, because the burlesque, which he is never able to resist, is constantly breaking into what ought to be serious situations.[20]

We are thus given yet another reading of the bulging B that comes to haunt the narrator of *The Haunted House*, this time as "burlesque:" what breaks into the serious situation or ghostly house is *laughter*, irrepressible, excessive writerly pleasure. The fine line separating the uncanny from the comic is constantly breached by Dickens, in Orwell's view, due to his "natural fertility" as a novelist, in other words his sheer libidinal investment in style.

We should thus in principal be able to map this formal opposition between novel and short story, burlesque-bodily B and restrained-spectral V, onto the two Dickensian ghost scenes we previously explored; since the first of these, the resuscitation of Riderhood, takes place in a novel, while the second, *The Signalman*, is framed as a short story. But in tracing the Deleuzean sense of the scene from *Our Mutual Friend*, we saw how the immanence of an ontological singularity there took place "beyond good and evil," as a suspension or parenthesis of ordinary diegetic sense; so that it is only when Riderhood comes back to himself, resumes his place as dubious "waterside character," that the signifying laws of the novel, momentarily eclipsed by the advent of the vocal-psychical ghost, are able to resume their normal "social" function. What we have identified as narrative hospitality—that which gives a novel's discourse its semantic consistency as well as its "natural fertility," making it a space of intersubjective rationality as well as of textual pleasure—is thus gravely troubled by the singular or "original" apparition of a life, of ontological immanence. The "double-barrelled" (*OMF* 195) voice of the ghost, as we saw, figures its double inscription, both inside the space of narrative, with all its rich intertextual resources of tradition and convention, and at the same time *beyond* that pleasurable space, at the level of an impersonal or inhuman being, a being impossible to draw out into meaningful, hospitable discourse.

It is not the Dickensian novel, then—at least not *Our Mutual Friend*—that makes the ghost legible and laughable, that smoothly includes it in a hospitable scene of rhetorical pleasure (like Master B's chamber in "The Haunted House"); and nor, of course, is it a textual fragment like *The Signalman*. What appears in and as the latter text can in fact be seen, as we argued, to be *figural*, in Lyotard's sense—that is, to be radically incommensurate with the interpretive space of discourse as such.[21] But if the true ghost can never inhabit a "fat" discourse of pleasurable dialogic proliferation, there remains the problem of the ghost story itself as established genre, with its "beaten track" of convention and artistic cliché. How can the ghost, as singular ontological manifestation on the edge of the void, in excess of consistent reality, be effectively hosted by a narrative conventionally defined through "accredited circumstances" or generic clichés that threaten to reduce its ghostly essence to a laughable travesty?

Part II
Guests ◊ Ghosts

3   Broken Lineage
M. R. James

UNSETTLING ONTOGRAPHY

"The prototypes of all the best ghost stories," claimed Montague Rhodes James (1862–1936), "were written in the [eighteen] sixties and seventies."[1] James's own stories, which he began to write a generation after those dates, do seem to bear an unmistakably Dickensian hallmark; although in fact the Victorian "tradition" of ghostly entertainment at Christmas they apparently recall was still then a fairly recent invention, dating only from James's own childhood and the popularity of periodicals such as Dickens's *Household Words* and *All the Year Round*. By the 1890s, however, Dr James, eminent biblical scholar and Dean of King's College Cambridge, certainly did not intend his ghost stories for a mass audience of the kind attracted by the Victorian magazines of his youth; indeed, the first of those stories (written around 1893) was meant merely as a bit of end-of-term fun, a Christmas entertainment for some college friends.[2] In due course, however, the Jamesian ghost story was to become a celebrated annual college institution, and its author's fame began to spread to the outside world; so in 1904 the first volume of the stories duly appeared under the donnish title *Ghost Stories of an Antiquary*. Though writing for a much smaller audience than his great Victorian predecessor, then, by the early twentieth century James had become an inheritor of the "traditional"—and thus the Dickensian— Yuletide ghost story. As we will see, however, the ostensibly retrospective, conservative nature of what James called the "antiquarian ghost story" belies some of its very "modern" preoccupations and techniques.

If we start by looking briefly at a story written long after *Ghost Stories of an Antiquary*, entitled "A Warning to the Curious" (1925), we will find an implicit recollection of the Dickensian origins or "prototypes" of James's stories. The narrator begins by presenting the tale's setting (Aldeburgh, on the Suffolk coast, disguised as "Seaburgh"), a place "not very different now from what I remember it to have been when I was a child;" and he mentions "Marshes intersected by dykes to the south, recalling the early chapters of *Great Expectations*" (CG 343). It is worth pausing over this allusion to Dickens, bearing in mind James's idea that the foundational texts of the ghost story genre come from the 1860s and 1870s (*Great Expectations* was published in 1861). What happens in the early chapters of Dickens's novel?

Almost immediately, with the protagonist having barely told us his name, we have one of the most famous scenes in Dickens: the encounter in the graveyard between the young orphan Pip and "a fearful man" who will turn out to be the escaped convict Magwitch.[3] But what is crucial to see is how this encounter, terrifying though it is for the young boy, radically differs from the ghostly encounters we have been exploring in *Our Mutual Friend* and *The Signalman*. What characterised the latter, as we saw, was a momentary eclipse of intersubjective reality—in the phantasmal apparition of Riderhood or the enigmatic zigzag posture of the signalman—that in effect jeopardised the very possibility of communication, cast into doubt the whole ontological basis of human community. It is by contrast precisely that basic communality which is repeatedly *affirmed* in the opening chapters of *Great Expectations*; as we can see from the very first appearance of Magwitch:

> "Hold your noise!" cried a terrible voice, as a man started up from among the graves at the side of the church porch. "Keep still, you little devil, or I'll cut your throat!"
>
> A fearful man, all in coarse grey, with a great iron on his leg. A man with no hat, and with broken shoes, and with an old rag tied round his head. A man who had been soaked in water, and smothered in mud, and lamed by stones, and cut by flints, and stung by nettles, and torn by briars; who limped and shivered, and glared and growled; and whose teeth chattered in his head as he seized me by the chin.[4]

The "terrible voice" is thus immediately identified by the narrator, tethered to the living body of a human being; and the phrase "a man" recurs like a leitmotiv all through the subsequent litany of sufferings, as the child's terror is gradually absorbed by an implicit narrative sympathy with the suffering body (and Magwitch will in the course of the novel emerge as a figure of Christ-like redemptive power). In other words, we should see this Dickensian scene as the very *antithesis* of the ghostly encounter: instead of disrupting the ontological space of human reality, the traumatic arrival of the guest or unknown apparition is "hosted" there, given a distinct legibility by the narrative and thus *identified*, in both a formal and a diegetic sense. Indeed, what Peter Brooks goes so far as to dub Pip's "original communion with Magwitch" is marked in the narrative as a kind of primal scene of hospitality, of the sharing of food, with the starving man devouring the single piece of bread he finds in the boy's pocket (clearly a pre-figurative symbol of the communion wafer or "body of Christ").[5] For M. R. James to recall the opening of *Great Expectations* at the start of one of his stories, then, was to invoke a scene where traumatic, supernatural apparition succumbs to manifest narrative hospitality.

The opening scene of an earlier James story, "Oh, Whistle, and I'll Come to You, My Lad" (1904), is deliberately set in "the hospitable hall of St James's College" (*CG* 76): from the outset, the author is clearly alive to the strange etymological roots of "ghost," and this story heavily implies the uncanny interconnectedness of ghosts, hosts and guests. But the initial scene in the hospitable college hall is far from an "original communion" of the sort implicitly linking Pip and Magwitch in *Great Expectations*; instead it bristles with rivalry, with the problem of the "neighbour" as an entity whose very proximity compromises or disturbs the relation of the self to itself: an unwanted guest or *parasite* (etymologically, "a person who eats at the table of another," as the OED puts it). Parkins, the young but rather old-maidish "Professor of Ontography," is telling the table about his holiday plans and fussing about the inconvenience of having to "rough it" in a hotel where the only room available has not one bed but, quite scandalously, two; then:

> "Do you call having an extra bed in your room roughing it, Parkins?" said a bluff person opposite. "Look here, I shall come down and occupy it for a bit; it'll be company for you."
> The Professor quivered, but managed to laugh in a courteous manner.
> "By all means, Rogers; there's nothing I should like better. But I'm afraid you would find it rather dull; you don't play golf, do you?"
> (CG 77)

The desire of the other, incarnated in "rude Mr Rogers" (77), disturbs the complacent "ontography" of the self, imposing a parasitic, interruptive element (an "extra bed") on the site of the ego's imaginary self-definition. If "company" is precisely what the professor wishes to exclude from his hotel room, he is momentarily checked by his "bluff" opponent's feint into restraining or disavowing that hostility (and note its *visceral* quality: the body "quivered") through a pretence of "courteous" communality. What is demanded by the discursive protocol of the "hospitable hall" (another of James's tales will feature a place called "Guestingly" Hall: *CG* 27) is an acknowledgement of the world as a neutral space of rational intersubjective co-existence, where my room, as it were, will always be shared by another guest, my ego obliged to play host to the parasitical other. But what this hospitable protocol disavows or veils, of course, is the ontological *singularity* of the other, the potential for the "neighbour on the other side" (76) to disrupt the fictional space of a communal rationality.

This fundamental ambiguity of the other—rational interlocutor or disruptive singularity—is highlighted by another of the professor's "parasitic" neighbours, who asks Parkins to reconnoitre "the site of the Templars' preceptory" (76) on the beach near where he'll be staying. The predictable formulaic courtesy of the professor's response is at odds, if we look closely,

with the textual "site" itself: for the word "preceptory," naming an institutional building of the Knights Templar (legendary guardians of mystical
relics) is also, in an archaic sense, an adjective meaning "commanding" or
"enjoining" (OED). In this latter sense, it is the *other* that is truly "preceptory," its insistent demand imposing disruptively on the controlled temporality and space of "my" narrative.

The problem of hospitality, in the sense of an ethical relation to the
other, is thus in question from the very outset of "Oh, Whistle, and I'll
Come to You, My Lad" (and even the story's title, adapting some lines from
Burns, seems to imply the advent of the other as uncanny moving spirit
or air, as "tremendous gust" [CG 83]). It is not hard to see that Professor
Parkins's disregard for his collegiate neighbours at dinner shows a degree
of complacent self-satisfaction, an attitude which the ensuing narrative will
duly unravel. As he trudges along the desolate seashore at Burnstow the
following day, Parkins glimpses "a prospect of company on his walk, in
the shape of a rather indistinct personage" (81) walking behind him; but
he chooses not to slow down and let this strange anamorphic blur enter the
legible scope of "his" reality. His next thought exposes the true inhospital-
ity of his ego: "For all that, company, he began to think, would really be
very welcome on that lonely shore, if only you could choose your companion" (81). The other, that is, would be very welcome to lodge as guest in
the house of the ego—provided that it remain entirely subject to my desire,
brings with it no actual trace of disruptive otherness.

Little does the Professor know, of course, how unsettling the "indistinct
personage" glimpsed on the beach will turn out to be for his self-centred
"ontography." The first glimpse of what we could call, using Lyotard's
term, the "figural" dimension of the text comes immediately after Parkins's
egoistic notion of "company" made acceptable to the ego by being purged
of any recalcitrant otherness; his thoughts dwell on the need for some pro-
tection against what may lie outside the bounds of the properly thinkable:

> In his unenlightened days he had read of meetings in such places
> which even now would hardly bear thinking of. He went on thinking
> of them, however, until he reached home, and particularly one which
> catches most people's fancy at some time of their childhood. "Now I
> saw in my dream that Christian had gone but a very little way when
> he saw a foul fiend coming over the field to meet him." "What should
> I do now,' he thought, 'if I looked back and caught sight of a black
> figure sharply defined against the yellow sky and saw that it had
> horns and wings? . . ."   (CG 81)

A misquoted fragment of Bunyan glosses the figure as dream vision:
it appears with a hallucinatory intensity grotesquely at odds with the
grown-up discursive rationality of Parkins's supposedly enlightened world.
There is something constitutively *unthinkable* about this mental picture,

this "black figure" of a demonic other: at once "sharply defined" sensory phenomenon and imaginary phantasm, it defies any ontological consistency or narrative logic.

The language of the eye, then, again disfigures the encounter with the other in the ghost story, making it an unthinkable or unspeakable event. Like the spectre in *The Signalman*, what appears in "Oh, Whistle, and I'll Come to You, My Lad" stands not just outside the self-enclosure of the protagonist's complacent ego, but outside the very space-time of narrative itself. Thus, when Parkins chooses most unwisely to blow on the mysterious whistle he has taken from the ruined Templars' preceptory, the "sound . . . seemed to have the power (which many scents possess) of forming pictures in the brain" (83). A hallucinatory dimension suddenly intrudes on the semantic orderliness of the professor's psychical space: a sensory "discourtesy" thrusts itself into the mental topography of the "I." And the otherness that appears there is far more radical than the merely potential otherness comprised by the unwelcome neighbour at the table or the hotel: indeed, it is disconcertingly *actual*, has already happened, taken the ego unawares.

Now, a discrepancy between the sensory and the semantic, or between the perceptual and the thinkable, was central to another exploration of psychical hallucination during the period when James was beginning to write his stories: namely Freud's *The Interpretation of Dreams* (1900). The dream, Freud wrote there, is a *Bilderrätsel*, a "picture puzzle" or rebus, its signifying elements couched in a "pictographic script" and thus encrypted, suspended in a medium inherently hostile to the laws of speech.[6] A late, brief James story, "The Malice of Inanimate Objects" (1933), includes a fragment of "Freudian" *Bilderschrift* that can be seen to cast retrospective light on "Oh, Whistle, and I'll Come to You, My Lad." A man called Mr Burton is given some news by a polite Mr Manners about a hated rival's death; and he proceeds to encounter the titular "malice of inanimate objects" at every turn. Clambering up a hillside, Burton absurdly trips on the string of a kite; and then

> As they approached, a puff of wind raised the kite and it seemed to sit up on its end and look at them with two large round eyes painted red, and, below them, three large printed red letters, I. C. U. Mr Manners was amused and scanned the device with care. "Ingenious," he said, "it's a bit off a poster, of course: I see! Full particulars, the word was."   (CG 399)

The kite is thus a kind of groundless pictograph, a fragmentary rebus whose letters spell out the ominous airborne message of the Freudian superego (common intellectual currency by the 1930s): "I see you." The kite speaks, that is, the language of the eye: its letters do not "represent" but *present* the gaze of the other, the very point where discursive language fails before, is deformed by, the sensory real in its "full particulars." Neither the eyes of the kite nor its letters can therefore simply be read (although they are, drolly enough, "printed red"): they do not signify but actually *figure* the haunting of the baffled eye, the puzzling of the ego.

It is this pictographic actuality that takes us back to Professor Parkins and his enigmatic whistle. The latter object is "shaped very much after the manner of the modern dog-whistle" (82)—and note that a dog-whistle, like the Dickensian signalman's spectral bell, would to human ears be *silent*—but it is also a *Bilderrätsel*, a crypto-pictograph:

> There were legends both on the front and on the back of the whistle. The one read thus:

FUR FLA PLE BIS

The other:

QUIS EST ISTE QUI UENIT

The first thing to note about this pictographic script—the "figural" quality of which is essential, irreducible—is the bewilderment it provokes in professional ontographer Parkins: he has to confess "after some earnest thought . . . that the meaning of it was as obscure to him as the writing on the wall to Belshazzar" (82). Now, as everyone in James's first audience would have known, the writing on the wall at Belshazzar's feast, as recounted in the Old Testament's Book of Daniel (5.1–31), spelt out *Mene, Mene, Tekel, Upharsin*: Hebrew words for different monetary units (a free translation might be "Pounds, shillings and pence"). And the prophet Daniel's interpretation of that pictograph was that it amounted to a final demand on the king of Babylon's unpaid divine account: he had been "weighed in the balances" by God and found wanting, his number was up.

The double inscription on the whistle therefore constitutes a kind of sum, written in what Lacan might have called an "algebra of letters," as well as a rebus or graphic puzzle to be solved. But before we join in with the collective effort of modern readers to decipher the enigma of the whistle, let us recall the first Freudian response to the pictography of dreams. The night before his father's funeral, says Freud (though it was actually, we learn from an editorial note, the night *after*), he dreamt of seeing "a printed notice, placard or poster—rather like the notices forbidding one to smoke in railway waiting-rooms," and this super-egoic pictograph comprised "two versions" of a message—which, as Freud puts it, "I usually write in this form:"

the

"You are requested to close   eye(s)."[7]

an

"The dream-work," writes Freud, "failed to establish a unified wording for the dream-thoughts which could at the same time be ambiguous:" the triple inscription of doubleness (non-unified, simultaneous, ambiguous) points to something in excess of the theoretical account, an element irreducible to the regime of conceptual formulation or calculation. The very logic of Freudian dream interpretation, it seems, is at stake here, with the dream's figural dimension as *Bilderschrift* intruding on the space of rationality, unsettling its very foundation.

It is this sense of an incalculable figurality, both central to the Freudian discovery and yet fundamentally in excess of its governing epistemic regime, that can shed light for us on the Jamesian writing on the whistle. Indeed, what characterises that writing corresponds, we could even say, to Freud's triple characterisation of the dream as *zweideutig*, double-meaning: its sense is non-unified, it occurs twice at one time, it points two ways. Let us look again at the front first:

FLA

FUR   BIS

FLE

There are (at least) two ways to construe the Latin here: either as three verbs, second person indicative future tense—*furbis, flabis, flebis*—meaning "you will go mad," "you will blow (i.e., whistle)," "you will weep;" or as a noun (*fur*, "thief") plus two imperative verbs and the adverb *bis*, "twice." The latter version would give either "Thief–whistle–twice–weep," if we read it clockwise; or "Thief–weep–twice–whistle" if anti-clockwise. But the total number of readings, the definitive sum, can never be reached, since the signifying elements can be interconnected with endless variations of sense or hermeneutic "spin." And although one reading certainly suggests itself as a possible *mise en abyme* or summary of the whole narrative—in which Parkins takes the whistle from the preceptory (making him a thief: *fur*), blows on it (*fla*) not once but twice (*bis*) and then gets very upset (*fle*)—this is by no means the end of the story: divergent strands of narrative meaning could be tied into other ways of rotating or notating the whistle (such as those for instance which might yield *furbis*, "you will rave, go mad"). Just as Freud cannot finally count how many eyes he is requested to close in his dream, neither the professor nor the reader can decipher, in a single and decisive interpretive act, the enigmatic legend on the whistle. The ghostly inscription therefore remains an essentially *unsettled* account, recalling the "pounds, shillings and pence" that marked Belshazzar's fateful insolvency.

If we turn to the legend on the reverse of the whistle, which the professor does have a stab at interpreting, we can see how that unsettling of the account is marked there in a way that has today become distinctly unsettling:

⚒QUIS EST ISTE QUI UENIT ⚒

Either side of the Latin inscription is a symbol, the swastika, which Parkins does not comment on, and which indeed we could see as emblematic of the whole non-discursive, figural or apparitional dimension presented in "Oh, Whistle, and I'll Come to You, My Lad." In 1904, of course, the swastika had not yet come to signify German Nazism (it would only begin doing so in 1920); instead it was a popular symbol in various religious cultures (including Hinduism and Buddhism) for well-being or success, for "things turning out well." But intriguingly, given our rotation-notation of the whistle, the swastika can also be given a topological sense, seen as turning either clockwise or anti-clockwise:

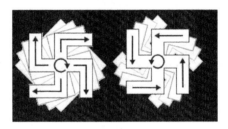

The pictographic swastika is therefore a perfect figure for the semiotic torsion or dynamic disfiguring of legibility at work in the story, the endless, restless movement of letters that troubles its narrative surface.

The writing on the whistle, then, like the biblical writing on the wall and the duplicitous *Bilderschrift* of the Freudian dream, should be seen as radically alien to the discursive regime of everyday life: it constitutes a figure that cannot be paraphrased or glossed, rendered comprehensible, re-presented as a single coherent message. We have seen this fundamental incalculability of the ghostly in earlier chapters as an eclipse of discursive "reality," the breach of the signifying network of a legible host-text by a fragmentary or anamorphic "guest" element appearing "on the edge of the void." What was visible in both the Homeric epigraph in *Melmoth the Wanderer* and the opening "telephoneme" of *The Signalman* was how this implausible breach of narrative propriety is fundamentally *sensory*: the audible-visible intrusion of ψυχὴ, of breath or voice, on the order of the text. When Parkins blows on the whistle, this sensory breach of narrative reality is vividly portrayed:

He blew tentatively and stopped suddenly, startled and yet pleased at the note he had elicited. It had a quality of infinite distance in it, and, soft as it was, he somehow felt it must be audible for miles around. It was a sound, too, that seemed to have the power (which many scents possess) of forming pictures in the brain. He saw quite clearly for a moment a vision of a wide, dark expanse at night, with a fresh wind blowing, and in the midst a lonely figure. . . .   (CG 83)

The vision is interrupted by a "tremendous gust"—that last word an obvious pun on "ghost," but only a letter away from "guest"—that embodies the hostile arrival of psyche, of spirit or breath as unmortified life-enjoyment, in the professor's tidily ordered mental topography. What is clear, once again, is that, like the Dickensian signalman's bell, when the psychical telephone whistles only *eye heard it*: the ghostly voice, that is, is also a spectre, a hallucinatory figure excluded from calculable discursive reality, where sensory things are "mortified," rationally sited in space and time, sound and sight. The spectral advent of the voice entails a nonsensical collapse of the intersubjective space supporting such a consistently presented reality; so that subject and object, "in here" and "out there," semantic host and sensory guest are thrown together in "tortuous confusion" (90). Just as, in "The Malice of Inanimate Objects," the kite bearing the letters "I.C.U." embodies an impossible gaze detached from any realistic site, so the voice of the ghostly whistle is extimate, both inside and outside, intimately close and with "a quality of infinite distance in it" (83). The voice and the gaze, those uncanny figural objects, indeed feature in "Oh, Whistle, and I'll Come to You, My Lad" in ways that are by now familiar to us as generic features of the ghost story: thus the "moaning" or "rustling" (83, 85) of a spectral-vocal presence and the "intensely horrible face of *crumpled linen*" (92), where the italicised text seems to mime the disfiguration of representation itself in contact with the ontological singularity of the apparition.

If the ghost story as reinvented by M. R. James, then, is "antiquarian," it comes with none of the retrospective consolation or formal conservatism that such a term might be thought to imply. The antique object found by Professor Parkins may be malicious but it is certainly not "inanimate:" on the contrary, it embodies a living vocal-graphic thing which can never be properly counted, which cannot be contained or made fully legible by the decorous host-narrative. Let us turn to another text from *Ghost Stories of an Antiquary* to see how we can link the extimate guest in the Jamesian narrative to what, I'm afraid, its author saw as most likely to spoil a good ghost story: that is, sex.

MEZZOTEXT

By 1929, M. R. James had become a kind of unofficial laureate of the ghost story, and at last felt able to impart some wisdom on what he saw as the genre's defining features. In "Some Remarks on Ghost Stories," published in *The Bookman* that year (in the Christmas edition, of course), he wrote:

> Reticence may be an elderly doctrine to preach, yet from an artistic point of view I am sure it is a sound one. Reticence conduces to effect, blatancy ruins it, and there is much blatancy in a lot of recent stories. They drag in sex too, which is a fatal mistake; sex is tiresome enough in the novels; in a ghost story, or as the backbone of a ghost story, I have no patience with it.   (CG 414–415)

On this view, the ghost story would essentially be the domain of the non-explicit, of signifying restraint, we might even say of repression. But James has more to say about the genre:

> At the same time don't let us be mild and drab. Malevolence and terror, the glare of evil faces, 'The stony grin of unearthly malice,' pursuing forms in darkness, and 'long-drawn, distant screams' are all in place, and so is a modicum of blood, shed with deliberation and carefully husbanded; the weltering and wallowing that I too often encounter merely recall the methods of M. G. Lewis.   (CG 415)

The proper ghost story, then, should not "drag in sex;" and if it must include bloodshed that resource should be "carefully husbanded:" what is discernable here, as that last phrase makes all but explicit, is that what James sees as the "reticence" of the genre in fact entails a thinly veiled sexual politics, which we could define as a "husbandry" of the signifier. For James, that is, the human body must be "in place," somewhere, in the ghost story—especially figured as stereotypical glare and scream, gaze and voice—but its full sensory goriness must be restrained, properly "husbanded," to ward off the unghostly, gothic (and by implication unmanly, feminizing) horrors or pleasures of "weltering and wallowing."

If we turn, then, to another text from *Ghost Stories of an Antiquary*, "The Mezzotint," written at the end of the 1890s, we can see how its author is already investigating the definition of the proper ghost story, probing the framework of what Dickens had mockingly called the "accredited ghostly circumstances." The story opens with a playfully "metafictional" framework, concerning "the pursuit of objects of art for the museum" at "another University" (CG 24)—the Ashmolean in Oxford, which M. R. James had no doubt visited while working for a while at the Bodleian Library in 1899—and thus aligns itself with a very *fin de siècle* motif: that of the artwork whose theme is none other than art itself. The story's protagonist is keen, we are told, to enlarge "the already unsurpassed collection of English topographical drawings and engravings possessed by his museum" (24). And in case the word "engravings" has not given us a sufficient clue, James is careful to remind us (a full fifteen years, note, before the appearance of the famous Freudian text on *unheimlichkeit*) that "even a department so homely and familiar as this may have its dark corners" (24). The homely English artwork, as engraving, may thus also be *un*homely, with some "dark corners" in its apparently familiar topography; and this of course will turn out to be the case for both the eponymous mezzotint and for its metafictional frame-narrative.

The first description of the mezzotint itself recalls our Lyotardian distinction in Chapter 2 between discourse and figure: "I cannot hope" says the narrator, "to put before you the look of the picture as clearly as it is present to my own eye" (25). There is thus something *un*presentable about "the look of the picture," a phrase deliberately chosen to waver semantically between gazing subject and object gazed at, as if the mezzotint, like the Lyotardian figure, refuses to conform to the ordinary grammar of identity. But if the picture is thus marked out as beyond the signifying space of the narrative, it is nevertheless "present to my own eye:" it has a haunting psychical temporality at odds with the time of interpretation. And what we might call its mezzo-textuality—being beyond representation and yet everpresent to the inner eye—is carried over to the problem of how to define this aesthetic object in relation to official, authoritative knowledge. Thus, holding the mezzotint in his hands, Williams is puzzled by the gap between its authorised value, which has been given by his ever-reliable dealer Mr Britnell, and the actual impression it makes on his own eye:

> The whole thing gave the impression that it was the work of an amateur. What in the world Mr Britnell could mean by affixing the price of £2 2S. [note that double numbering] to such an object was more than Mr Williams could imagine. He turned it over with a good deal of contempt; upon the back was a paper label, the left-hand half of which had been torn off. All that remained were the ends of two lines of writing; the first had the letters—*ngly Hall*; the second,—*ssex*.   (CG 26)

So the mezzotint is mislabelled, or half-labelled: not only is its official evaluation in the catalogue dubious—to be counted twice in both pounds and shillings—but its very topographical site has been damaged, remains only half-legible. The purloining of letters here takes us to the central trope or figure of "The Mezzotint:" that is, the incalculability of the artwork corresponds to the fragmentation of the proper name and the interruption of patrilineal transmission (of authority, of proper identity). And as the second mutilated line irresistibly suggests with 'the second,—*ssex*,' this combination of textual interruption and perturbed authority has everything to do with "the second sex:" in other words, woman.

In what sense, though, if we turn it back the right way around, can the mezzotint in "The Mezzotint" be considered unaccountable or incalculable? At the diegetic level, marked by M. R. James's characteristic camp black humour, we are shown various dons and college servants struggling to cope with the fact that the picture *keeps on changing*: what first appears as the faintest blur in the foreground subsequently materialises, a few hours later, as a hunched figure creeping across the lawn toward the house; then a closed window is seen later in the evening to be in fact open; and finally the ghostly intruder is seen, when the picture is viewed the following day, scuttling back across the lawn with a child in its arms. And this spectral narrative of child abduction that appears and disappears in the mezzotint turns out, after some research, to be the story of an interrupted male lineage; featuring a poacher with the ludicrous name of Gawdy who was "the last of his line: kind of *spes ultima gentis*" (34), and who, having carelessly shot someone in a wood, is caught by the landlord and strung up, only subsequently to creep back as a ghost to steal the landlord's son and "put an end to *his* line, too" (34).

Now, apart from the sheer preposterousness of this scenario (we recall that the mezzotint "gave the impression that it was the work of an amateur"), the obvious thing to note about it would be the double motif of the *two interrupted lines*: on one side, the childless outlaw and landlord; on the other, the mezzotint itself (of its titular label, we recall, "All that remained were the ends of two lines"). And it is here that the incalculability of "The Mezzotint," what we might call the loophole or window in its textual topography, becomes more interesting. Let's go back to the conversation between Williams and his colleague; their topic, as they fill in the background narrative of the mezzotint, is patriarchal decline:

> '. . .Well, this man that was left was what you find pretty often in that country—the last remains of a very old family. I believe they were Lords of the Manor at one time. I recollect just the same thing in my own parish.'
>
> 'What, like that man in *Tess o' the Durbervilles*?' Williams put in.
>
> 'Yes, I dare say; it's not a book I could ever read myself. But this fellow could show a row of tombs in the church there that belonged to his ancestors, and all that went to sour him a bit;'   (CG 33)

The allusion to Hardy's *Tess of the d'Urbervilles*, published in 1891, thus barely a decade before *Ghost Stories of an Antiquary*, adds a subtle intertextual twist to "The Mezzotint." We need to examine more closely this intertextual relocation, this shift from "either. . .Sussex or Essex" to Hardy's Wessex. First of all who, precisely, does Williams mean by "that man in *Tess o' the Durbervilles*"? The ironic disparagement of Hardy's novel—"it's not a book I could ever read myself"—both reminds us of its scandalous reputation (it was very definitely not on the Cambridge syllabus in the 1890s) and subtly links it to the mezzo-modernist theme of "The Mezzotint," that of illegible or incalculable textuality: "it's not a book I could ever read." Now, both of these aspects can be clarified if we follow the citational lineage back to Hardy's text; where once again we find ourselves at a scene of *engraving*. Towards the end of the novel, Angel Clare has gone back to the Vale of Blackmoor, guiltily searching for his abandoned wife Tess. Haunted by remembered scenes of desire, he arrives at the village of Marlott and takes a short cut through the churchyard, "where", amongst the new headstones, he saw one of a somewhat superior design to the rest. The inscription ran thus:

> In memory of John Durbeyfield, rightly d'Urberville, of the once powerful family of that name, and Direct Descendant through an Illustrious Line from Sir Pagan d'Urberville, one of the Knights of the Conqueror. Died March 10th, 18—

> HOW ARE THE MIGHTY FALLEN.[8]

What Angel thus sees is the grave of his father-in-law, Tess's father, that vain and foolish "haggler" or jack-of-all-trades; and Angel then learns from the sexton that the headstone, for all its rhetorical flourish, has not in fact been paid for, since Jack Durbeyfield, of course, died in extreme poverty. The engraved text has been left by a local stonemason as a well-meaning attempt to re-inscribe the "Illustrious Line," to restore the name of the father both to its correct form and its rightful Anglo-Norman lineage. And Angel Clare duly joins in with this archival restoration of the name and the line by immediately calling at the stonemason's house and himself settling the bill for the headstone, as if to repay the dead, deficient father's debt.

So "that man in *Tess o' the Durbervilles*" recalled in "The Mezzotint" is the dead, impotent father, whose improperly inscribed name is a symptom of decayed patriarchal power and whose death leaves his sons impossibly burdened with debt (and Angel's repayment of the stonemason's bill is a vain attempt to assuage his own guilt at the abandonment of Tess with her "interrupted" line, to rectify her damaged d'Urberville name).

The central trope of "The Mezzotint," then, the disruption of the male lineage corresponding to a fragmentation of the proper name and an unfinished memory, unpaid debt or still-living, unmortified and thus incalculable inscription—all of this can be seen recapitulated (or rather *pre*capitulated) in a scene from *Tess* cryptically inscribed in the corner of James's text. But what the title of Hardy's novel reminds us is that this citational lineage is haunted by a figure in excess of M. R. James's text: that of woman.

At first sight, however, the mention of *Tess of the D'Urbervilles* in "The Mezzotint" takes place in an entirely masculine discursive scenario: first, it forms an intertextual node between two male authors (M. R. James and Thomas Hardy); and then, within the diegesis, it occurs in a conversation between two men for whom "that man" (Tess's father) metonymises a problem of male lineage or patrimony. So where is the woman in all this? To understand this we need to see the appearance of *Tess* in "The Mezzotint" in a special, slanted light: to see it as an anamorphic stain, an enigmatic hinge between two incompatible registers or genres of writing. To see the anamorphic stain in Holbein's celebrated portrait *The Ambassadors* for what it 'represents'—a skull as *memento mori*—we need to relocate, displace our viewpoint from a consistent realist epistemology. In one sense, this anamorphic switch of perspective corresponds to the switch from "The Mezzotint" to *Tess of the D'Urbervilles*, in that Hardy's text, for all its mythological resonance, centres on what is held to be a real problem of human existence—how sexual difference ultimately entails divergent modes of being and representing the self—a problem which is warded off or repressed from the archly stylised, knowingly ironic world of M. R. James. Indeed, compared with the traumatic, nightmarish events of *Tess*, a ghost story like "The Mezzotint" looks positively twee, its gestures toward the uncanny constantly toppling over into mock-Dickensian horror-comedy.

But if we take a more detailed look at Hardy's text, it becomes clear that the repression or negation in M. R. James's story of an incalculable ontology Hardy emphatically links to femininity might be seen as indicative of a more general kind of patriarchal violence in Victorian culture. What is at stake is what Hardy calls in one of his poems "a presence more than the actual:" an ontological immanence irreducible to any actual situation, any existence presentable within the matrix of discourse.[9] In "The Mezzotint" we can see this irreducible excess inscribed in two contrasting ways: first, on the front of the picture, on its diegetic surface, as the ironic, stylised conceit of the mutable artwork, with its ghostly but essentially light-hearted metafiction of child abduction. But if we subsequently turn to the back of the picture or consider its 'subtext,' we find a very different trace of a "presence more than the actual:" the "ends of two lines" which, we have argued, can be linked to the broken lineage and fractured name that spells out the tragic dimension of *Tess of the D'Urbervilles*. The "poor wounded name" in the Shakespearean quote Hardy uses as the novel's epigraph already suggests something analogous: what exceeds the representational protocol of a given culture—and Hardy associates that excess with Tess herself, her body and her innermost being—such an ontological excess cannot be narrated properly, given a new and more accurate representation, but must appear in a narrative as a wound suffered by that narrative, an unaccountable blot or stain at the edge of an otherwise legible page.

It is here that we need to turn to Hardy's text in conclusion. How does *Tess of the D'Urbervilles* figure forth an excess (coded 'feminine') haunting representation as such, without making it into an ironized metafiction à la M. R. James? This is how the innocent landlady Mrs Brooks first perceives the event of Tess's terrible "fulfilment," her murder of Alec d'Urberville:

> In reflecting she leant back in her chair.
> As she did so her eyes glanced casually over the ceiling till they were arrested by a spot in the middle of its white surface which she

had never noticed before. It was about the size of a wafer when she first observed it, but it speedily grew as large as the palm of her hand, and then she could perceive that it was red. The oblong white ceiling, with this scarlet blot in the midst, had the appearance of a gigantic ace of hearts. (471)

And of course the bloodstain on the ceiling really *is* an ace of hearts, since it has been caused by a single knife wound straight to the heart of Alec d'Urberville, that devilish "card" who had earlier broken Tess's heart and raped her, causing her own blood to flow across her white skin. The "wounded name" is again at stake, as the penetration of Alec by the knife, repeating and reversing his earlier violation of Tess, even cuts up the letters of the name "Alec," making it "ace."

First of all, then, Hardy dramatizes Tess's act as unaccountable—as, properly speaking, unrepresentable—by presenting in the image of the "oblong white ceiling, with this scarlet blot in the midst" a clear allegory of the writer's page disfigured by an illegible singularity or absolute otherness. The bloodstain is anamorphic, in that it confronts the interpreting eye with something against the rules of meaningful symbolization (the macabre image of the "gigantic ace of hearts," connected like an obscene pun to a whole network of signifiers throughout Hardy's text, aptly encapsulates this illegal or transgressive dimension).

The reference to *Tess of the D'Urbervilles* in "The Mezzotint" therefore opens another window, suggests a new problem of the non-closure of textual meaning, which gravely troubles the world of M. R. James. It is clear that all of the story's preoccupations—with interrupted patrilineal transmission, damaged names and missing children—must be reread through Hardy's text (or rather, his *Tess*). What this rereading shows is that the Jamesian ghost story as mezzotext, with its carefully contrived effects of veiled suggestion and half-disclosure, is haunted by something unspeakable, like a gigantic ace of hearts. Hardy's text shows how this central bloodstain disfiguring the space of textuality is unacceptable to, and must therefore be negated or repressed by, 'normal' subjects, perhaps especially men. Here is how Angel Clare reacts to the news that his wife has just committed murder:

By degrees he was inclined to believe that she had faintly attempted, at least, what she said she had done; and his horror at her impulse was mixed with amazement at the strength of her affection for himself, and at the strangeness of its quality, which had apparently extinguished her moral sense altogether. Unable to realize the gravity of her conduct she seemed at last content; and he looked at her as she lay upon his shoulder, weeping with happiness, and wondered what obscure strain in the d'Urberville blood had led to this aberration—if it were an aberration. (475)

The very phrase Angel conjures to account for Tess's unaccountable behaviour—the "obscure strain in the d'Urberville blood"—is an uncanny echo of the bloodstain or "scarlet blot" of d'Urberville blood that disfigured the white ceiling a few pages earlier, as if Hardy's text has to count the "aberration" twice (note the repetition of the word in the last line quoted). Both the "obscure strain" and the obscure stain of the noble or ignoble blood mark something impossible simply to count, to make decisively legible or reduce to an authoritative discourse. If "The Mezzotint" suggests, with its still-living artwork and its torn labels, that its author may have glanced momentarily into this phantasmatic breach of patriarchal authority, it is no accident that he decides to end the story by shutting away the engraving in a museum, where it will cause no trouble to anyone.

What we see in M. R. James's work, then, is a divergence we could see as characteristic of the transition from the Victorian to the modern ghost story. On the one hand, James is fully invested in the ghost story as a literary tradition defined by "reticence," by an anti-gothic stylistic restraint. This emphasis can be linked to the Dickensian institution, as it were, of the ghost story, with its framework of festive hospitality and sceptical mockery of stylistic excess (although, as we saw, Dickens's *The Signalman* is utterly at odds with such a framework). What the anti-gothic 'hospitable' ghost story offers is an implicit structure of intersubjective rationality as psychological defence against the traumatic ontological instance, the incalculable figure, of the apparition. James's allusion to *Great Expectations* at the beginning of "A Warning to the Curious" is exemplary here, since the ostensibly ghostly encounter staged by Dickens at the opening of that novel is controlled and comprehended by the redemptive hospitality of the novel's structure, emblematized by the ultimately paternal figure of Magwitch. But on the other hand, as we have shown, James's stories themselves actually centre on a disturbing vitality figured in textual elements that keep on disrupting the supposedly reticent, decorous host-narrative—the whistle found by Professor Parkins, its vocal-graphic inscription twisting like an uncanny swastika, or the cryptic allusion to the highly non-reticent "scarlet blot" of an incalculable femininity as seen in *Tess of the D'Urbervilles*.

If the ghost story in the hands of M. R. James, then, appears split between the anti-gothic and the gothic, between "antiquarian" hospitable discourse and traumatic ghostly figure, how does that split anticipate the rewriting of the literary ghost in the twentieth century? To start our response, we should turn to James's more famous namesake, the subject of the next chapter.

4 Ineffaceable Life
Henry James

All art constantly aspires towards the condition of music. For while in all other kinds of art it is possible to distinguish the matter from the form, and the understanding can always make this distinction, yet it is the constant effort of art to obliterate it.

—Walter Pater

A TALE OF TWO HOUSES

Had Henry James glanced—a highly unlikely eventuality—at *Ghost Stories of an Antiquary* when it was published in 1904 by his ghost-writer namesake, he might well have been struck, and no doubt bitterly amused, by a phrase at the beginning of "Oh, Whistle, and I'll Come to You, My Lad:" "the hospitable hall of St James." For, almost a decade earlier, it had been a similar-sounding "hall"—St James's Theatre in London's west end, to be precise—that had hosted what James must have felt to be one of the most *in*hospitable moments of his literary career: the infamous opening night of his play *Guy Domville*, an event given a bravura treatment by Leon Edel in his 1962 biography of James (as well as featuring in an uncanny coincidence of recent works by Colm Toibin and David Lodge).

What makes this oft-rehearsed scene so fascinating? As Edel presents it (not uncontroversially, of course), it is an exemplary scenario of uncanny symmetry, of mirroring or imaginary rivalry, indeed of what Lacan would have called "primordial jealousy."[1] On the evening of Saturday, 5 January 1895, James's play *Guy Domville*, produced by and starring the celebrated George Alexander, opened at the St James; while less than a mile away at the Haymarket Theatre another premiere took place, that of *An Ideal Husband* by Oscar Wilde. Without going through yet again the whole pantomimic performance—which culminates, of course, in Oscar's inevitable triumph and Henry's abject humiliation (a result, one might say, shortly to be reversed offstage)—we can identify its key features as a scene of literary and theatrical rivalry. First, there are two authorial protagonists, Wilde and James, competing for pre-eminence, rival contenders for the public's adoration; then within each play a male protagonist seeks to have his identity accepted, confirmed by the gaze of the (implicitly female) Other. The key stake for the hero of each drama is the ability to control the agency of the signifier: for in the event the two houses on that evening in 1895 host very different theatrical works, one in which laughter is in the script, as it were, seductively manipulated by the dramatist; while in the other, comedy intrudes on, makes a mockery of, the play's authorial meaning.[2] Whereas at the Haymarket the pleasures of the body are effectively deployed by the signifier, at the St James the efficacy of the signifier is spoilt, deformed by the sensory actuality of bodily performance (the audience started to giggle, Edel tells us, when the actress playing Mrs Domville entered wearing "an enormous hat, made of velvet and shaped like a muff" which "towered on her head under nodding plumes").[3]

Henry James's response to this spectacular debacle is as well known as the event itself: he completely withdrew from the theatre, and indeed from the whole rivalrous literary scene of London, to dedicate himself in the ensuing decade to a strenuous artistic self-reinvention as the great novelist of the early twentieth century. The two stories we will be reading—"The Jolly Corner" and "The Beast in the Jungle"—clearly form part of this transitional phase, this literary self-transformation. While I will not enter into the psychobiographical complexity of that transition, in one sense I want to see these stories as a writerly response by James to his moment of rivalry with Wilde in 1895: above all because that rivalry entails a host of questions about identity, about the ego in its relation to the other, to sexual difference, and to the equivocal presentation of narrative events; questions of hospitality that will return to haunt the remainder of James's work.

If Edel's biographical account of the James/Wilde rivalry, then, is a tale of two houses, shot through with uncanny symmetries and odd coincidences, so clearly, on both counts, is "The Jolly Corner" (1906). The opening Jamesian *donnée* of the tale is the "so strangely belated return" (*THJ* 341) of its protagonist Spencer Brydon to his native New York, which immediately gives us a first contrast between the city of his childhood and the new place where "[p]roportions and values were upside-down" (342): the things remembered as having been ugly have become "uncanny phenomena" since Brydon now finds them charming; while his full horror is reserved for the gigantic "monstrosities" thrown up by the modern city.

There is much more to say about this initial opposition between modernity and tradition, as we could swiftly label it, if we are to grasp its central significance for James's writing. The new, twentieth-century American city is "the mere gross generalisation of wealth and force and success" (343), a public, crowded site of productive economic activity, an efficient, heedlessly ahistorical and unremembering mechanism of capitalist progress; and such a city, as all of this implies, is figured as essentially *masculine*. By contrast the space of Brydon's memory and historical selfhood, thus in one sense the site of "his" personal New York, is a private, fragile domain, organized by a self-reflexive syntax of almost unfeasible complexity (". . . my 'thoughts' would still be almost altogether about something that concerns only myself:" 341). The latter is a site of reflection, of inwardness, of imaginary and remembered potential, as opposed to the ruthless and reductive "actuality" busily at work in the urban world outside.

The implicitly gendered subtext of this contrast between subjective interiority and worldly actuality comes into sharper focus once the opposition is mapped onto the two houses in the story, the two New York properties owned by Brydon. First, we have the "house within the street" which is "in course of reconstruction as a tall mass of flats" (342) and is metonymically linked to all the "dreadful multiplied numberings" (343) of the modern city. The very *convertibility* of this house is precisely the point here: because Brydon has no emotional investment in the property, because it is a "mere number" with no authentic ontological significance, it is fully consistent with "the modern, the actual" (359), the domain of meaningless, depthless multiplication or equivalence. The rather unexpected effect of visiting this place on Brydon is to make him look quite masculine, or to be more precise, quite "masculine:"

> At present, in the splendid autumn weather . . . he loafed about his "work" undeterred, secretly agitated; not in the least "minding" that the whole proposition, as they said, was vulgar and sordid, and ready to climb ladders, to walk the plank, to handle materials and look wise about them, to ask questions, in fine, and challenge explanations and really "go into" figures. *(THJ 343)*

If the conversion of the property thus seems to make a man out of Brydon, it is nevertheless a strange sort of man. He only mimes "work" instead of actually working, since all he is really doing is some Whitmanesque loafing about; and he is "undeterred, secretly agitated," a peculiar frame of mind in which his experience has to be constantly disavowed with secret scare quotes, thus rendered theatrical or mimic, turned into a game of builders or pirates who climb ladders or "walk the plank."

The childish masquerade of male "authority" thus performed by Brydon when at his modern property clearly results from the fact that in that location he feels wholly alienated from his true identity, as if on stage in someone else's play, a Broadway production where he has been mistakenly cast as an unreflective manly hero. His true self, meanwhile, is invested elsewhere, in the titular house on the "jolly corner," figuratively linked to his female counterpart Alice Staverton whose own subjectivity the text immediately glosses as a mere supplement to Brydon's, his indispensable "resource" (341). We should pay close attention to how James constructs, by means of this feminine supplement, an antithesis between the two houses or scenes:

> If he knew the way to [Alice Staverton's house] now better than to any other address among the dreadful multiplied numberings . . . it was really not a little because of the charm of his having encountered and recognised, in the vast wilderness of the wholesale . . . a small still scene where items and shades, all delicate things, kept the sharpness of the notes of a high voice perfectly trained, and where economy hung about like the scent of a garden. *(THJ 343)*

While the city outside comprises a busy, meaningless circuit of representation, a mechanical and essentially superficial system of inscription, inside the house, as if sealed off in some gothic crypt, the singular real of sensory experience is conserved in all its ontological plenitude, and figured by that signature-trope of the ghost, the disembodied voice. Hence, the "shades" or aesthetic nuances that inhabit Alice's house are also ghosts, as is the "spirit" (that term set off with scare quotes) which she and her house embody, the spirit of an "antediluvian" social order destroyed by the mindless onslaught of urban modernity. What is crucial is the ultimately *indefinable* quality of her "small still scene:" while the city outside corresponds to a ceaseless economy of signifying difference, what occurs *chez* Alice—as haunting impression, ambience, voice or scent—is an aesthetic fragment not fully caught up in the negativity of the signifying chain, thus retaining its own unique "feminine" mystery.

The opposition between masculine signifier and feminine "spirit" structures the underlying narrative topography of "The Jolly Corner." What is a "mere" signifier or number, a replica or reproduction able to be adopted or adapted at will, is marked in the text as having no real significance (like the charade of "manly" behaviour at the building site) and is consistently associated with an economy of discursive exchange and multiplication coded as masculine and exterior. Against this is implicitly posed another kind of "knowledge," a wholly separate ontological domain centred on an unmortified sensory thing or private enjoyment, and figured by the uncanny voice with its feminine or boyish *punctum* or "sharpness."

The ghostly essence of this latter dimension becomes apparent in the episode when Alice accompanies Brydon on a visit to the "apartment-house" (another phrase set off by quotes). Impressed by his "standing-up" (in scare quotes yet again) to "the man in charge" of the site—indeed she is sexually aroused, "ever so prettily flushing" at this theatrical show of manliness—Alice comments that if Brydon had stayed in New York he "would have anticipated the inventor of the skyscraper" (344): that is, he would have been a rich and successful American tycoon, a real man with his own skyscraper for a metaphorical phallus. This idea of another potential self, an extra "I," is of course what will supposedly determine the ghostly encounter as the tale unfolds; but what is essential to see is that at this originary point it is *produced by the feminine voice*—not merely as an idea situated at the level of the signifier (where it is deliberately ironic and nonsensical) but as a figure corresponding to a haunting, sensory vocal thing:

> He was to remember these words, while the weeks elapsed, for the small silver ring they had sounded over the queerest and deepest of his own lately most disguised and muffled vibrations.   (*THJ* 344)

Just as a "small silver ring" wavers between the visible and the audible, naming either a heterosexual exchange-object or a doorbell (perhaps an echo of the "spectre's bell" heard by Dickens's signalman), so the voice of Alice is weirdly apparitional: her ringing words make not just an idea but a "thing" become present. This unlikely spectrality of the female voice is the key to the problem of reading "The Jolly Corner." "The late James," writes Jeremy Tambling

> . . . attempts to turn language into a series of folds or corners, or to realise its existence as such, and to locate a doubleness or uncanniness inside narrative prose; to find the presence of something haunting, something different, that can only be tracked through pushing grammar to its limits, and turning it round on itself.[4]

It is, to recall the Dickensian signalman's words, very difficult to impart how this spectral "existence as such" can be thought of—it is again a problem of "a presence more than the actual," to recall Hardy's phrase, involving the reflexive torsion of language, its folding-over upon itself. Here we see the critical response to Jamesian writing struggling to formulate what is haunting the text, the vocal "ring" that both resonates through and echoes beyond the narrative agency of signifiers. It is precisely a question, in the end, of the difference between a metaphorical reading and one through which something appears that *exceeds* metaphor, something no longer fully determined by the logic of signifying equivalence.

If we concentrate again on the difference between Brydon's two properties, we can see how the Jamesian text begins to unsettle the very concept of literary metaphor. During their visit to the old house, Alice Staverton and Spencer Brydon hear from the cleaning woman, the comical Mrs Muldoon, of how she fears being in the house "in the ayvil hours" (346). Brydon reflects that "the question of the "evil" hours in his old home had already become too grave for him," and he tries to deflect ordinary discourse away from it, first laughing and then "quickly however changing the subject:

> for the reason that, in the first place, his laugh struck him even at that moment as starting the odd echo, the conscious human resonance (he scarcely knew how to qualify it) that sounds made while he was there alone sent back to his ear or his fancy;   (*THJ* 346)

The sound of laughter resonates uncannily in the house where the topic of "evil," another signifier kept at bay with scare quotes, is too "grave" to be allowed to pass into the realm of ordinary discourse. What is crucial here is Brydon's bewilderment, combined with his powerful sense—part imaginary and part *sensory*: an effect of "his ear or his fancy"—of something real which is incompatible with everyday conversational exchange. Whatever is there inhabits an ontological domain not available to the communicational subject, the master of the social signifier who knows how to deal with builders and can boldly walk the plank. This contrast between trivial and "grave," chit-chat and "resonance" develops into the structural rhythm of Brydon's double life:

He was a dim secondary social success—and all with people who had truly not an idea of him. It was all mere surface sound, this murmur of their welcome, this popping of their corks—just as his gestures of response were the extravagant shadows . . . of some game of *ombres chinoises*. He projected himself all day, in thought, straight over the bristling line of hard unconscious heads and into the other, the real, the waiting life; the life that, as soon as he heard behind him the click of his great house-door, began for him, on the jolly corner, as beguilingly as the slow opening bars of some rich music follow the tap of the conductor's wand.   (*THJ* 352)

The cork-popping social scene has all the theatrical extravagance and superficial glamour of a Wilde premiere; whereas the "other life" is fundamentally private—indeed, essentially secret or asocial, impossible to open up to an outside gaze or rational interpretation. The key to the difference here hinges on a shift in the status of metaphor. Just as Brydon's identity is a mere masquerade when he is at the convertible "apartment house" where he only play-acts at being manly, so in New York society he is fully caught up in a shadow-theatre: his "gestures of response" are mere simulacra, his "success" a mere effect of the discourse swirling around him; thus his inner essence, his ontological core, is left intact. Whilst inside such a theatre, in other words, Brydon's "self" is nothing but a metaphor, fully determined by the Other, by signifying substitution; and thus the game of *ombres chinoises* is a truthful—coherent, fully legible—representation of his identity.

Now, the first problem in trying to formulate the difference between this metaphorical-social fictive self and another kind of self, the one that for Brydon can only emerge secretly in the house on the jolly corner, is that the presentation of the latter is still *ostensibly* metaphorical; its life, we are told in what seems an obviously rhetorical analogy, begins "as beguilingly as the slow opening bars of some rich music" (352). The key word here, however, is "beguilingly:" unlike the "gestures of response" mechanically enacted by Brydon in everyday society—signs wholly determined by the rational teleology of the signifying Other—this other life comes with no origin or end to support the semiotic logic of the subject. Instead, its advent beguiles, fascinates, *possesses the site of* that subject, unravelling the signifying masquerade that normally makes subjectivity legible and thus socially convertible or acceptable. Hence, Brydon is beguiled or entranced by another life, another language no longer alienated by the social gaze— and thus no longer divided, gendered, symbolically mortified—but instead able to voice itself as such, persist in its own irreducible being, fold in on itself "at home." This other life, where a singular ontology emanates in the interval or parenthesis of social discourse, is of course the life of the ghost—a life before which metaphor fails, and which therefore demands a new kind of figurativity:

... he put his stick noiselessly away in a corner—feeling the place once more in the likeness of some great glass bowl, all precious concave crystal, set delicately humming by the play of a moist finger round its edge. The concave crystal held, as it were, this mystical other world, and the indescribably fine murmur of its rim was the sigh there, the scarce audible pathetic wail to his strained ear, of all the old baffled forsworn possibilities. What he did therefore by this appeal of his hushed presence was to wake them into such measure of ghostly life as they might still enjoy.   (*THJ* 352–353)

The sign is attenuated to a sigh, its signifying utterance now inoperable, incomprehensible. Having abandoned "noiselessly" the conventional signifier of phallic authority, Brydon enters the forbidden domain of the uncanny voice, of pure ghostly enjoyment: he divests himself, that is, of his actual discursive "self" in order to embody, not the life he might have lived had he stayed at home (a notion which is a pure MacGuffin or imaginary narrative lure[5]) but rather everything foreclosed—"baffled, forsworn"—by the ordinary discursive agency of the signifier. What is allowed to resonate, "set delicately humming," there is "a presence more than the actual:" something irreducible to the symbolic disposition of a coherent narrative with its consistent topography of gender and identity. This ghostly hum is the voice of an obscene, asocial, autistic enjoyment—and as such it is unspeakable, taboo. Indeed, what is crucial about this ghostly music—"the scarce audible pathetic wail"—is that it does not "represent" such enjoyment but rather *renders* it, as Žižek writes, in "sounds that penetrate us like invisible but nonetheless material rays [which are] the real of the 'psychic reality'."[6] What is forbidden, in other words, by the intersubjective rationality of worldly social existence is allowed, inside the "concave crystal" of the ghostly house, to take shape as an obscene phantasmal entity, an uncanny vibration at once invading the real of the body and embodying the ontological singularity hosted by the psyche. The music of ghostly life comes in place of the subject, as a guest in discursive reality, an extimate vibration at odds with the logic of the signifier.

Now, the Jamesian text itself, it would seem, remains sharply conscious of the implausible, indeed the potentially ludicrous, aspect of this notion of an imaginary manifestation of an essential psychical reality that is impossible to "represent," to put into proper, wide-awake language:

That was the essence of his vision—which was all rank folly, if one would, while he was out of the house and otherwise occupied, but which took on the last verisimilitude as soon as he was placed and posted. He knew what he meant and what he wanted; it was as clear as the figure on a cheque presented in demand for cash.   (*THJ* 353)

Once again, the Lacanian figure of anamorphosis provides us with a useful gloss on the topographical shift here. Looked at from the outside, that is, where superficial adult masculinity must be dutifully enacted for the Other, the "vision" remains an unaccountable anomaly, a meaningless blot or psychotic hallucination. But once the viewpoint has been adjusted, once the internal drama has been set in motion by the initial plosive, visceral click, that illegible blot is transformed into a hypersensitive "verisimilitude," a resonant surface attuned to all the subtle shades of psychical reality closed off, "forsworn" by the semiotic logic that governs subjectivity in the external world. What was bizarre or singular has become as clear as a bank statement: a new, radiant or revelatory figure embodying an ontology beyond "mere words."

It is here that an unlikely analogy suggests itself, which may help us to grasp the problem of narrative ending that bedevils "The Jolly Corner," producing its odd, in my view decidedly un-Jamesian, conclusion. The two houses in the story correspond, as we have seen, to the divergent poles of Brydon's existence—one modern, actual, discursive, convertible; the other traditional, phantasmal, unique or "consecrated" (346)—but at the same time they constitute contrasting scenes of gender or sexual identity. If we compare these scenes to another pair of contrasting houses, the parallels are striking. Here is Žižek discussing Hitchcock's *Psycho*:

> . . . the architectural locale of the two murders [carried out by Norman Bates] is by no means neutral; the first takes place in a motel which epitomizes anonymous American *modernity*, whereas the second takes place in a Gothic house which epitomizes the American *tradition*;. . . This opposition (whose visual correlative is the contrast between the horizontal—the lines of the motel—and the vertical—the lines of the house). . . In consequence, the very duality of desire and drive can be conceived as the libidinal correlative of the duality of modern and traditional society: the matrix of traditional society is that of a 'drive,' of a circular movement around the Same, whereas in modern society, repetitious circulation is supplanted by linear progress.[7]

It should be clear from what we have argued that the opposition between Brydon's two houses can be similarly linked to the duality of American modernity and tradition; and there is even a parallel sense in James of the modern city being horizontal—a "vast ledger-page. . .of ruled and criss-crossed lines and figures" (343)—while the gothic house, with its "intricate upper rooms" (357), its "fine large descent and three spacious landings" (362) is figured as vertical. Thus while the "apartment-house" is in the course of being modernized—that is, made horizontal: turned into flats—the essential feature of the "jolly corner" house is its steep staircase, on or near which (just as in *Psycho*) the traumatic apparition reveals itself. If the mother's house in *Psycho* is a libidinal crypt, an asocial fantasy realm hosting the endlessly circulating ghostly drive, it is easy to see in Brydon's secret nightly bouts of repetitious circulation around the rooms of his old home a parallel figure of "ineffaceable life" (348), of an ontological singularity encrypted, foreclosed from the "linear progress" of everyday signification and (especially masculine) identity. This is vividly illustrated by a moment when we see Brydon and Alice poised on the very threshold of the house:

> . . . the next moment he had opened the house-door and was standing with her on the steps. He closed the door and, while he re-pocketed his key, looking up and down, they took in the comparatively harsh actuality of the Avenue, which reminded him of the assault of the outer light of the Desert on the traveller emerging from an Egyptian tomb.
>
> (*THJ* 348)

The couple are emerging, in other words, from the mummy's house, the towering receptacle of ancestral tradition with its illegible hieroglyphs of encrypted *jouissance*, and going out into the flat, "enlightened" emptiness of modern reality. Seen in the "outer light" of the street, the family pyramid remains an inscrutable, monolithic mystery; only from within, where its spectral gloom makes it a "watery under-world" (362), can the special inner "verisimilitude" of the house be imbibed or sensed without recourse to empty signifiers.

What the "small silver ring" of the female voice in "The Jolly Corner" makes appear, then, may at first seem a beguiling alternative to the Wildean theatre of modern social discourse where identity is always predetermined as a "gesture of response" to the Other, an iterative performance of "self" with no inner plenitude or originality. But when it comes to the final "harsh actuality" the thing conjured up by the voice emerges as a monster, something forbidden from external reality—or more precisely, something *incompatible with the signifier*. Hence, when Brydon at last comes face-to-face with what he calls his "awful beast" (367)—that phrase re-echoing James's description of Oscar Wilde in a letter—he has to *disappear* as the controlling protagonist or host of the narrative, just as at the end of Dickens's *The Signalman* or Poe's "Valdemar" the encounter with the apparition coincides with the eclipse of the signifier, a collapse of narrative rhetorically masked, given a sheen of diegetic "meaning," as the death of its central character. Narrative discourse, in short, cannot deal with the apparition in the real: "No words," as Dickens wrote of the event at Staplehurst, "can describe the scene."[8]

If what emerges in the apparitional scene is therefore fundamentally at odds with narrative signification as such, how does "The Jolly Corner" manage the appearance of that scene at the end, the dramatic culmination, of its narrative? The encounter between Brydon and the "vivid truth" (364) of the apparition is staged, in three rapid paragraphs, as a catastrophic clash between the rich ambiguity of metaphor and the overwhelming self-identity of the literal, with the subtle complexity of Brydon's inner "vision" collapsing before a "blatant, vulgar" (365) materiality. Brydon, that is, is unable to *identify*, and thus affirm his habitual sense of epistemological expertise, the thing that confronts him; he cannot hang on to the controlling, manly narrative centre of the scene, so he becomes a mere onlooker, his gaze reduced to an empty or infantile "gape" (364). Indeed, as the text suggests most subtly, its protagonist can hardly believe in this castrating "drop," this usurpation of his masterly consciousness by the crude physicality of a male body:

> Then harder pressed still, sick with the force of his shock, and falling back as under the hot breath and the roused passion of a life larger than his own, a rage of personality before which his own collapsed, he felt the whole vision turn to darkness and his very feet give way. His head went round; he was going; he had gone.   (*THJ* 365)

"His very feet:" not only did his beautiful metaphor unravel, *he even fell over*, the text seems almost (but not quite) amused to have to tell us. The essence of Brydon's "vision" and his self-conception, it has been clear throughout, lies in a sense of psychical reality as sacrosanct, as a precious, intangible (and implicitly feminine) inner world wholly distinct from the external domain of mere "reality," historical accident. Thus the frequent use of scare quotes in passages concerning Brydon's interiority: mere signifiers are inadequate, it is implied, to convey the rich specificity of his psychical world, where even thoughts have to be marked as citational: "my 'thoughts'" (341). And so the terrible catastrophe awaiting Brydon on the Hitchcockian staircase is not some awful narrative disclosure (of the kind occasionally dreamt up by critics[9]) but consists rather in the absolute triumph of mere exteriority, the failure of a poetic, metaphorical self-projection in the face of the sheer otherness of a "bare life" in its radical impersonality.

What is particularly striking about "The Jolly Corner," though, is that the tale does not end here, at the epiphanic point marking the displacement of inner vision by the apparitional real (and here it contrasts, as we shall see, with James's earlier story "The Beast in the Jungle"). Thus, instead of ending like M. Valdemar with "he had gone," James's text adds a strange coda or narrative supplement. When Brydon wakes up, we learn, he is lying on the "ample and perfect cushion" of Alice Staverton's lap (365). And this is how he tries to make sense of this unexpected state of infantile passivity:

> What he most took in ... was that Alice Staverton had for a long unspeakable moment not doubted he was dead.
>
> "It must have been that I *was*." He made it out as she held him. "Yes—I can only have died. You brought me literally to life. Only," he wondered, his eyes rising to her, "only, in the name of all the benedictions, how?"
>
> It took her but an instant to bend her face and kiss him, and something in the manner of it ... somehow answered everything. "And now I keep you," she said.   (*THJ* 366)

The Jamesian text has died, we may at first think, and gone to heaven with Mills and Boon. Although the feminine is again plainly figured as a supplement to masculine subjectivity, an embodiment of the plenitude or "life" it lacks, what has apparently vanished is the whole delicate interaction of self and other that made "The Jolly Corner" a complex Jamesian meditation on questions of identity, memory and fantasy. For if those questions are to be closed down by a mother's kiss (and it is clearly in the role of mummy that Alice has triumphed, brought life back to Brydon's Egyptian tomb), something strange must have happened to Jamesian writing. The haunting presence of what is irreducible to mere discourse, a fragile and quintessential inward-otherness excluded from the rapid, vapid circulation of modern identities—this precious "feminine" spirit, as we saw, was the secret key to Spencer Brydon's self-narrative, as well as to his house. But this elusive spirit poses an interpretive problem in that, while it is consistently figured as "ineffable" (356), beyond the reach of mere denotative language, it is in effect wholly determined by the reflexive contortions of literary style; a style which, as Tambling puts it, rather than naming a worldly entity, twists language back on itself "to locate a doubleness or uncanniness inside narrative prose."[10] In other words, the haunting otherness of the Jamesian text is a product, a kind of spectral double, of the constitutive self-reflexive consciousness of narrative; and if it ever comes to be "represented," exposed as an identifiable form in a specific narrative scenario, that representation must always entail a bathetic collapse. Let us examine the moment when Brydon at last comes face to face with "his" ghost:

> Horror, with the sight, had leaped into Brydon's throat, gasping there in a sound he couldn't utter; for the bared identity was too hideous as his, and his glare was the passion of his protest. The face, that face, Spencer Brydon's?—he searched it still, but looking away from it in dismay and denial, falling straight from his height of sublimity.
>
> (THJ 364–365)

The rhetorical figure of bathos, a fall from sublime distance to banal proximity, is at the root of what horrifies Brydon and what puts him (anticipating modern psychobabble) "in denial." His protest is a disavowal—with its alternating pulse of gazing and looking away, representing and abolishing—the disavowal of "bared identity," of the collapse of infinite "ineffable" signifying potential into mere actuality. Now, at the level of Brydon's "romantic" life, an insistent implied subplot of the whole story, it would seem that we are dealing in the final section with the same figure of a fall from the "sublimity" of pure potential (playfully invoked by Alice's fantasy of Brydon as a rich, husbandly American kitted out with a big manly skyscraper); a fall, that is, into mere embodied actuality, into a relationship with a real person (who happens to be a woman). Why then, if the ghost's "fall" into diegetic reality is so horrific, does Brydon seem so cheerful about having fallen at the very end of his story into the "ample and perfect cushion" (365) of a real woman's lap?

The answer, as indeed we might suspect, is *not* that James is simply content to let his narrative slide into the complacent finale of a sentimental romance. The end of "The Jolly Corner" is in fact a deeply troubling vision of how a subject can refuse to relinquish the sublime *jouissance* of the fantasy-apparition, can disavow its mortifying reduction to signifying actuality and thus preserve it as eternal transcendent negation of all mere discursive versions of the self. And what is most disturbing of all about this psychotic refusal of signifying reality is how it hypnotically entrances the other, binds her in as partner to a *folie à deux*:

> She was beside him on her feet, but still holding his hand—still with her arm supporting him. But though it all brought for him thus a dim light, "You 'pitied' him?" he grudgingly, resentfully asked.
> "He has been unhappy, he has been ravaged," she said.
> "And haven't I been unhappy?"   (*THJ* 369)

It is a conversation between Norman Bates and his mother. Within a penumbral private world locked away from the harsh "masculine" light of the city outside, an imaginary twin is granted existence as both Spencer's rival and his naughty self, both the banished negation and the welcome re-affirmation of his ego. And the uncanny game of hide-and-seek involving mother, son and ghost can even revise history, undo its humiliations:

> "Ah I don't say I like him *better*," she granted after a thought. "But he's grim, he's worn—and things have happened to him. He doesn't make shift, for sight, with your charming monocle."
> "No"—it struck Brydon: "I couldn't have sported mine 'downtown.' They'd have guyed me there."   (*THJ* 369)

Here the couple are deep in the fantasy crypt, speaking their own private, telepathic language. To an external eye—that of the non-entranced reader, say—the exchange borders on the ludicrous, since it seems to involve a comparison between a monocle worn in reality by the son and an imaginary "pince-nez" worn by his spectral double (shortly followed by details of the latter's annual ghostly salary). But—and this is the key—what this nonsensical comparison allows is a textual fissure in which the filial protagonist, for a precious phantasmatic moment, can avoid ever having appeared ridiculous 'downtown,' those scare quotes designating a hostile urban space of masculine predators; can avoid, that is, ever having been "guyed."

It is on this last signifier that the mutual fantasy hinges. To "guy," according to the OED, is a transitive verb that emerged in the nineteenth century from an intransitive form meaning to exhibit an effigy of Guy Fawkes on 5 November; the verb thus, according to the dictionary, came to mean "make fun of," "ridicule by innuendo" or "trifle with (a theatrical part)." It is clear from this that "guyed" has connotations linking it to theatrical exhibition and specifically to London (the scene of Guy Fawkes's failed *coup d'état* and Henry James's failed *coup de théâtre*). I am tempted to hear inscribed in Spencer's fate—having avoided being 'guyed downtown' or, we might say, 'guyed *en ville*'—a cryptic echo of *Guy Domville*: as if James's text is somehow still haunted by the disastrous opening night of his play in 1895. Then, James had certainly felt himself to be 'guyed downtown,' exposed to public ridicule and made into an effigy of the cultural outsider: one way to interpret the strange mad coda of "The Jolly Corner" might be to see it as a cryptic phantasmatic undoing of that fate.

But we would nevertheless be wrong to conclude that the whole aim of "The Jolly Corner" is merely to present a fantasy of full, 'non-guyed' selfhood sustained by an imaginary union of man and woman; even if we were to identify such a fantasy of uncastrated masculinity as the basis of a "telepathic" or psychotic bond. If the Jamesian ghost story, as we suggested at the start of this chapter, is in one sense a medium for artistic self-reinvention, and as such can be seen partly as a response to the failure of *Guy Domville*, we cannot in the end reduce it to being no more than an imaginary cancellation of that failure, a phantasmatic reparation of the ego. For the imaginary scene of theatrical rivalry that took place in January 1895, in which *An Ideal Husband* seemed to 'triumph' over *Guy Domville*, was wholly governed by the gaze of the Other, determined by a specular discursive matrix of social and sexual identity. By contrast, in "The Jolly Corner," as we have shown, the theatrical scene of social identity is framed as a domain of non-knowledge, of an inauthentic performative self or masculine charade; and contrasted with another scene where what emerges is another kind of self, another ontological register irreducible to the logic of the signifier, a spectral presence adumbrated in the complex "ramifications" (354) of both the old house and the narrative style.

It is both the location and the very *sense* of the self, in other words, that have shifted between *Guy Domville* and "The Jolly Corner;" and what emerges in the latter text cannot simply be reconnected to the earlier scene: it eludes the consistent domain of signification governed by the gaze of the Other, is no longer socially recognisable or "realistic." This other self, no longer constrained by the imaginary social topography of the socially conditioned ego, can be glimpsed as a ghostly blur in the story's final moments:

> "Ah!" Brydon winced—whether for his proved identity or for his lost fingers. Then, "He has a million a year," he lucidly added. "But he hasn't you."
>
> "And he isn't—no, he isn't—*you!*" she murmured as he drew her to his breast. (*THJ* 369)

On the one hand, we might read this last line might as a plea for sanity (the ghost is non-existent, we have imagined it: only you, as an ordinary discursive self, are real); but on the other hand—the one with the missing fingers, so to speak—the ghost is still there, haunting the uncanny syntax of the couple's embrace. For there are (almost) three persons in that embrace: "he isn't you" opens up a gap between two alternative versions of Brydon: then "he" (that is, not you) "drew her to his breast." The emphatic double negation of the first ghostly "he," in other words, surreptitiously unsettles the other, supposedly real "he," as if the pronoun still bears an echo of the spectral murmur: "he isn't—*you.*" At the very closure of the story, in other words, at an apparently conventional generic moment of heterosexual satisfaction that ostensibly sets a seal on the story's vertiginous inquiry into the subject and its sexual identity, Jamesian writing subtly but insistently keeps those questions alive through the occult vibration of its oscillating syntax.

THE PASSION OF THE OTHER

Let us look once again at the precise moment of the encounter with the apparition in "The Jolly Corner." When Brydon enters on the "preposterous secret thrill" (351) of his nightly adventure on the jolly corner, his entry to the house of *jouissance* is accompanied, we recall, by a distinct figure: that of an uncanny music. But we need to attend carefully to what this music actually entails. The other life, we are told, begins for Brydon "as soon as he had heard behind him the click of his great house-door" and it emanates "as beguilingly as the slow opening bars of some rich music follow the tap of the conductor's wand" (352). These 'sounds degree zero,' the click and the tap—minimal rhythmic or acoustic indices—are followed by the "first effect" of Brydon's stick on the marble floor, a "dim reverberating tinkle as of some far-off bell" (352). The entry into the domain of secret *jouissance* is marked, in other words, by a soundtrack of pure percussive noises, acoustic splinters that echo, become rich and strange, through the medium of reflective consciousness. But the key point about these piercing sonic shards is that they derive neither from the outside nor from the inside; they are not "normal" external noises nor are they merely psychical hallucinations.[11] The click of the door can be taken as the perfect rendition of this acoustic 'extimacy,' since it is sited on the very *limen* or edge between outer reality and the forbidden domain of "preposterous thrill," the phantasmatic *Innenwelt*.

The other key feature of these spectral acoustic splinters is that, as Žižek writes in a discussion of sounds in cinema, they "penetrate us like invisible but nonetheless material rays."[12] Although for Brydon being penetrated or possessed by the sounds in the house is initially part of the secret thrill of his nocturnal experiments, he later comes to suffer a very different spectral-acoustic deprivation of masculine self-possession. In the final nightmarish encounter with the ghost, it suddenly drops its hands from its face "and left it uncovered, presented;" and then "Horror, with the sight, had leaped into Brydon's throat, gasping there in a sound he couldn't utter. . ." (364). The speed of the writing may blur the precision of what it is being spelt out here: for the eclipse of the signifier by the apparition is not just a matter of the subject being 'dumbfounded,' lost for words in a supposedly familiar way; but consists rather in his body being possessed by something alien to discourse. What leaps into his throat to dispossess Brydon of his voice is "horror, *with the sight*" (italics mine): that is, a hallucinatory gaze-voice, a thing unspeakable because couched in the figural language of *Bilderschrift*.

What becomes manifest, then, in the sounds and the sight of the apparitional thing in "The Jolly Corner" is written in an incalculable language of the eye. It is this figural ghost-speech that usurps the consistent site of social, discursive subjectivity, opening—"as beguilingly as . . . some rich music" (352)—the dimension of the hypnotic, of psychical invasion, trance or possession. It is that dimension which Henry James, in "The Jolly Corner" and especially in "The Beast in the Jungle," thinks above all in relation to the enigmatic crux of sexual difference.

"The Beast in the Jungle" was written in 1902, two years before James began the long trip to America that would inform the narrative background of "The Jolly Corner." Although the earlier story is sometimes seen as a preliminary, less developed version of the later text, I will argue on the contrary that it is the earlier narrative, away from the later preoccupation with questions of nationhood and cultural identity, that presents a more focused picture of the essential link between the enigmatic real of sexual difference and the status or possession of psychical reality.

What probably first strikes readers today about this story is how it initially presents the feminine partner in the quasi-amorous relationship as a mere resource for the masculine subject, a kind of non-actualized passive repository of all that the hero-protagonist may lack or require. Thus, here the equivalent of Alice Staverton in "The Jolly Corner" is May Bartram (with her forename implying potential, passivity); and she is pictured waiting for, nay waiting *on*, the protagonist John Marcher, like some dutiful maid or useful bit of technology, an attendant robot whose job is merely to assist his heroic discourse:

> Her face and her voice, all at his service now, worked the miracle—the impression, operating like the torch of a lamplighter who touches into flame, one by one, a long row of gas jets. (*THJ* 305)

What is superficially at stake for the couple here is the sharing of memory, the extension of their separate consciousnesses back in time through an intersubjective negotiation; but in fact it is a question of who *owns* psychical reality, which of the partners is able to control and re-animate that "spiritual" gaseous resource. And it is clearly May who holds the conductor's wand, to recall the metaphor used by James in "The Jolly Corner," whose gaze and voice command the resource of consciousness, can work the miracle of its illumination or actualization. In other words, the question of power in the relation between male and female subjects—which at first seemed so clearly biased in favour of Marcher, with May's body and soul "all at his service"—turns out to be much harder to discern. For the whole premise of Marcher's future-anterior project, in which his everyday existence is constantly sublated (in true Hegelian fashion: at once negated and ennobled) by "the thing that waited" (321), the great imaginary event that supposedly will have made his life truly significant and worthwhile—that whole premise, it becomes clear, is fully invested in a trope of femininity which the text constructs as a thing-like resource (so much so that "the thing that waited" could almost be a description of May Bartram herself). Just as it will be in "The Jolly Corner," in this story Jamesian femininity is closely linked to psychical reality itself, defined as a realm of pure potentiality, of a semantic subtlety irreducible to the stark either/or demanded by the hard-nosed realism of the "masculine" world outside. It is this nebulous, dubious realm, therefore, that hosts the "great accident" (322) ceaselessly projected by Marcher as his future-anterior redemption, a phantasmatic supplement that will one day have elevated the meagre actuality of his former existence to a higher plane of meaningfulness and ontological dignity.

If the "thing that waited" is thus in one sense a woman, though, it is also, as the title of the story reminds us, a beast in the jungle: in other words, like many a good metaphorical supplement, its advent will be dangerous, will threaten the ontological integrity of the "host" element it supposedly supports. The multiple of Marcher's experience, to use Badiou's terminology, is only constituted or made consistent by the subtraction of one element, the signifier of the event (as "the beast in the jungle") being "necessarily supernumerary to the site" (*BE* 181). If the beast were ever to spring, the future-anterior truth-event to take its place as an ordinary element within the multiple, the very ontological consistency of Marcher's world would collapse.

The most subtle stylistic device in "The Beast in the Jungle" is the reflexive transposition of this opposition between signifying actuality and redemptive or apocalyptic truth-event onto the reader's own engagement with the narrative. Thus the possibility of Marcher's grand existential project simply dissolving, resulting in no more than "an abject anti-climax," is at the same time always an implicit possibility for the very tale we are being told: will anything finally have happened in this text, or will it all amount to nothing, to an empty discourse, a signifying multiple without the key master signifier? What supports our interest in John Marcher's story, in other words, both at the level of diegetic content and of narrative form, is the possibility of the "thing" promised being eventually delivered by the text, of the great future-anterior event continually foretold by the narrative finally taking a comprehensible shape and rewarding our readerly patience. Indeed, it is this that gives "The Beast in the Jungle" its status as an anticipation of modernist literary experimentalism—for what is fundamentally at stake in the story of Marcher and May is the *eclipse of content by form*: the possibility, we might say, of an absolute writing (one famously envisaged by Flaubert as a "writing about nothing"). What becomes clear in the end is that Marcher's desire for an ontological substance to give shape to his life is completely abstract; it is not invested in any specific content—that is to say *anything*, provided it is not nothing, will do:

> He didn't care what awful crash might overtake him, with what ignominy or what monstrosity he might yet be associated . . . if it would only be decently proportionate to the posture he had kept, all his life, in the promised presence of it. He had but one desire left—that he shouldn't have been "sold." (*THJ* 323)

The only unacceptable fate for this man is therefore the travesty of form, the inconsistency of the multiple or the non-correspondence of signifying response (from the Other) and imaginary "posture" (assumed by the self as demand addressed to the Other). Marcher's fundamental desire not to have been "sold" recalls the fantasy of not being "guyed" in "The Jolly Corner:" as long as the basic demands of formal consistency are met, as long as the gaze of the Other is satisfied by a minimal convergence of authorial posture and meaningful event—and the author therefore not exposed as ludicrously incapable of delivering on his own "promised presence"—all will be well, the artwork of the self will be saved. What serves to guarantee that dubious self in "The Jolly Corner," what enables the "rich return of consciousness" (365) after the humiliating encounter with mere spectral exteriority, is, we recall, the comforting receptacle, the "ample and perfect cushion" (365) of feminine subjectivity. And it is the feminine domain, implicitly figured by the architectural complexity and otherworldly interior of the house on the jolly corner, that can encrypt or host the "rich music" of the relation, the psycho-telepathic bond between man and woman adumbrated in the last section of the story. Only that secret music of spectral femininity is able to render—not, of course, merely to "represent"—a different kind of life, an ontology not exclusively determined by the specular exteriority of signifying proportion or consistency.

What happens, though, to this redemptive feminine receptacle-host in "The Beast in the Jungle"? After May Bartram has had the indecency to die, John Marcher is suddenly left alone to contemplate what to do

> . . . now that the Jungle had been threshed to vacancy and that the Beast had stolen away. It sounded too foolish and too flat; the difference for him in this particular, the extinction in his life of the element of suspense, was such in fact as to surprise him. He could scarce have said what the effect resembled; the abrupt cessation, the positive prohibition, of music perhaps, more than anything else, in some place all adjusted and all accustomed to sonority and to attention. (*THJ* 334)

The disappearance of the Beast becomes a bathetic figure for the demise of the shared fantasy, the humiliating solo awakening from a *folie à deux*. And what has been suddenly prohibited, as if by some puritan superego, is something quite specific: namely *music*—that ultimate aesthetic dimension, according to Pater, the pure coalescence of form and matter where form becomes "an end in itself."[13] In other words, the space of fantasy constructed by the couple Marcher/May was a kind of musical performance, a sublime duet in which what was shared, what truly *counted*, was supernumerary to the multiple, exceeded the semiotic constraints of ordinary discourse, with its formal perfection a pure "element of suspense" in which the closing bar of meaning could be ceaselessly deferred, always written in the future anterior.

Deprived of this redemptive-ontological phantasmal music by May's untimely demise, Marcher is left to ponder the transformation of his own subjective position in relation to the signifying Other:

> If he could at any rate have conceived lifting the veil from his image at some moment of the past . . ., so to do this today, to talk to people at large of the jungle cleared and confide to them that he now felt it as safe, would have been not only to see them listen as to a goodwife's tale, but really to hear himself tell one.   (*THJ* 334)

Only while he was safely ensconced in the secret phantasmatic marriage could he have "conceived" or lifted his bridal veil to reveal the truth; whereas now, in the cold light of the Other's gaze, his discourse no longer merely *seems* like empty "female" twittering but—lacking the female partner who could privately avow it, turn it into fantasy music—it really *is* that demeaning stereotype. Thus, after such a castration or phantasmatic deprivation, Marcher's future-anterior project has to rapidly reinvent itself: as another kind of (implicitly phallic) hunt, no longer for a lurking beast but now for "the lost stuff of consciousness" (334). It is this precious "stuff" that will return in the closing section of "The Jolly Corner," with the phantasmatic rebirth of the hero in the consoling embrace of a feminine being—a being not governed by the reductive contingency of the signifier, but rather one imbued with a translucent certainty, an ontological groundedness as indubitable as that of consciousness sensing itself.

We have seen, then, that psychical reality, the "stuff of consciousness," which can never be reduced to any specific textual manifestation, is figuratively linked in these two Jamesian stories both to feminine characters and to a "feminine" space of phantasmal interiority and "sonority" (334) or musical self-identity located away from the site of mere discursive actuality. If this phantasmatic "stuff" pervades the house on the jolly corner and seems almost to loom larger than mere reality in the story's surreal coda, a very different fate greets it in "The Beast in the Jungle." The earlier

story, indeed, is far less "jolly:" while the end of "The Jolly Corner" offers
a phantasmatic celebration of a psychical embrace implicitly at odds with
the narrative medium itself (although, as we argued, subtle doubts are suggested by the closing syntax), at the end of "The Beast in the Jungle" the
untimely death of May Bartram seems likely to preclude the possibility of
any such redemptive apocalypse.

The ghostly "lost stuff of consciousness" for which Marcher vainly
searches does not, however, simply disappear; instead it returns from the
Other as a devastating rebuke to the narcissistic self which both of these
stories so mercilessly portray. Marcher's response to May's death, to what
has deprived him of his fundamental fantasy project and reduced him
to "nothing" (336)—in other words to an ordinary subject with no tele-
psychopathic "gift"—is to start a new relationship, "oddly enough," with
her gravestone:

> What it all amounted to, oddly enough, was that, in his now so simpli-
> fied world, this garden of death gave him the few square feet of earth on
> which he could still most live. It was as if, being nothing anywhere else
> for anyone, nothing even for himself, he were just everything here. . .
> The open page was the tomb of his friend, and *there* were the facts of
> the past, there the truth of his life, there the backward reaches in which
> he could lose himself.   (*THJ* 336)

The woman's grave thus becomes "a positive resource" for the hero, a
kind of metonymic shard or souvenir-fetish of the fantasy life in which his
ego is still fully invested. Indeed, once reduced to a fetishistic totem—a
stone page on the tomb revered at regular intervals like an altar—his relationship with May actually becomes far more convenient as a fantasy receptacle than it was during her lifetime (note how the change frees Marcher
from the tedious limitations of linear time: the page on the tomb is no
longer fixed in the future anterior, but can be opened at will to access "the
backward reaches in which he could lose himself"). If "The Beast in the
Jungle" were to end with this image of the man by the gravestone, an ironic
yet still affecting tableau of "true love," we might see the final note of the
story, not unlike that of "The Jolly Corner," as a possibly redemptive recu-
peration of the psychical "stuff" which served as support for the couple's
peculiar fantasmatic bond.

What happens at the very end of the story, though, gives "The Beast
in the Jungle" a final twist that radically displaces any such 'redemptive'
reading. Marcher has happily settled into his complacent routine of visits
to May's grave as his psychological "resource," "feeding only on the sense
that he once *had* lived, and dependent on it not only for a support but for
an identity" (337), when something occurs which is figured, in an extraordinary prolepsis of modernist writing, as a kind of terrorist attack:

The incident of an autumn day had put the match to the train laid
of old by his misery. . . . And the touch, in the event, was the face
of a fellow-mortal. This face, one grey afternoon when the leaves
were thick in the alleys, looked into Marcher's own, at the cemetery,
with an expression like the cut of a blade. He felt it, that is, so deep
down that he winced at the steady thrust. The person who so mutely
assaulted him was a figure he had noticed . . . absorbed by a grave a
short distance away. . . .   (*THJ* 337)

The mute assault of the other's gaze is a spark that lights the trail of gun-
powder to blow apart the illusory structure of the ego (with a distinct whiff
of Guy Fawkes, who re-appears, as we saw, at the end of "The Jolly Corner;" and a prefiguration of the London bombers of Conrad's 1907 novel
The Secret Agent). At the same time, the gaze is "like the cut of a blade,"
like a fatal act from Strindberg or Dostoyevsky, a pure transgression that
shatters the imaginary ontological consistency of reality. What is at stake
is the horrific proximity of the *Nebenmensch*, in the Freudian term, the
"fellow-mortal" with his own intractable pathology; and the effect of the
sudden intrusion of the other's passion into the ego's world amounts to a
brutal awakening from a feeble-minded dream:

His neighbour at the other grave had withdrawn . . . and was advanc-
ing along the path. . . This brought him near, and his pace was slow, so
that—and all the more as there was a kind of hunger in his look—the
two men were for a minute directly confronted. Marcher felt him on
the spot as one of the deeply stricken—a perception so sharp that nothing else in the picture lived for it . . . nothing lived but the deep ravage
of the features that he showed. . . . What Marcher was at all events
conscious of was . . . that the image of scarred passion presented to him
was conscious too—of something that profaned the air; and . . . that,
roused, startled, shocked, he was yet the next moment looking after it,
as it went, with envy.   (*THJ* 338)

What expresses the radical force of the apparitional gaze here is the transition from the metaphorical economy of ordinary subjectivity to an overwhelming "ravage" of non-metaphorical affect (the transition, in Lyotard's
terms, from discourse to figure). And this transition is presented by James in
an almost explicitly anamorphic mode: compared with the sharp *punctum*
of the gaze (which absorbs Marcher's own gaze and erases its subjectivity,
giving "a perception" its truly Deleuzean sense as impersonal immanence),
compared with this vital apparition "nothing else in the picture lived." All
of the discursive ingredients that ordinarily make up an identity—dress,
age, character, class—*no longer count*: they are reduced to an illegible
blur, to mere dead letters, by the anamorphic revelation or truth-event,
the making-visible of "life itself" (note how by the end of the encounter

Marcher is witnessing no longer "him" but "it"). This falling-away of the tissue of subjectivity and of the whole interpretive framework of human reality gives the scene its proto-modernist intensity, makes it a matter of "rendering"—of an unspeakable graphic "image of scarred passion"—and thus of the traumatic fracture of a consistent ontology still supported by an epistemologically stable or "realistic" discourse.

This, then, is the ultimate response to Marcher's mock-heroic project, his search for "the lost stuff of consciousness." The "spring" of the Beast comes not in response to any specific action on the part of the ego, but as a radical surprise (and even the autumnal setting seems to mock the romantic "spring" embedded in the names of May and Marcher). The text spells out quite deliberately how the apparition that demolishes the fantasy actually possesses the secret treasure, the psychical thing-in-itself, which has passed from Marcher's existence with May's death: "the image of scarred passion presented to him was conscious too—of something that profaned the air." Marcher's lifelong future-anterior fantasy, his self-conscious "consciousness" of how special his own destiny will one day have been, can therefore no longer serve to protect him; he suddenly confronts a rich depth of consciousness before which his own sham subjectivity shrivels up, appearing as an obscene profanation. Indeed, a quasi-religious subtext in this scene is readily apparent: the face of the Other is given a Levinasian spiritual power, with its "scarred passion" a thinly disguised version of a transcendent sacred passion.

If "The Jolly Corner," then, seems to present at least some redemptive potential in the final embrace of the couple (however ironized we may take that to be by its equivocal presentation, its textual duplicity), by contrast "The Beast in the Jungle" ends on an unequivocal note of savage pessimism. The ontological annihilation of John Marcher is complete and devastating: the bitter sense that only a fleeting, meaningless encounter with another's passion has given him "something of the taste of life" (339) leaves him with nothing but psychotic hallucination to fill the void—leaves him, in other words, utterly beyond the domain of narrative signifiers: like M. Valdemar, outside the multiple of his own experience.

We should pause, in conclusion, over the anamorphic quality of the final truth-event of "The Beast in the Jungle" to see how the ghostly life figured there recalls the Dickensian "spark of life" with which we began our argument; and how it prefigures the conflagration, the radical narrative transformations, of modernist writing.

We have seen that what destroys John Marcher, what bursts the lifelong bubble of his phantasmatic identity, is the "raw glare" of a stranger's gaze: an encounter with vital intensity in "a perception so sharp that nothing else in the picture lived for it" (338). The notion of "the picture" here is essential: the entire scene is in question, not as a representation grasped and controlled by the external gaze of the narrative protagonist, but as an enigmatic epiphany where the whole discursive structure of subjectivity—that

of Marcher's as much as the stranger's—is struck out, rendered insignificant, by the pulsing radiance of the gaze (we might envisage this scene best,
perhaps, as a picture by Munch such as *The Scream*). There is nothing in
the scene that *involves* the spectator, in other words, that draws the eye to
its centre, except this unbearable emanation of bare life.

We may recall something similar taking place in *Our Mutual Friend*,
when what Deleuze saw as the absolute immanence of a life became visible
in the resuscitation of the "ghost" Rogue Riderhood. What was crucial
in that Dickensian scene was the subtraction of that apparition from the
consistent multiple of narrative reality, in that neither Riderhood's well-
known villainy nor any of the other characters' various individual qualities
counted for anything during the episode: beside the anamorphic "spark of
life," nothing else in the picture lived. Just as Marcher's masterly gaze, the
site of his subtle, self-aware reflexive consciousness, is overwhelmed by the
chance apparition of a stranger's vital gaze, reduced to a dumb "gape," so
the onlookers in *Our Mutual Friend* when confronted by Riderhood's vacillating spirit are absorbed into something impersonal, an event beyond any
merely narratable interest or meaning: life itself stripped of all its worldly
constituents, reduced to its pure ghostly event or figure.

In both a Victorian novel and an early twentieth-century short story, then,
an anamorphic spectral apparition of life radically jeopardizes the narrative
structure and ontological consistency of the everyday world. In fact even the
basic generic difference involved here already encapsulates something of what
has changed between the moment of Dickens and that of Henry James. In
Our Mutual Friend, that is, the vital ghostly apparition can still be termed by
the narrator a "short-lived delusion" (*OMF* 506), set apart as a momentary
suspension of the narrative laws that determine the fictional world; and is
thus something which can be quickly forgotten, like a dream, by the characters as soon as the story proper resumes. By contrast, in "The Beast in the
Jungle" the apparition that occurs emerges in a true "Valdemar" moment,
in the sense indicated by Barthes or Lacan: the terminal collapse of narrative
into an obscene, unaccountable figure, something "empty of all plausibility,"
impossible to include in the ontologically consistent multiple of reality .

What the Dickensian text still has, of course, is a good old-fashioned
narrator, one fully equipped with a god-like omniscience; and so that text
is able to offer, at least on a first reading, a reassuring sense of authorial
control and an implicit guarantee of narrative continuity and coherence.
In the Jamesian text, by contrast, the absence of any such powerful, quasi-
paternal host-narrator makes the apparitional text almost by definition a
"tale of terror" in Poe's radical sense: an enigmatic, incalculable fragment
of *jouissance*. For the thing that appears there, in all its unmortified intensity, remains impossible to interpret, to treat as an ordinary element in the
set of narrative discourse.

What the close of "The Beast in the Jungle" vividly reveals, in fact, is how,
once the omniscient narrator has disappeared, the apparition of bare life, of

a pure immanence unconstrained by narrative sense or teleology, becomes explosive: its mute assault is a threat to the very structure of subjectivity, the social-discursive bond itself. The "lost stuff of consciousness" figured in the epiphanies and enigmas of James's stories will return in the ensuing decades to drive the fundamental modernist challenge to predominant ways of thinking and living the social bond: a challenge caught between creative exuberance and haunting nightmares. One of the first writers to embody the hallucinatory force of that writerly challenge to social-discursive form was May Sinclair, the subject of the next chapter.

Part III
Hosts of the Living

5 A Loop in a Mesh
May Sinclair

> Horror is in no sense an anxiety about death.
>
> —Levinas

THE PERFECT HOSTESS

Steven Connor has argued that although the 'other world' of the Victorian occult has often been seen as a 'spiritual' flight from the pragmatic dominance of scientific modernity, it was in fact thoroughly "entangled with the 'real world' of science and progress . . . in its mirroring of the communicational technologies of the second half of the nineteenth century."[1] Thus, when in 1894 W. T. Stead reports to the public on "progress in telepathic automatism," he can find no better way to communicate what he has discovered than by invoking the most new-fangled technological wizardry:

> The more I experiment with telepathy the more is the conviction driven in upon me that the mind uses the body as a temporary two-legged telephone for purposes of communication at short range with other minds, but that it no more ceases to exist when the body dies than we cease to exist when we ring off the telephone.[2]

But if the mind uses the body as a mobile phone, the connection may at times be faulty; and Stead has to admit as much in the same article when, having "asked mentally" for a message about the health of a sick friend and duly received telepathic news of her recovery, he is still troubled by doubts:

> I feared to believe the good news. I read the messages to my friend, who signed them as confirmation, and remarked that if this turned out right it would be a great score for the spooks, but I feared my own strong desire for better news had vitiated the accuracy of the despatch.[3]

"I feared my own strong desire:" Stead's phrase encapsulates what May Sinclair (1863–1946), for her part, will write as the "flaw in the crystal"— the notion that desiring subjectivity poses a constant threat to the supposed "accuracy" of the telepathic link; that, in other words, the two-legged telephone can only be imagined as a reliable mechanism if the dimension of desire could be suspended entirely. A moment later, Stead unwittingly reduplicates the same problem of the relation between subjectivity and

telecommunication: "I quote from memory the contents of letters and tele-
grams" (those documents having been sealed in an envelope and delivered to
the Society for Psychical Research), so that "I cannot lay hands upon them
at the moment of writing" (285). The "accuracy of the despatch," the reli-
ability of the psychical transmission, is thus again jeopardized by the particular disposition of the subject, its contingent, desirous being-in-the-world.
The only truly reliable telepath, the only crystal without a flaw, would therefore be a subject wholly subtracted from the worldly mesh of interests and
emotional relations. The very medium of the "despatch"—that which Freud
posited as a distinct register called "psychical reality"—is at odds with the
logic of telecommunication with its ostensibly scientific verifiability.

Addressing the Society for Psychical Research in 1896, William James
suggested a possible link between subjects' gender and their responses to
paranormal phenomena; so that things registered as real entities by the "feminine-mystical mind" remained invisible to the "scientific-academic mind"
supposedly characteristic of the Victorian male.[4] Invoking this venerable rhetorical gender-doublet was one way to explain the high number of women
attracted to Madame Blavatsky's Spiritualist movement, and conversely the
entrenched resistance shown by the patriarchal edifices of Victorian culture
to their supposed discoveries. But it also sheds light on Stead's own sense of
the dubious medium of desiring subjectivity in psychotelegraphy: for what, in
his view, constitutes a threat to the efficacy of psychical transmission (itself
figured in very "scientific-academic" language: "experiment," "communication at short range," "accuracy of the despatch"), this supposed threat bears
all the characteristics of the "feminine" mind: impulsive reversals, contingent
vagaries of desire, utter lack of "objective" scientific rigour.

Here one of the central ironies of psychical research, often noted by critics, comes into view: namely, how its language internalizes an implicitly
gendered opposition between scientific knowledge and mystical intuition,
thus reproducing in its own discourse the very rhetoric that was busy elsewhere condemning the enterprise of psychical investigation itself as dubious
"feminine" frivolity.[5] In Stead's notion of his own desire posing a threat to
the accuracy of telepathic transmission, we see an instance of this mim-
icry of naturalist scientific knowledge, with its implicit denigration of the
"feminine-mystical mind." The very space of psychical reality, as site of
singular desire or subjective bias, is coded as a dubious (implicitly feminine)
interiority in opposition to an objective (implicitly masculine) "external"
mechanism, here supposedly that of telepathic "transmission."

It was not William James, of course, but his brother Henry who at the
end of the nineteenth century was to transfer the "scientific" question of the
psychical to literature in his reinvention of the Victorian ghost story. To recall
our discussion of "The Jolly Corner" in Chapter 4 we could now re-envis-
age Spencer Brydon's two New York properties—the horizontal-discursive
"house within the street" and the vertical-figural "Egyptian tomb" on the
jolly corner (*THJ* 342, 348)—in terms of William James's opposition between

the "scientific-academic" and the "feminine-mystical." In that story, Henry James tropes this doublet in the same gendered terms his brother had used, with on one side the "harsh actuality" of a modern, phallic city, on the other the "small still scene" of a fragrant, delicately feminized tradition (348, 343). The very language in which James describes the feminine "mystical other world" encrypted in the house on the jolly corner may indeed have echoed, like some "dim reverberating tinkle" (352) on the 'telepathic' airwaves, in May Sinclair's mind when in 1912 she chose to call her own tale of psycho-telegraphic connection "The Flaw in the Crystal." To trace this intertextual 'telepathy,' we should return to the scene where James's protagonist Spencer Brydon is tiptoeing into the hall of the house on the jolly corner:

> . . . he put his stick noiselessly away in a corner—feeling the place once more in the likeness of some great glass bowl, all precious concave crystal, set delicately humming by the play of a moist finger round its edge. The concave crystal held, as it were, this mystical other world, and the indescribably fine murmur of its rim was the sigh there, the scarce audible pathetic wail; to his strained ear, of all the old baffled forsworn possibilities. (THJ 352–353)

A Jamesian crystal thus appears in a text published only six years before Sinclair's own story; and that crystal has all the "feminine-mystical" quali-ties of a telepathic portal onto a "ghostly life" (353) foreclosed from the everyday world of patriarchal rationality. Likewise Sinclair's heroine Agatha Verrall is blessed or cursed with an ambiguous telepathic gift that makes her not so much a two-legged telephone as a kind of mobile crystal receiver:

> She went down with slow soft footsteps as if she carried herself, her whole fragile being, as a vessel, a crystal vessel for the holy thing, and was careful lest a touch of the earth should jar and break her.[6]

In "The Jolly Corner," though, James has his hero Brydon evade any actual relation with the other sex, as his passion for the fantasmatic 'feminine' space of the old house displaces any real sexual encounter; until, that is, the story's strange coda that sees him reabsorbed into an ostensibly conventional hetero-sexuality (although the text is still haunted by the cryptic crystalline music, the "indescribably fine murmur," of another life, an alternative self or different narrative teleology). We could see May Sinclair's own "crystal," a story writ-ten by a financially independent suffragist in 1912, as in part a veiled rebuke to the ghostly Master who had so influenced her. While in James, that is, the "concave crystal" remains a numinous "feminine" symbol contemplated by a self-explorative male protagonist, Sinclair makes pointedly clear her hero-ine's psychological suffering under the patriarchal regime of sexuality, as Agatha's "whole fragile being" becomes the telepathic supplement to a defec-tive masculinity.

But at the opening of "The Flaw in the Crystal" we see something distinctly reminiscent of Henry James's stories: that is, the figure of woman as hostess, as actively passive recipient of a male subject in flight from the ties of his ordinary existence. Those ties include marriage, of course, and Sinclair's feminist critique of that heterosexual institution takes a strange twist as her narrative seems deliberately to displace the flaw in male identity away from masculinity itself:

> To be wedded to a mass of furious and malignant nerves (which was all that poor Bella was now) simply meant destruction to a man like Rodney Lanyon. Rodney's own nerves were not as strong as they had been, after ten years of Bella's. It had been understood for long enough (understood even by Bella) that if he couldn't have his weekends he was done for; he couldn't possibly have stood the torment and strain of her.   (*US* 59)

The non-relation between man and woman is depicted here as the pathological juncture of host and parasite. If Bella is merely a "thing" without proper access to the symbolic register of human subjectivity (as Agatha's free-indirect narration implies), that thing has inflicted its own pathology on the male subject it is "wedded" to, making him not merely less masculine, but more like *it*—in other words *less human*. So Rodney's Friday visits to Agatha are much more than a bit of weekend fun: his "escape to Agatha" (59) offers him the sole chance to evade, not just the tedium of a loveless marriage but the "torment" of an overwhelming feminine Thing that threatens to eclipse his very subjectivity. It is here that the apparent misogyny of Sinclair's portraying a woman as "a mass of furious and malignant nerves" can be seen in a different light. For the key to Sinclair's representation of sexual difference in "The Flaw in the Crystal" is the sense that masculine subjectivity is caught up in a discursive network that fails to account for, that cannot transact symbolically with, a pathological bond or connection that opens, beyond the fixed forms of socio-cultural exchange, onto a radical ontological dimension glimpsed as an unnameable otherness. Thus, although Bella is dismissed by the narrator as a somatic parasite, she is at the same time presented as a figure of undeniable power: her host-husband's masculine identity is defenceless against her pathological influence, which acts through a direct, hypnotic transference of affect. It is the women in Sinclair's writing, however much they seem to be disparaged on the surface of the narrative, that are imbued with real *savoir faire* concerning pathological transference, whether as dangerous telepathic parasite or as healing psychical hostess.

Sinclair's trope of the telepathic "crystal"—a creative and dangerous portal onto the inner ontological essence of the other, sited beyond the deceptive, insulating surfaces of discursive protocol—finds its clearest manifestation in the tale as Agatha's "uncanny, unaccountable Gift" (60).

It is this telepathic gift that saves her from the sordid realities of ordinary sexual relations, with her ontological centre withdrawn from the external world into a transcendent-hypnotic zone of multiple interiority. But at the same time, as the plot of the story unfolds, this opening of her subjectivity beyond the normative defences of discourse, makes her especially vulnerable to psychical invasion by the other.

To engage further with Sinclair's text, we need to start by looking again at the rhetoric of its title. Does the "crystal" of that title still have the status of a literary symbol, serving as a quasi-poetic figure for the otherwise unaccountable psyche of the feminine-telepathic medium? In "The Jolly Corner," James had resolved this rhetorical uncertainty by clearly associating the idea of the mystical crystal with Spencer Brydon's own penumbral thoughts: "The concave crystal held, *as it were*, this mystical other world . . ." (*THJ* 352; my italics) With a touch as light as "as it were," James is able to suggest his character's self-conscious, slightly arch interior monologue and thus make the "crystal" a matter not of authorial opinion but of a character's self-aware discursive world. In the following passage from near the start of Sinclair's story, we see her free-indirect narration doing something altogether different. Agatha is tensely awaiting the possible arrival of Rodney:

> There was no need to prepare her. She was never not prepared. It was as if by her preparedness, by the absence of preliminaries, of adjustments and arrangements, he was always there, lodged in the innermost chamber. She had set herself apart; she had swept herself bare and scoured herself clean for him. Clean she had to be; clean from the desire that he should come; clean, above all, from the thought, the knowledge she now had, that she could make him come. (*US* 60)

As in James, the narrative voice is thoroughly enmeshed with the character's psyche; but in contrast to "The Jolly Corner," here there is no implied reflexive acknowledgement of the rhetorical nature of the language being used: used, that is, as a figure of speech, as someone's way of picturing the world to themselves. Instead, we enter a strange borderland between objective and psychical reality where the sense of Agatha being a psychical chamber to accommodate a desiring masculine being is no longer understood as *simply* metaphorical. In what precise sense, we might therefore ask, has Agatha "swept herself bare and scoured herself clean for him"? As the short, crisp phrases of Sinclair's writing mime the repetitive strokes of domestic drudgery, we are reminded that the woman's active passivity is not simply an idea, a mere effect of signifiers, but a real product of conscious psychical work. Agatha's "preparedness" as cleansed and stripped-bare chamber, in other words, has the objective force of a distinct psychical reality.

The central writing-problem of "The Flaw in the Crystal" is how to represent the equivocal ontological dimension of a transitional zone between the external world and the psychical. Agatha's self-scouring can indeed almost be seen as a reflexive figure for what happens to literary language in this text: its metaphorical surface is stripped away to reveal "naked thought" in its fully dangerous, fully transgressive state. This is made more explicit in another exchange between Agatha and Rodney. She has just told him that she has shared their "secret" with another woman (although what that secret actually entails is not disclosed to the reader; nor is it ever clear to the characters themselves):

> 'Good God.' As he stared in dismay at what he judged to be her unspeakable indiscretion, the thought rushed in on her straight from him, the naked, terrible thought, that there *should* be anything they had to hide, they had to be alone for. She saw at the same time how defenceless he was before it; he couldn't keep it back; he couldn't put it away from him. It was always with him, a danger watching on his threshold.
>
> (*US* 64)

"The thought rushed in on her straight from him:" the failure of the couple to communicate at the level of discourse is accompanied by its spectral reversal—a direct, telepathic transference of "naked, terrible thought." But the interpsychical vector is drastically skewed in Agatha's favour: while he can only gape uncomprehendingly (and the platitude "Good God" will prove heavily ironic), she with her telepathic gift can both grasp his misunderstanding and observe his psychical vulnerability to "it," to a liminal or extimate presence riddling his identity with an internal otherness: "And still his thought, his terrible, naked thought, was there. It was looking at her straight out of his eyes" (64).

The asymmetry of psychotelegraphy thus has everything to do, in Sinclair's writing, with that of sexual difference. Masculine subjects, and behind them a line of decayed patriarchal institutions like the church and matrimony, can no longer (if they ever could) cope symbolically with, produce a consistent discourse on, what is now coming though on the medium of Agatha's telepathic crystal: a bare life or absolute ontological otherness intermittently visible to her inner eye. Traditional forms of ethno-cultural transmission, all the rites and ceremonies that throughout history were supposed to mediate between sensory experience and ideology, thus providing at least a possible structure for a relation between social reality and the "spiritual"—all those institutional forms are no longer viable in the face of what is becoming manifest (an ontological immanence vaguely hypostasized in the narrative as "it" or "the Power").

Sinclair's text is shot through with traces of failed symbolic ritual, couched in the obsolete language of patriarchal tradition, from the "unrestrained communion" (92) that now designates a perilous and ecstatic psychosexual intercourse; to the "unthinkable sacrament" (98) of partaking in the "nameless, innermost essence" (93) of another psyche, imbibing its forbidden psychotic opiate. This blasphemous spillage of religious language into a world it can no longer redeem or comprehend marks a traumatic point of failed ideological transmission, a dangerous collapse of social-discursive connections. We see this most clearly in Agatha's problem of trying to explain her "gift:"

> There was a long silence. At last Milly's voice crept through, strained and thin, feebly argumentative, the voice of a thing defeated and yet unconvinced.
> 'I don't understand you, Agatha. You say it isn't you; you say you're only a connecting link; that you do nothing; that the Power that does it is inexhaustible; that there's nothing it can't do, nothing it won't do for us, and yet you go and cut yourself off from it—deliberately, from the thing you believe to be divine. [. . .]
> 'Yes. It's divine and it's—it's terrible. It does terrible things to us.'
> 'How could it? If it's divine, wouldn't it be compassionate?'
>
> (*US* 104)

The psychological enigma of "transference" (to use the psychoanalytic term which Freud himself, in the same year Sinclair wrote her story, was explicitly linking to hypnotic suggestion[7]) is just visible here, but it remains submerged in a defunct liturgical vocabulary; what results is a nonsensical discursive compromise that impedes the transference of the "secret," the theoretical solution of the enigma. A vague, quasi-divine "Power" is all these women can conjure as name for an occult, intuitive manifestation that can no longer be contained or mediated by traditional forms of cultural transmission, and whose energy now overflows language itself, so that the very signifiers caught up in its current vacillate and vibrate, failing to designate a coherent entity. The key word here is "compassionate"—not of course in its Christian sense, which has nothing to do with the intransigent, anonymous force in question here, but in an almost punning sense, to encapsulate the "nameless, innermost essence" (93) of telepathy (itself a Greek variant of the Latinate "compassion:" both words designate "feeling with" the other). If this "thing you believe to be divine" is thus no longer governed by any consensual, connective framework of shared terms or values, it is very much rooted in the event of com-passion, of the "connecting link" or transference between affective psychopathological singularities.

As the phrase "connecting link" implies, by 1912 there were certainly other ways to attempt to think about affective transference than the obsolete trope of "communion." The following passage takes us to Sinclair's central metaphor (if that still remains the right term) of psychical telecommunication, confirming Steven Connor's link between the "evolution of ghost phenomena and the developing logic of technological communications:"[8]

> She had found out the secret of its working and had controlled it, reduced it to an almost intelligible method. You could think of it as

a current of transcendent power, hitherto mysteriously inhibited. You made the connection, having cut off all other currents that interfered, and then you simply turned it on. In other words, if you could put it into words at all, you shut your eyes and ears, you closed up the sense of touch, you made everything dark around you and withdrew into your innermost self; you burrowed deep into the darkness there till you got beyond it; you tapped the Power, as it were, underground at any point you pleased and turned it on in any direction.   (*US* 73)

Here it is as if Sinclair has adopted and updated Stead's two-legged telephone: the "connection," with its underground wires, mobile receiver and on-switch, now connotes the most dazzling modernity, giving the "secret" that has been discovered a sheen of twentieth-century technological novelty. Agatha's switching-on of this "current of transcendent power" is not, though, merely some painless luxury of modern civilization, like the telegram she sends after an easy stroll to the village; rather, it entails a crucial ordeal, a withdrawal into the "innermost self," a kind of Cartesian *epochê* or suspension of worldly subjectivity that opens a domain of absolute cogitation, of what Michel Henry terms "thought's essential self-sensing."[9] Only the flawless crystal ontological centre of the cogitating subject can tap into the Power, successfully turn its telepathic beam onto an object; any trace of mere worldly desire, any emotional investment in the perceptual fabric of everyday reality, and the line goes dead.

It is this quasi-Cartesian aspect of Sinclair's psychotelegraphy that allows us properly to gauge its rhetoric of techno-modernity. What is key to the *epochê*, the reduction of Agatha's thinking "I" to nothing but its "innermost self" is the reduction of signification to an inhuman, mechanical degree-zero: a buzz or click that marks the difference between on and off, absence and presence. We recall how in "The Jolly Corner" Henry James inscribed a liminal *jouissance*—a phantasmal extimacy neither objectively present nor merely imaginary—by means of spectral acoustic splinters, taps and percussive noises, which could "render" (in Michel Chion's sense) what the text could not signify as such.[10] The same figural, non-discursive logic is at work in the self-suspension of Agatha's subjectivity as she makes her psychotelegraphic "connection:" since mere words cannot survive the ascetic rigour of the Cartesian *epochê*, all that is left is the non-metaphorical event of liminal noise, the punctual switching-on of the "current" of *jouissance*. That event, when it comes, is appropriately liminal, even if it involves a quaintly old-fashioned bit of technology:

At two o'clock, the hour when he must come if he were coming, she began to listen for the click of the latch at the garden gate. [. . .]
     When the click came and his footsteps after it, she admitted further . . . that she had had foreknowledge of him.   (*US* 62)

As she spoke she heard the sharp click of the latch as the garden gate fell to; she had her back to the window so that she saw nothing, but she heard footsteps that she knew, resolute and energetic footsteps that hurried to their end. She felt the red blood surge into her face. . . .

(*US* 106)

Each time, the click of the latch occurs when the eye is veiled, the specular-representational ego partly suspended; and it triggers a telepathic connection, an intuitive *Gefühlsbindung* (Freud's term for the "affective link" uniting a crowd and its leader or a hypnotist and his subject).[11] The withdrawal of the self from the ordinary social site of discourse, and its concomitant opening to a radical ontological otherness, is marked by the *acousmatique*, to recall Chion's term: a "sharp click of the latch" that does not "represent" but *embodies* the unspeakable incidence of *jouissance* at the anamorphic margin extimate to the field of signifying representation.

This figural-acousmatic dimension of psychotelegraphy, of course, reminds us that it is an event impossible to re-present, to frame and comprehend within a metanarrative. The telepathic event, we might say, *departs from the Other*: it does not belong to the realm of consistent space-time where I recognize and remember myself. And even if Agatha feels she has "controlled" (73) the Power, with the next phrase—she had "reduced it to an *almost intelligible* method" (73; my italics)—Sinclair subtly re-inscribes its alterity, its "nameless innermost essence" (93). What can be made "almost intelligible" must remain, it is ironically implied, essentially opaque, must not properly inhabit the ego's signifying reality. Thus the ego can precisely only play *host* to the "mystical" advent of what it cannot properly identify or comprehend: the acousmatic voice of the spectral guest, a ghostly vibration announcing its arrival.

It is here that we can return to the question of Sinclair's text as host, receptacle or "crystal" vessel, which is also bound up with the problem of psychical transmission raised at and through its diegetic level. Just as her heroine Agatha is happy to imagine herself as a chamber "scoured clean" (60) for a visiting male psyche, so in her writing Sinclair seems openly to play hostess, at the intertextual level, to two powerful literary-psychical guests: not only James's "The Jolly Corner," linked as we have seen to Sinclair's text by the figure of the mystical-telepathic crystal, but also another master-text of psychotelegraphy, namely Stevenson's *The Strange Case of Dr Jekyll and Mr Hyde* (1886). By exploring the intertextual *Gefühlsbindung* or affective-textual loop between Sinclair's text and Stevenson's, we will be able to see how her writing exceeds and interrogates the traditional gendered split between rationality and intuition (which we saw emblematized in William James's distinction between the "scientific-academic" and the "feminine-mystical").

What, then, links "The Flaw in the Crystal" to the *Strange Case*? The answer, it could be said with an ironic twist, is *linkage itself*. The first sign of this comes in the second paragraph of Sinclair's story, where we learn that Agatha's visitor is called "Rodney Lanyon" (59)—and we immediately recall that "Dr Lanyon" was a principal character, indeed one of the main narrators, in Stevenson's famous Victorian thriller. It may initially seem preposterous to hear that name as a near pun on "lanyard" (i.e., rope, lash or tether); until, that is, we look more closely at the texts by Stevenson and Sinclair. The former opens with a dedication to Stevenson's beloved cousin Katherine De Mattos, beneath which we read "It's ill to loose the bands that God decreed to bind."[12] And if, as this proverbial epigraph suggests, one of the novella's central themes will be the very Freudian topic of *Entbindung*, of the traumatic unbinding of psychical and social bonds, it is Dr Lanyon's character, above all, that is associated with those bonds, as his lanyard-like name suggests. Thus, when Jekyll-Hyde addresses Lanyon in a letter, he asserts the permanent solidity of their *Gefühlsbindung*: ". . .I cannot remember, at least on my side, any break in our affection" (*JH* 48). Having read the letter, Lanyon reflects "I felt *bound* to do as he requested" (49; my italics); and then later Jekyll-Hyde, having tried to bind him with "the seal of our profession," upbraids Lanyon for having "been *bound* to the most narrow and material views" (53; my italics). It is clear, in other words, that in Stevenson's text Dr Lanyon stands as a kind of one-man embodiment of "the bands that God decreed to bind," an exemplar of that very social-psychical bondedness which the tale's protagonist unwisely tries to loosen.

If we then turn to Sinclair's text, another tale of psychical bondage and *Entbindung*, it quickly becomes clear that Rodney Lanyon's surname has not been selected at random, but is bound into the rigging, as it were, of Stevenson's vessel. Just as Jekyll-Hyde feels an unbreakable affective bond with Lanyon, so Agatha sees herself linked by "the safe, the intangible, the unique relation" (*US* 66) to her own Lanyon. But she begins to suspect there might be another side to this psychical bond:

> She was reminded that, though there were no lurking possibilities in her, with him it might be different. For him the tie between them might come to mean something it had never meant and could not mean for her. . . .   (*US* 67)

"The tie between them:" once sexual difference inhabits the psychical relation (as it notoriously never does in Stevenson's novella), the homosocial solidity of the affective lanyard disappears, leaving "lurking possibilities" of misunderstanding and interpretive discrepancy. What is crucial here is the incidence of doubt, of signifying equivocation: nothing is certain in the relation; no meaning is safe from the shifting sands of interpretation. In other words, because Agatha's "tie" to Lanyon is a matter of sexual desire, it is essentially governed by the signifier: the antagonism of the partners takes the form of a ceaseless semiotic negotiation of terms, of the contractual basis of their relationship. It is clearly her desire for Lanyon that entails the "flaw" in Agatha's psychical crystal, the imperfection that jeopardizes the efficacy of telepathic connection (just as desire had caused W. T. Stead to cast doubts on that efficacy). But we need to understand this desire in the psychoanalytic sense as desire of the Other: that is, the relation is caught up in the equivocal texture of the symbolic order, subject to the law of the signifier (it is indeed tempting to read in "flaw" a punning inscription "of law").

To successfully embody a flawless telepathic crystal would entail, as we saw clearly implied by Stead earlier, transgressing the signifying law of desire, moving beyond its constitutive symbolic alienation. It is here that Agatha's other psychosexual entanglement comes into play, her relationship with the psychotic Harding Powell. The asemic ontological essence of the *Gefühlsbindung*, warded off, jeopardized or dissembled by the shifting matrix of interpretations in her equivocal relation to Lanyon, now threatens to impinge directly on Agatha's psychical topography, and thus gravely endanger the imaginary stability of her ego. The psychical link can be seen as fundamentally resistant to the signifier, an energy or mobility working against the alienating but logical structure of psychical topography. Here Sinclair's text closely recalls a passage from the *Strange Case* where Jekyll is contemplating his own psychical transformation as his self-representing subjectivity is engulfed by the unspeakable oneness of *jouissance*:

> I became, in my own person, a creature . . . solely occupied by one thought: the horror of my other self. But when I slept . . . I would leap almost without transition (for the pangs of transformation grew daily less marked) into the possession of a fancy brimming with images of terror, a soul boiling with causeless hatreds, and a body that seemed not strong enough to contain the raging energies of life.   (*JH* 68)

This being-possessed by the other "almost without transition," the breaching of the equivocal topographical membrane of the "own person," is powerfully re-animated by Sinclair:

> There could be no doubt as to what had happened, nor as to the way of its happening. The danger of it, utterly unforeseen, was part of the very operation of the gift. In the process of getting at Harding to heal him she had had to destroy, not only the barriers of flesh and blood, but those innermost walls of personality that divide and protect, mercifully, one spirit from another. With the first thinning of the walls Harding's insanity had leaked through to her, with the first breach it had broken in. It had been transferred to her complete with all its details, with its very gestures, in all the phases that it ran through. . . .   (*US* 98)

Doubt, *dubium* or semiotic duplicity, is expelled from the quasi-Cartesian "operation of the gift," its destruction of difference, its topographical obliteration. Mimetic-affective transference has no truck with the semantic vagaries of the signifier; in transit, the psychotic "spirit" remains intact, "complete with all its details:" nothing divides it from itself.

The intertextual dimension of "The Flaw in the Crystal," then, has some surprising features if we examine it closely enough. To take our initial opposition between "masculine" reason and "feminine" telepathic mysticism, as proposed in theory by William James and implied in his brother Henry's fiction, we might expect that archaic opposition to map neatly onto the Freudian dualism of binding and unbinding, and so provide a key to the imbrications of gender and subjectivity, the mystical connections and "real" social bonds, in Sinclair's text. But nothing so reassuringly schematic emerges from the telegraphic network linking Sinclair and Stevenson. Although, as we have argued, the name Lanyon serves in the *Strange Case* to emblematise the "bands that God decreed to bind," a putatively stable network of social-discursive relations, in Sinclair's narrative that patriarchal formula can no longer sustain the uncertain experience of modern sexuality. Agatha's bond to her Lanyon is no longer protected by a divine law; rather it is subject to a divisive law, the signifying law that both opens the sexual relation and prevents it from being one, "true" or unequivocal. The only indubitable bond in Agatha's story is her transgressive involvement with Harding Powell, which closely resembles the psychical annexation of Jekyll by Hyde, the obliteration of any coherent psychical topography by the "raging energies" of untrammelled *jouissance*. The question of sexual difference, along with every other semiotic distinction, is erased, made illegible, by this topographical obliteration. While in Stevenson's text that question is in effect suppressed by the absence of any female characters, in Sinclair there is no sense that we should look to Agatha's femininity to explain, according to some misogynist stereotype, the mystical bond or "unrestrained communion" (*US* 92) uniting her with Powell.

What becomes clear in Sinclair's writing is ultimately that the *Gefühlsbindung*, the mimetic-affective link that in its most radical form destroys the "innermost walls of personality," will not submit to the binary logic of the signifier; and that it therefore entails an ontological threat to the whole economy of representation, along with all habitual ideological oppositions like that of "masculine" rationality and "feminine" mysticism. This ruination of the law of the signifier takes the form, in Sinclair, of a proto-modernist epiphany, a hallucinatory vision of a world infested, swarming with an obscene, infernal vitality:

> Out of the wood and the hedges that bordered it there came sounds that were horrible, because she knew them to be inaudible to any ear less charged with insanity; small sounds of movement, of strange shiverings, swarmings, crepitations; sounds of incessant, infinitely subtle urging, of agony and recoil. Sounds they were of the invisible things unborn, driven towards birth; sounds of the worm unborn, of things that creep and writhe towards dissolution. She knew what she heard and saw. She heard the stirring of the corruption that Life was; the young blades of corn were frightful to her, for in them was the push, the passion of the evil which was Life. . . .   (*US* 95–96)

Agatha's ear and eye have been opened by her telepathic bond, her psychical merging with psychotic *jouissance*, and she finds herself suddenly exposed to the microbiotic chirruping of a manifold life-force normally kept silent, subdued and deadened, by the signifying fabric of human reality. It is this acousmatic ontological "stirring"—the uncanny anamorphic phenomenalization of voice and gaze as forbidden, unrepresentable objects—that marks the event of the ghost, as we have seen from the "vague vibration" of the Dickensian signalman's trench to the "indescribably fine murmur" of the Jamesian crystal.

In 1911, just before she wrote "The Flaw in the Crystal," Sinclair produced what she thought "the best short story I ever wrote or shall write:" a ghost story she entitled "The Intercessor."[13] And in the same period, while creating what she described to a friend as "stories of all queer lengths and all queer subjects; 'spooky' ones," Sinclair wrote ("partly as a ghost story," as Suzanne Raitt sees it), a critical biography she entitled *The Three Brontës* (MS 129). An exploration of these texts will take us closer to the uncanny inventiveness at the heart of Sinclair's distinctive writerly response to "the passion of the evil which was Life."

LANGUAGE OF JOY

Sinclair's contemporaries did not hesitate to identify her with the Brontës. Janet Hogarth, an old school-friend aware of the many parallels between Sinclair's life-story and that of the Brontës, wrote that "aspects of Miss Sinclair's work . . . almost suggest a Brontë reincarnation;" while a jovial reviewer of Sinclair's first novel described it as a posthumous work by Charlotte Brontë (MS 115). In the years before the First World War, as Raitt observes, Sinclair took this identification vigorously to heart, writing a number of prefaces to new editions of the great novels, as well as to Gaskell's *Life of Charlotte Brontë*; and responding in 1912 to a request from the publisher Constable to write a full-length monograph, which she chose to entitle *The Three Brontës* (MS 116). One of her principal concerns in that work was to challenge what she saw as the ideological distortion of Charlotte Brontë's genius by a series of patriarchal critics and biographers, for whom the unfeasible creativity that had produced *Jane Eyre* was, as Sinclair put it, "the thing that irritated, the enigmatic, inexplicable thing:" a thing which therefore had to be explained away in terms of a supposed (and supposedly heterosexual) "tragic passion."[14]

But if Sinclair's central feminist aim in *The Three Brontës* was to insist on the autonomous space of women's writing, she also made use of her critical intervention to explore a new set of aesthetic ideas bound up with her "spooky" stories and with her own developing interests in psychoanalysis and the paranormal (she joined the Society for Psychical Research in 1914).[15] We can see these ideas clearly emerging through Sinclair's different portraits of the various Brontës, all of which can be seen as in some sense 'portraits of the artist,' in other words versions of Sinclair herself. First of all we are shown the much-maligned author of the "Vision of Hell," the Reverend Patrick Brontë, who like many a Victorian father "thought himself more important than his children" (*TB* 22). But, Sinclair insists,

> . . . . he *was* important as a temporary vehicle of the wandering creative impulse. It struggled and strove in him and passed from him, choked in yards and yards of white cravat, to struggle and strive again in Branwell and in Anne. As a rule the genius of the race is hostile to the creative impulse, and the creative impulse is lucky if it can pierce through to one member of a family.   (*TB* 22)

Sinclair's burgeoning interest in the ghost story—a literary genre marked, we have argued, by a consistent figurative topography of host and guest—is distinctly legible here. The tragicomic father of the Brontës, that is, is *possessed* by a visiting spirit that is later to animate the works of his daughters, with his ridiculous clothing an apt figure for what is "hostile to the creative impulse," what represses and binds up an uncomprehended life-force it nonetheless hosts and somehow transmits. But it is of course Charlotte—partly through her sheer ability, like May Sinclair's, to survive her siblings—who will prove the best hostess for this penetrative vital impulse. Sinclair's account of this successful union of ghostly creativity and worldly embodiment, though, is far from a simple celebration of Brontë's literary achievement:

> Somehow the years passed, the years of Charlotte's continuous celebrity, and of those literary letters that take so disproportionate a part in her correspondence that she seems at last to have forgotten; she seems to belong to the world rather than to Haworth. And the world seems full of Charlotte; the world that had no place for Emily.   (*TB* 46)

Literary letters, a kind of redundant excess of letter at the expense of spirit, loom too large, become disproportionate, and thus lead Charlotte astray into an oblivious worldliness that denies the placeless ontological authenticity of Haworth and Emily. But there were other letters, as Sinclair is quick to remind us, written by Charlotte to her non-literary friend Ellen Nussey; and these unliterary letters

> . . . come palpitating with the life of Charlotte Brontë's soul that had in it nothing of the literary taint. You see in them how, body and soul, Haworth claims her and holds her, and will not let her go.
>   Nor does she desire now to be let go. Her life at Haworth is part of Emily's life; it partakes of the immortality of the unforgotten dead.
>   (*TB* 46–47)

Letters, then, the very medium of discourse, are a site of unstable equivocation. While the spiritual domain, that of pure Brontësque life or soul, is incompatible with "the literary taint," the worldly rhetoric of literary texts, there is nonetheless another kind of writing that emerges pulsating with Brontë-life (a strange life, since it corresponds to "the immortality of the unforgotten dead"). And for Sinclair the *unheimlich* home of that otherworldly life-death-writing is Haworth, a site of telepathy, of a compassionate shared interiority just like that of Agatha's crystalline trance.

What the contrasting pictures of Charlotte and her sister Emily in *The Three Brontës* show most clearly, however, is a new literary-psychical topography that Sinclair is developing, and which in turn will determine the uncanny textual landscape of "The Intercessor." Parodying Sir Wemyss Reid's hapless effort to "lighten the gloom" of the Brontës' biography, Sinclair sketches a tableau of the various siblings on their way to a picnic. The loquacious Branwell is holding forth while his sisters Charlotte and Anne attempt to compete; meanwhile,

> Emily Brontë does not talk so much as the rest of the party, but her wonderful eyes, brilliant and unfathomable as the pool at the foot of a waterfall . . . show how her soul is expanding under the influences of the scene. If she does not, like Charlotte and Anne, meet her brother's ceaseless flood of sparkling words with opposing currents of speech, she utters a strange, deep guttural sound which those who know her best interpret as the language of a joy too deep for articulate expression. (*TB* 59–60)

Emily is thus given a special place, set apart from the others in an ontological distinction equivalent to that between the register of discourse and the fascinating objects—gaze and voice—that exceed or impede discursive transmission. Sinclair takes up the same contrast later in the book when, having noted the frenzy of critical and biographical texts around Charlotte Brontë, she adds "[a]round the figure of Emily Brontë there is none of that clamour and confusion. She stands apart in an enduring silence, and guards for ever her secret and her mystery" (167). Emily is thus a *figure beyond speech*, the site of an ontology "too deep for articulate expression" (60), immune to the superficial play of competing worldly discourses. Georges Bataille, in his 1957 study *Literature and Evil*, was struck in a similar way by Emily as the embodiment of an ontological silence:

> We know that in the austerity of the vicarage, the three Brontë sisters lived in a frenzy of literary creativity. They were bound together by a day to day intimacy, though Emily nevertheless continued to preserve that moral solitude in which the phantoms of her imagination developed. . . . She lived in a sort of silence which, it seemed, only literature could disrupt.[16]

The key to this sense of Emily's separateness and solitude for Sinclair, however, is that it corresponds not to silence of a meekly 'feminine,' submissive kind but to the act of a radical "creative impulse" unconstrained by the laws of discursive protocol (and this resonates with Bataille's idea of her psyche hosting "phantoms"). The index of this disturbing creativity is the "strange, deep guttural sound" emitted by Emily, the *voix acousmatique* (to recall Chion's term) or pure voice beyond discursive structure. Now, that indecorous sound, "the language of a joy too deep for articulate expression," recalls a far more famous Brontësque noise:

> . . . it was not fated that I should sleep that night. A dream had scarcely approached my ear, when it fled affrighted, scared by a marrow-freezing incident enough.
> This was a demoniac laugh—low, suppressed, and deep—uttered, as it seemed, at the very key-hole of my chamber door.[17]

The insomniac is Jane Eyre, of course, and what wakes her is a pure vocal object, a liminal acousmatic thing: "Something gurgled and moaned" (175). The uncanny laugh of the madwoman in the attic, in other words, for all its overdetermined ideological significance in the eyes of modern critics, is given by Sinclair to Emily Brontë as the figure of an unconstrained creative language of joy, a wordless musical *jouissance*.

If this idea sounds at first far-fetched—to link what Sinclair imagines as the guttural sound of Emily's rapture to the gurgling laughter of Bertha Mason in *Jane Eyre*—it turns out, in fact, to be fully consistent with Sinclair's overall reading of the Brontës. Indeed, beyond her general sense of telepathic connectivity among the denizens of Haworth, Sinclair proposes a specific correlation between *Wuthering Heights* and the genesis of *Jane Eyre*. Arguing against what she sees as the prevailing patriarchal account of the latter—according to which Charlotte Brontë's breakthrough to authorship is to be related to her supposed passion for a professor she met on her trip to Brussels—Sinclair offers her own theory: that Charlotte's literary *passage à l'acte* was triggered, not by the everyday banality of desire, but by an extraordinary encounter with her sister's work: "As for Charlotte, her genius must have quickened in her when her nerves thrilled to the shock of *Wuthering Heights*" (*TB* 131).

The psychical relation between Charlotte and Emily Brontë, then, is for Sinclair more than a matter of literary or sibling rivalry. Her sense of Emily Brontë is as an intransigent force, a "spirit" inhabiting an ontological space set apart from that of ordinary discursive communication. But if that spirit is somehow 'behind' *Jane Eyre*, its "germ of the real" (to use Charlotte Brontë's phrase), this does not, in any direct sense, offer an explanation of what becomes manifest at Jane Eyre's key-hole. What emerges, rather, from Sinclair's contrast between the two sisters—on one side the successful Victorian novelist and literary celebrity; on the other the "unearthly" (169) figure or untimely spectre—can be presented, in a revised version of our host/guest schema, as follows:

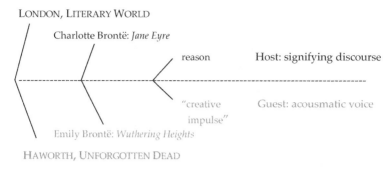

LONDON, LITERARY WORLD

Charlotte Brontë: *Jane Eyre*

reason   Host: signifying discourse

"creative   Guest: acousmatic voice
impulse"

Emily Brontë: *Wuthering Heights*

HAWORTH, UNFORGOTTEN DEAD

Figure 5.1

Here the point is not simply to endorse Sinclair's speculative notion that Charlotte Brontë's encounter with *Wuthering Heights* provided the inspirational shock that awakened *Jane Eyre*; but rather to see that notion as a mere side-effect of a systematic set of oppositions between the 'host' and the 'guest' domains that, we have argued, forms the double-loop topology of the literary ghost. It is clear that Charlotte Brontë, as the most successful, most fully 'socialized' family member and the famous author of *Jane Eyre*, can be identified with the domain of the signifier, where legible texts and identities are produced and circulate, a domain governed by a rational enlightened subject (who probably inhabits a modern imperial urban control-centre like London). Although in fact for Sinclair only one *side* of Charlotte's identity is associated with that domain, which Sinclair portrays as a world of false, posturing rhetoric where—just as in the parties detested by Spencer Brydon in "The Jolly Corner"—the hidden truth of the self is erased by the superficial gestures and "literary taint" of celebrity; while elsewhere another side of Charlotte remains "palpitating" with an authentic life—an authentically *asocial* life—at one telepathically with the cultic Brontë soul, thus possessed by Emily and Haworth (and by *Wuthering Heights*).

For Sinclair, in other words, there are two quite incommensurable Charlotte Brontës: the 'hostess' or successful bearer of the discursive signifier who can form legitimate relations with the patriarchal world, who like Jane Eyre herself can manage to embrace the master without jeopardising the integrity of her own innermost soul; and by contrast a 'guest' or vagrant "creative impulse" that will remain forever outside the patriarchal bounds of literary identity, an ontological immanence beyond social-discursive compromise. It is clear that in Sinclair's eyes only the latter side of the Brontë identity reflects the true spirit or genius struggling to emerge in all its shocking, baffling novelty and force; and for her, as for Bataille, the ultimate avatar of that "demoniac" spirit is Emily Brontë.

Given its date of composition, then, it is hardly surprising to find that "The Intercessor" is everywhere marked by signs of Sinclair's Brontësque preoccupations. *The Three Brontës* begins with Sinclair claiming that

[i]t is impossible to write of the three Brontës and forget the place they lived in, the black-grey, naked village, bristling like a rampart on the clean edge of the moor; . . . the small oblong house, naked and grey, hemmed in on two sides by the graveyard. . . .   (*TB* 19)

And the same vision of Haworth returns, very lightly modified, to describe the house approached at the beginning of "The Intercessor" by the protagonist Garvin:

At the end of the last field a wild plum tree stood half-naked on a hillock and pointed at the house. All that Garvin could see was a bald gable-end pitched among the ash trees. It was black grey, like ash bark drenched with rain.

It stood, he now saw, in a little orchard of dead trees, shut in from the fields by walls, low and loose-piled, a plot so small that it showed like a loop in a mesh of the stone network.   (*US* 177)

Each house is given a distinct set of Brontësque features: bare, ash-coloured and surrounded by death, the building is at once vertiginously exposed and enclosed by a stifling ominous atmosphere. As Garvin enters the house in "The Intercessor," he notices "its date graved above the lintel of its door: 1800, and the initials of its founder: E. F" (178); while at the threshold of Wuthering Heights, Mr Lockwood had "detected the date '1500,' and the name 'Hareton Earnshaw'."[18] The three-hundred-year difference between the dates perhaps sounds a note of subdued irony, as if Sinclair is acknowledging her story as a piece of mock gothic, a renovated or updated version of the Brontësque style. Throughout "The Intercessor," at any rate, a whole network of signifiers insistently recalls *Wuthering Heights*, from the setting to the plot to the names of the characters (with "Falshaw" a faulty or 'fallen' version of "Earnshaw"). But the key to Sinclair's story, as we shall see, lies in how it makes that intertextuality into a reflexive aspect of its ghostly language, its tale of memory and awakening, of cryptic hosting and haunting.

In the first place, though, we need to clarify in what specific sense the narrative events of "The Intercessor" can be considered Brontësque. The opening scenario, with the arrival at an isolated rural house of Garvin, a researcher from London working on a county history (of Yorkshire) for an aristocratic patron, has many generic features of the ghost story. Like one of M. R. James's dons, Garvin is an academic 'ontographer,' a writer-up of "old things, of old houses, old churches, old ways and superstitions" (*US* 177). Like one of Henry James's bachelors, he is a willing exile from the family, stipulating as the primary condition for his residing anywhere the complete absence of children. But what gives the scenario its properly Brontësque dimension is the enigmatic *sexual* aspect of the hostility encountered by the modern urban interloper in the rural-gothic scene. In his search for peaceful accommodation, Garvin enquires whether there are any children at Falshaw's:

> No (this time it was palpable, the sidelong, sinister intention), there wouldn't be; leastways not in August nor yet in September—if all went well with Falshaw's wife. Garvin judged that the state of Falshaw's wife had acted somehow as a deterrent to tourists. It had kept Falshaw's empty. (*US* 178)

The anamorphic grimace of the local peasantry speaks, for Garvin, of an insidious equivocation to do with "the state of Falshaw's wife," something indeterminate and hostile, thus at odds with the ordinary laws of hospitality (and in "Falshaw" we might also hear an echo of "false law"). What is palpably "sinister" here, what impedes the movement of signifiers as well as of bachelor tourists, appears to be a femininity no longer effectively governed by the paternal signifier; and the result is a "world of a hostile sovereignty," to quote Bataille's description of *Wuthering Heights*.[19] Indeed, when Garvin subsequently enters the Falshaws's house what he finds shows this dereliction of the signifying law in full force: an enigmatic atmosphere of "gloom" (182) that warps the normal economy of intersubjective relations. Having been seated at the family hearth as a guest, Garvin begins to realise that something is very wrong with his host:

> He did not look at Garvin when he spoke to him. He had not looked straight at him since he had brought him into the house. He seemed unable to face another man fairly and squarely in the presence of his wife. (*US* 182)

Falshaw, the supposed bearer of the paternal signifier, clearly falls short (in yet another surreptitious pun on the name); while his wife emanates a "forbidding" (182) power that disrupts the patriarchal regime of authority, the unconscious rules governing eye-contact and utterance. With gaze and voice no longer constrained by the signifier, they become manifest as material things within diegetic reality and so effectively eclipse it as neutral space, disfigure its 'realistic' transparency. The narrative is fraught with acousmatic traces left behind by defective signifiers—as bizarre perspectives or unearthly cries seem to make reality itself come alive, bristle with uncanny enjoyment:

> She sat in twilight and slantwise from the doorway, so that she had her back both to them and to the light. The sound of the lifted latch had been answered by a loud and sudden scraping of her chair; it was like a shriek of fright. (*US* 180–181)

This unravelling of voice and gaze from the signifying fabric of reality is what will determine and inform the apparition of the ghost. When Garvin first hears it, what he finds most strange about the sound is its fundamentally 'unrealistic' quality:

> There was no petulance in it and no anger; it had all the qualities of a young child's cry, except the carnal dissonances and violences. The grief it uttered was too profound and too persistent, and, as it were, too pure; it knew none of the hot-blooded throes, the strangulated pauses, the lacerating resurgences of passion. . . . He lay and listened to it till he knew all its changes and inflections, its languors and wearinesses, its piteous crescendos and amazements, as of a creature malignly re-created, born again to its mysterious, immitigable suffering.   (*US* 186)

What becomes manifest in this uncanny radio broadcast is thus voice as pure musical object, "a thing empty of any plausible appearance" (to recall Lacan's comment on Poe's "Valdemar").[20] The voice is detached from any realistic carnal host and from the ordinary logic of temporality: an eternal cyclical operatic aria rendering, without 'meaning,' psychical suffering. Likewise, when the ghost becomes visible outside the door of Garvin's bedroom, its apparition is something radically at odds with the signifying grid of everyday reality:

> Its face was so small, so shrunken and so bleached, that at first its actual features were indistinct to him. What *was* distinct, appallingly distinct, was the look it had; a look not to be imagined or defined, and thinkable only as a cry, an agony, made visible.   (*US* 188)

Just as Falshaw's gaze is telepathically disabled by his wife's forbidding presence, so the uncanny apparition at Garvin's threshold annihilates the ordinary topography of intersubjective relations. Its gaze is figured as an unaccountable singularity, a black hole in representation that causes signifiers to collapse inwards onto an impossible sensory paradox: the acousmatic obverse of meaningful consciousness. The thing that appears—or rather that precisely *fails* to appear as something with "actual features," an identifiable entity—thus constitutes a gap in knowledge, an indiscernible anamorphic opening of human experience onto its inner outside, its radical ontological otherness.

This indiscernible apparition allows us another approach to the intertextual dimension of "The Intercessor." As we have seen, during the composition of the story Sinclair was heavily involved with the work of the Brontës, and there are a mass of implicit references in the story to their writing, above all, to *Wuthering Heights*. But to grasp the full significance of this intertextuality in Sinclair's work we need to move beyond the standard 'anxiety of influence' reading which would see her as a belated heir struggling to negotiate the powerful legacy of the Brontës through a strategic rewriting of their major tropes.[21] Something far more disturbing, far closer in fact to the indiscernible apparition that confronts Garvin, is at work in the link between Sinclair's work and the Brontës, a link we can best describe as a *Gefühlsbindung*, to recall Freud's term for the affective-hypnotic bond uniting the crowd and its leader.

To grasp how Sinclair's writing deals with this hypnotic Brontësque bond, we need to return to her opening description of Falshaw's house:

> It stood, he now saw, in a little orchard of dead trees, shut in from the fields by walls, low and loose-piled, a plot so small that it showed like a loop in a mesh of the stone network.   (*US* 177)

The phrase "like a loop in a mesh of the stone network" is our key (our key*hole*, to be precise) to the textual and intertextual topology of Sinclair's story. Throughout the narrative the figure of an anamorphic *gap in a partition* keeps returning: the approach to the house is "sideways through a little gate in the low wall" (178); "its wall was broken halfway" (178); "a gate in the wall" (180); "there were gaps in its borders" (193) and so on. The clearest version of this "loop in a mesh" comes in a kind of epiphany experienced by the protagonist towards the end of the story:

> Garvin's gaze followed the network of stone walls flung over the country. He had a sense of the foregoneness of the things he saw. He saw the network as a system of lines that, wherever you picked it up and followed it, led in some predestined way to the house as its secret and its centre.   (*US* 197)

Just as each "loose-piled" wall is itself a stone mesh whose coherence is breached by a loophole, so the network of walls forms a system of lines whose topographical structure is warped by the uncanny 'strange attractor' of the house, "its secret and its centre," at once unavoidably visible and, like an anamorphic stain, impossible to discern or decipher. The house is thus a loop in a multiple sense, a self-enclosed anomaly both outside the system of lines or signifiers and at its cryptic centre; and thus impossible to situate either in space or time: "What it did was to throw back its century into some tract of dark and savage time" (178).

"A loop in a mesh" is thus Sinclair's principal trope for an anomaly in a textual system, a paradoxical *punctum* at once enclosed by a network of signifying relations and anamorphically skewed away from its logical structure. As such, of course, this anomalous loop is radically alien both to conscious reflection and to discursive communication—exactly as Effy's apparition is "not to be imagined or defined" (188). And this is the crucial point: it is only through this figural loop or keyhole that we can grasp how Sinclair's text communicates with the work of the Brontës. In other words, the extensive network of signifiers we can trace from "The Intercessor" to *Wuthering Heights* and its overlapping Brontësque contexts is in effect no more than a mesh or border within and against which the telepathic "spiritual tie" itself can take effect as cryptic, uncanny ontological opening.

If the house in "The Intercessor" thus recalls Haworth as described by Sinclair in *The Three Brontës*—as well as recalling Wuthering Heights and other *unheimlich* Brontësque houses such as Thornfield or Wildfell Hall—that recollection takes shape as "a loop in a mesh:" not, that is, merely as a "system of lines" (197), a set of identifiable features or signifiers, but at a point that coincides with that system's *suspension*, a "secret" that can only be uttered outside discourse, as acousmatic voice (scrape, shriek or laugh), through what critic Paul Fry calls the "ostensive hum" of literature .[22] The same suspension of the signifying network occurs in both the apparition and the pure vocal utterance of Effy's ghost, and in turn the "strange, deep guttural sound" imagined by Sinclair as Emily Brontë's "language of a joy too deep for articulate expression" (*TB* 60). We could even see the "vivid and ineffaceable idea of Emily" (236) that dominates *The Three Brontës* as an element unconsciously re-inscribed by Sinclair, condensing "Emily" and "ineffaceable," in the name "Effy." What speaks in this ineffable language of joy does not in fact speak at all but creaks, gurgles or moans at the keyhole of the signifying space inhabited by humans; if it cannot be recollected as proper experience, recognized by the Other as a legitimate act of signification, nor can it be forgotten or effaced: it remains as a haunting trace of ontological inconsistency.

To understand the intertextual link between Sinclair and the Brontës, then, we need to dwell further on the relation between possession or haunting and the 'pure,' acousmatic or ostensive, figure—the voice or gaze exposed as such, stripped bare of identifiable literary features. The persistent rhetoric of "naked life," of things stripped back to an uncompromising essence, in Sinclair's engagement with the Brontës, takes a new, uncanny turn in the decisive scene of Garvin's hosting of the other:

> He couldn't say what it was that happened. He only knew that it was bound to happen; it had been foreshadowed by his fear. He knew what the sudden shifting in his brain meant. He had simply gone over the borderland of fear and was in the gripping centre.
>
> There were two there, a man and a woman. He did not discern them as ordinary supernatural presences; the terror they evoked

surpassed all fear of the intangible. . . . He couldn't say whether he really saw it, or whether he apprehended it by some supreme sense more living and more horrible than sight. It was monstrous, unintelligible; it lay outside the order of his experience. He seemed, in the shifting of his brain, to have parted with his experience, to have become a creature of vague memory and appalling possibilities of fear. . . . The feeling was unspeakable. Its force, its vividness was such as could be possible only to a mind that came virgin to horror.   (*US* 200)

The unforgettable impact of the primal scene—in the term used by Freud to designate the infant's decisive, traumatic first encounter with the incomprehensible otherness of the sexual—is vividly evoked here. The crucial constituent of the trauma is the non-relation between the empirical subject—the specular, self-recognizing ego—and the event suddenly thrust before its eyes. Because the thing that happens before Garvin "lay outside the order of his experience" in one sense *it did not happen*: it lacks all of the formal properties of real events which can be consistently presented and remembered (and thus repressed and 'forgotten').

What "The Intercessor" reveals, then, is an extraordinary—we might almost say a *telepathic*—sense, in Sinclair's writing, of the central problems to be theorised by the psychoanalytic concepts of transference and the primal scene (concepts she cannot, incidentally, at the time of writing the story, have simply learnt about from Freud, since in 1911 the major Freudian texts on those concepts had yet to be published).[23] It is clear in this story—as also in "The Flaw in the Crystal," where Agatha's "pulses of compassion" open her up to a "swimming darkness" (*US* 74) of Being beyond the divisive walls of personality—that for Sinclair the mystical transcendence of self is always a state of *transition*, a loop of affective transference to and from the Other. The Levinasian account of the enigmatic bond between witness and spectacle in mystical experience offers a useful gloss on this transferential dimension:

Mystical participation is completely different from the Platonic participation in a genus; in it the identity of the terms is lost. They are divested of what constituted their very substantivity. The participation of one term in another does not consist in sharing an attribute; one term *is the other*. The *private* existence of each term, mastered by a subject that is, loses this private character and returns to an undifferentiated background; the existence of one submerges the other, and is thus no longer an existence of the one. We recognize here the *there is* [*il y a*].[24]

The *il y a*, the manifestation (or horrific "rustling," as Levinas puts it) of Being when it is no longer hosted by the consistent ontology of an individual subject, corresponds to a withdrawal of the signifier as symbolic matrix of identity, the collapse of the coherent empirical ego into an "undifferentiated background" or swimming darkness. What appears is a telepathic buzz or gleam, apprehended, in Sinclair's brilliant phrase, by "some supreme sense more living and more horrible than sight:" the very capacity of the speaking subject to host itself and its world is obliterated, overridden by the force of what Lacan writes as *plus de jouir*, an affective event beyond the limits of what a subject can enjoy (or even, as a signifying subject, endure).[25]

If the encounter with the other as radical loop or *il y a* is thus for Sinclair always transitional, an uncanny participation of existences in something that essentially undoes the basis of their subjective difference, it is at the same time figured as fundamentally resistant to the hospitable order of the signifier, the domain of communicable or 'liveable' reality. What Garvin sees when he plays host to the ineffaceable spirit, the ontological absolute, of Effy is, he senses, "outside the order of his experience" (200), incompatible with the signifying mesh that makes sense of the world and structures his narrative experience of it. And what is involved in that epiphany, the manifestation of something indiscernible that eclipses the signifying agency of the subject, finds an equivalent in "The Intercessor" at the level of the visible surface of Sinclair's writing.

Here it is a question of something analogous to what Jacques Derrida calls the "living tableau" of crypto-textual symptoms at work in Freud's "Wolf-man" case history, where semantic or formal "rhymes" point towards, while never precisely naming, a radically excluded, silent "magic word."[26] The central word in Sinclair's text is not, in the same way as the Wolf-man's was, an inscription of psychical trauma covered up by overlapping layers of cultural and linguistic sediment; although it certainly signifies something unspeakable, something whose prohibition, in Lacan's view, is "the condition sine qua non of speech."[27] Let us examine the following "mesh" of signifiers from "The Intercessor:"

interest (179, 181, 185, 190)	instinct (187)	indistinct (188)
sinister (189)	INTERCESSOR	intenser (193)
insisted (213)	iniquitous (199)	inquest (207–8)

Figure 5.2

What Garvin discovers in the Falshaws' garden—the trampled fragments of a child's world, the broken vessel of her lived-in enjoyment—makes him realise that something there has been "ruined beyond remembrance" (193). What is thus indicated, what lies at the ruined site beyond memory, can be neither re-presented nor forgotten: it thus has an *incessant* status, returning in an endless loop at odds with the logic of narrative closure that governs the textual mesh around it. This incessant figural loop is not subject to the teleological structure of the symbolic order, the semiotic-temporal matrix that generates and constrains human identity; and so it can only appear in the discursive texture of reality as a figural breach, an anamorphic blot warping the signifying surface of things. This recalls the anamorphic split between incompatible temporalities we saw in James's "The Jolly Corner," where Spencer Brydon, once inside the "Egyptian tomb" of the ghostly ancestral house, could dwell in an incessant, ever-returning ontological domain that, when seen in the "harsh actuality" of the light outside, appeared as nothing at all, a non-event. (*THJ* 348)

Now, in "The Intercessor" the crucial "magic word," which is clearly discernable in the network (Figure 5.2) as the phonographic combination *in + cs*, has two faces, we might say: while the word *incest* is clearly legible there (though the text never inscribes it as such), at the same time the semic fragment *incess* embodies the Latin root of a cluster of terms for endlessness, temporal non-closure ('incessant,' 'unceasing'). Is what does not cease, what returns in an endless figural loop, thus being implicitly linked in Sinclair's text to incest?

As we saw, at the diegetic level "The Intercessor" centres on the "unspeakable" force of what Freud was to call the primal scene—that is, the child's originary encounter with an enigmatic "language of passion" (to use Sándor Ferenczi's term for the visible figure of a radical sexual otherness)[28] which it can never translate into the cognitive order of experience. Garvin's attempt to mediate (as quasi-therapeutic "intercessor") between the incessant loop of ghostly "passion" left behind by this encounter and the inadequate symbolic register of the Falshaw family, leads him to reconstruct a narrative that hinges on the key feature of the primal scene—the child's observation of adult sexual intercourse as something "monstrous, unintelligible" (200). But this "family romance," as Freud might have called it, is far from conforming to some standard pattern of child development, where the primal scene might be seen as the fantasmatic cause of unconscious symptom-formation, of fantasy scenarios and so on. Instead, what warps the "normal" Oedipal matrix of development, what forestalls the foundational act of repression which would have subjected the primal scene to the signifying economy of the unconscious—and thus made it possible for the ego to *forget* that scene—is the unconstrained, lawless desire of the mother.

It is this emphasis on female, and specifically maternal, desire that gives the "passion" at stake in Sinclair's writing its singularity. This is made explicit in the diagnostic interview between Garvin and the authoritative

Dr MacKinnon, where Sinclair seems (just as she does in "The Flaw in the Crystal") pointedly to shift the location of the cause of psychical trauma from male to female. Thus, according to Dr MacKinnon, Falshaw's act of adultery is fairly trivial, his "one bright spot of immorality" (205); while by contrast his wife's traumatised reaction to that act is "the ugliest thing on God's earth—the hard, savage lust that avenges its frustration on its own offspring" (207).

This ostensibly patriarchal diagnosis is perhaps surprising, even today disturbing (since we hardly expect an avowed feminist like Sinclair to simply 'blame it on mame'). But Sinclair's burgeoning interest in psychoanalysis, which was a crucial factor in the writing of "The Intercessor," allows her a new sense of how displacing attention from the supposedly normative Oedipal family onto the less 'legible' relation between mother and child might entail a corresponding shift in her own writing (and this stylistic shift is especially important for her "spooky" tales). For what is at stake in this shift is a fundamental encounter with a "passion" hosted by the mesh of signifiers that determine existence, an encounter that illuminates and inspires the human subject while remaining secret to it, impossible to articulate with its 'Oedipal' signifying topography. Thus the only way to 'experience' this mysterious affective bond hostile to the network of signifiers is to be *possessed* by it. This is what Garvin discovers, as he gazes at the Brontësque house that had once seemed to him "intolerably secret, intolerably remote:"

> And now he knew its secret. 'Their evil' saturating the very walls, leaking through and penetrating those other walls, the bounds of Garvin's personality, starting in him a whole train of experience not his own.
>
> (*US* 209)

By quoting the doctor—who has used the phrase "their evil"—Garvin can begin to re-appropriate what has happened to him, to identify in language what has possessed him and thus restore the signifying integrity of his subjective structure. Dr MacKinnon therefore occupies a position of symbolic paternity, providing the infantilised Garvin with a set of signifiers to alienate and so 'comprehend' the traumatic real he has encountered; but those signifiers are shown to be strikingly impoverished and restrictive, allowing only the crudest of binary moral judgements. In contrast to this limited juridico-medical patriarchal 'solution,' the secret experience "not his own," lying outside the ontological register of Garvin's empirical cognition but part of his psychical reality, is figured as a domain of inexpressible vitality:

> The doctor had watched the outside of events; whereas he, Garvin, had been taken into the invisible places, into the mystic heart of suffering. He knew the unnamed, unnameable secret of pity and fear.   (*US* 209)

It is Garvin's mystical participation in what happened, then, his absorption in the incessant loop of Effy's passion, that opens his eyes to the "unnameable secret" of the narrative, its non-signifying affective ontological core (note how Sinclair has the mother, with her regional accent, rename her undead child "Affy" as if to half-utter her affective essence). And if that participation in the mystery has robbed Garvin, as according to Levinas it should, of his very identity as speaking subject, his re-awakening to the real world of juridico-medical rationality is presented as a dispiriting, diminishing transition. Of course Garvin's subsequent intervention—his symbolic "intercession"—is *meant* to be 'dispiriting,' in other words to dispel the troubled spirit that haunts the bond between mother and daughter. But the conventional restoration of patriarchal rationality at the end of the narrative leaves intact—this is the "unnameable secret" of Sinclair's writing, and perhaps of the ghost story itself as genre—the incessant music of the apparition:

> What really possessed him and remained with him was Effy's passion. Effy's passion (for the mother who had not loved her) was *the* supernatural thing, the possessing, pursuing, unappeasably crying thing that haunted the Falshaws' house. Effy's passion was indestructible. It was set free of time and mortality. (*US* 210)

The ghost story, for Sinclair, thus resonates above all with a moment of writerly *transition*, of the breakthrough to a new field of aesthetic possibilities and risks. Garvin's encounter with "Effy's passion" is a truth-event, in Badiou's sense. What is revealed offers no solution to the mystery, has none of the juridical veracity of Dr MacKinnon's diagnosis, but instead it "bores a hole in knowledge," as Badiou puts it: that is, it remains essentially indiscernible, irreducible to the differential economy of the sign.[29] The consistent ontology that structured the whole world of realism so meticulously catalogued by the nineteenth century novel is fractured, traumatized by this indiscernible "crying thing," just as Garvin's professional activity as archival researcher "sifting the dust of oblivion for a clue to some forgotten family" (*US* 177) is exposed as a trivial waste of time in comparison with the ethical power of Effy's "indestructible" passion. That passion is the only thing that *counts*; and Sinclair makes this algebraic pre-eminence clear by emphasizing the definite article: it "was *the* supernatural thing."

"Nothing else in the picture lived for it:" we recall the anamorphic displacement of discursive reality in John Marcher's ravaging encounter with "scarred passion" at the end of Henry James's "The Beast in the Jungle" (*THJ* 338). The truth-event is a narrative catastrophe, ripping open plausible or legible narrativity by suddenly breaking with the proper logic of signifying structure, making knowledge of the narrative world—the very currency of the underlying contract between writer and reader—impossible to sustain for a moment (but that moment is anamorphically skewed away from realistic temporality, "set free of time and mortality:" *US* 210). It is this ontological eclipse of the mortifying agency of the letter that both James and Sinclair, each at a crucial point of aesthetic re-invention or transition to a new kind of writing, present as a ghostly epiphany that lays waste to the known, narratable world. How, then, did those self-conscious innovators born a generation after James and Sinclair, the modernists, take up the challenge of this ghostly truth-event?

6 Distant Music
Woolf, Joyce

> When the loop in time comes—and it does not come for everybody—
> The hidden is revealed, and the spectres show themselves.
>
> —T. S. Eliot, *The Family Reunion*

GUST OF LIFE

"—What is a ghost?" asks Stephen Dedalus, tingling with energy (and after a few drinks) in Dublin's National Library.[1] And although the ensuing "farrago," as Hugh Kenner puts it, of half-baked Joycean bardology has not always seemed entirely convincing to critics, that initial question still remains as a critical challenge—the challenge, that is, of thinking of modernism, habitually defined by Pound's famous poetic exclamation "MAKE IT NEW," in terms of ghosts.[2]

What we have already learnt about the literary ghost from the texts we have been reading by Dickens, M. R. James, Henry James and May Sinclair (to name only the writers of the supposedly fictional texts) should allow us, if not yet to supply a definitive answer to Stephen's question, at least to see why the question of the ghost should prove so directly relevant to modernism (and we understand that term to correspond, at least in part, to an originary desire to write 'life itself' beyond the constraints of traditional literary decorum). For the ghostly encounter, as we have explored it, marks above all a point of contact with life in its properly *indiscernible* ontological otherness, as something irreducible to the logic of discourse—whether that thing be voiced in the impossible hypnotic utterance of Poe's Valdemar or by the dying man Dickens hears declaring "I am gone," or else is breathed as pure spectral object-voice in Maturin or M. R. James. In essence, the immanent life-thing that appears—to be named 'naked' appearance, appearance itself: *apparition*—always does so *in breach of* discourse, in a hush or lapse of speech that is somehow telepathic, luminous, phantasmal, a point which Sinclair writes as "an agony, made visible" (*US* 188). It is this punctual anamorphic encounter, as we saw at the end of Henry James's "The Beast in the Jungle," that devastates John Marcher, as a glimpse of the "deep ravage" (*THJ* 338) of a stranger's grief-stricken face annihilates Marcher's complacent self-image, suddenly shows him his own narrative world as an empty semblance, a mere signifying charade.

The literary apparition, then, can be seen as a 'truth-event,' to use Badiou's term: an event, that is, which "bores a hole in knowledge" (*BE*

525). This means, in the first place, that the apparition does not confirm or conform to the representational language of the narrative self; instead it remains fixed unforgettably in a language of the eye or the ear, an unspeakable spectral *punctum* or uncanny music. We saw how in Sinclair's work this phantasmal-ontological music took the figure of the "wuthering" spectre of Emily Brontë or else the "unappeasably crying thing" (*US* 210) that embodied Effy's passion, each figure giving voice to an affective intensity skewed anamorphically away from legible narrative reality, and so indecipherable or, as Sinclair brilliantly puts it, "withdrawn in the secret of its suffering" (*US* 188).

It is probably the intertextual dimension of Sinclair's work that appears its most obvious link to the stylistic experimentalism of the modernists. Her personal association with, and critical advocacy of, Ezra Pound and T. S. Eliot, can be easily assimilated to an account of her work that would see it essentially redefined by her encounter with modernism, as the conventional Edwardian realism of *The Divine Fire* (1904) yields to the more experimental 'free indirect' style of *Mary Olivier: A Life* (1919).[3] But in 1914, shortly after she published the two "spooky" stories we discussed in Chapter 5 and with the Brontës still very much on her mind, a remark of Sinclair's makes it clear that the intertextual aspects of her work in fact owed little to her recent contact with the young Turks of modernism. Writing in the preface to a new collection, *The Judgment of Eve and Other Stories*, she notes that her book contained "tales of a transition period, the passing to a more intense and more concentrated form."[4] The Brontësque style of Sinclair's ghost stories, that is, should be seen not as some playful modernist experiment (such as the flagrant pastiche of literary styles which Joyce will stage in the 'Oxen of the Sun' episode of *Ulysses*) but rather as part of her search for "a more intense and more concentrated form:" for a more forceful—therefore perhaps in one sense a *less* 'literary'—rendition of life.

If, as we have argued, the literary ghost corresponds to an unbearable affective encounter that withdraws ("in its own secrecy") from the textual and diegetic ontology of the host-narrative, then it may have been sensed as such—whether consciously or not—by those at the beginning of the twentieth century in search of a more direct, more vital way of writing (and Virginia Woolf's early criticism, as we will see, strikingly confirms this). In this sense, modernism is indeed haunted by the ghost story, but crucially not as a mere 'style' or set of mock-gothic tropes to parody and recycle. Rather, what the ghost story offered to the modernists was an exemplary *fracture* of narrative consistency, an uncanny telepathic fissure of textual topography that opens onto what Sinclair writes as the "unthinkable sacrament" (*US* 98) of mystical participation in an otherness beyond the ontological boundaries of the ego. Indeed, this question of haunting as mystic-telepathic connection makes the whole critical notion of authorial 'influence' extremely problematic here; in tracing the ghostly intertextual networks occupied

by Woolf and Joyce, we will see the supposed integrity of an authorial 'I'
incessantly breaking apart.

A good starting point is Woolf's emphatic declaration in 1916 (a mere
five years, that is, since May Sinclair had published her *The Three Brontës*)
that "there is no 'I' in *Wuthering Heights*."[5] In Woolf's view, Emily Brontë's
revolutionary work differed essentially from her sister Charlotte's, since
Jane Eyre still remained largely consistent with the traditional form of the
novel; whilst *Wuthering Heights* broke wholly with that form and with its
implicit metaphysics of self-presence:

> It is as if she could tear up all that we know human beings by, and
> fill the unrecognizable transparences with such a gust of life that they
> transcend reality. . . . She could free life from its dependence on facts;
> with a few touches indicate the spirit of a face so that it needs no body;
> by speaking of the moor make the wind blow and the thunder roar.
>
> (CE 190)

If Sinclair had turned the tale of the Brontës into a ghost story, to recall
Raitt's remark, we can see a ghostly language haunting Woolf's account
too: "unrecognizable transparences" are spectral apparitions filled with
"a gust of life" (we recall the "tremendous gust" at Professor Parkins's
window in the M. R. James story, with "gust" suggesting both "guest"
and "ghost"); while the bodiless "spirit" conveyed by Brontë's clairvoy-
ant "touches" speaks in the *voix acousmatique* of the trance-possessed
medium. The spectral violence of Brontë's writing is for Woolf nothing
less than a triumphant assault on the official patriarchal regime of "fact,"
of "all that we know human beings by," the stifling doctrinal languages of
science, history and religion that had been dutifully aped by the Victorian
literary establishment. This Brontësque "gust of life" is therefore enough,
in Woolf's eyes, to expose the meticulous verisimilitude of nineteenth-century realism as a sterile tissue of familiar discourses and rhetorical clichés,
the ideological recitation of a non-transcendent ontology that could host
an implacable patriarchal self-identity wholly untroubled—or so it imagined—by spirits.

Now, the trouble with the Victorian ghost story, as Woolf writes in a
later article of 1921, is that it often risks falling back on its own repertoire
of generic conventions and stylistic clichés, and so turning the potentially
creative shock of the ghostly encounter into a mere stylistic conceit (and, as
we saw in Chapter 2 something very similar was already a concern of Dickens in 1850 when he wrote of the "accredited ghostly circumstances" that
had turned festive entertainment into a mock-gothic pantomime). Thus,
Woolf profoundly distrusts the beautiful rhetoric which she finds sugaring
the ghostly pill in Henry James's 1900 story *The Great Good Place*: "All
the characteristic phrases are there in waiting—the silver bowls, the melted
hours—but there is no work for them to do. The story dwindles to a sweet

soliloquy" (*CE* 287). A contrast between Henry James and Emily Brontë, a contrast charged with personal and political significance for Woolf, is very near the surface in the following implicitly gendered meditation on aesthetics:

> But beauty is the most perverse of spirits; it seems as if she must pass through ugliness or lie down with disorder before she can rise in her own person. The ready-made beauty of the dream world produces only an anaemic and conventionalized version of the world we know. And Henry James was much too fond of the world we know to create one that we do not know. The visionary imagination was by no means his.   (*CE* 287)

A perverse, elusive Brontësque feminine spirit is set against a realistic world of facts emblematized by the solid figure and double-masculine name of Henry James. Whereas Emily Brontë had succeeded in abolishing reality as a closed patriarchal set of "facts," and so could set loose the "gust of life" in all its timeless visionary power, James (at least on this view) seems to Woolf fatally overinvested in the known legible world, with his precious style ultimately no more than a meticulous reproduction of that familiar legibility. In a letter of 1917, Woolf complains to her friend Saxon Sydney-Turner about her disappointment on reading James's posthumous *The Sense of the Past*:

> What is there to say about The Sense of the Past? I'm afraid my old image must still hold good as far as I'm concerned—the laborious striking of whole boxfulls of damp matches—lovely phrases of course but—but—but.[6]

James's title itself becomes an ironic jest for the modernist Woolf: the smooth beauty of the writing, lacking the vital spark or spiritual gust of actuality, consigns it irredeemably to a bygone era. In this, again, the implicit contrast with Emily Brontë is stark: while her writing, unconstrained by the laborious rhetorical cleverness of a Jamesian ego, still roars with disembodied intensity, James's ornate style has already made his work seem in Woolf's eyes a faded period piece. Here, though she may not have known as much, Woolf's perspective was very close to May Sinclair's, who (as we saw in Chapter 5) wrote in 1911 of the "literary taint" (*TB* 47) that she sensed disfiguring the work of Charlotte Brontë, in contrast to that of her sister Emily, where disregard for conventional stylistic propriety had liberated the true Brontë spirit from the patriarchal enclosure of Victorian literary culture.

But to create a world we genuinely do not know, to re-animate the strange vital intensity of the ghostly encounter was not, as Woolf was very well aware, a mere matter of avoiding the niceties of fine prose. And indeed, as she also knew, the subtle cadences of Jamesian writing were sometimes quite capable of producing distinctly uncanny effects. Woolf struggles in her article to rein in and conceptualize her ambivalent response to James:

> The stories in which Henry James uses the supernatural effectively are, then, those where some quality in a character or in a situation can only be given its fullest meaning by being cut free from fact. Its progress in the unseen world must be closely related to what goes on in this. We must be made to feel that the apparition fits the crisis of passion or of conscience which sent it forth. . . .   (*CE* 291)

The cutting-free of life itself from facts, that distinction between vital spark and mundane reality Woolf had earlier associated with Emily Brontë, returns here; but in the next sentence the factual world seems to come back as a model for the supernatural, as if to reconnect the feminine-vital and the masculine-factual. If a ghost should now behave plausibly, like a character in a realist novel, how then can it still be an "unrecognizable transparence," a vagrant spirit from an unknown world? Woolf uses the figure of music, which we have seen so often linked to the ghostly, to attempt a resolution of these divergent ideas:

> The use of the supernatural draws out a harmony which would otherwise be inaudible. We hear the first note close at hand, and then, a moment after, the second chimes far away.   (*CE* 291)

The crude distinction between life and facts can thus be refined—in a distinct echo of the "indescribably fine murmur" (*THJ* 352–353) or spectral voice of the Jamesian otherworldly in "The Jolly Corner"—and restated as a ghostly revelation of another ontology concealed in and as ordinary reality. The unworldly strangeness of life is thus no longer to be cut free from facts but rather exposed as already hosted by them, awaiting only the magic Jamesian "tap of the conductor's wand" (*THJ* 352). And what the musical analogy allows Woolf to capture in a moment of acute insight is the constitutive *temporality* of the uncanny: it is not the first note "close at hand," safely embedded in the realist text, but its repetition "a moment after" and "far away" that estranges familiar things, produces the spine-tingling *unheimlich* harmony.

It is this secret musical art of uncanny temporality, then, that can open up, even in so gentlemanly a stylist as Henry James, an otherworldly vision of "the ghosts which are living within ourselves" (*CE* 294), as Woolf puts it: the apparition of ontological otherness masked off by the signifying shroud of our personal identities. In an earlier article of 1918, Woolf had taken James's *The Turn of the Screw*—a text whose haunting power over Woolf's imagination sheds some ironic light on her jovial talk of James's "damp matches"—as an exemplary manifestation of this uncanny possession of the self by another self, a more vital inner-psychical being, which she nervously refers to as a "state of mind:"

> It is a state of mind; even the external objects are made to testify to their subjection. The oncoming of the state is preceded not by the storms and howlings of the old romances, but by an absolute hush and lapse of nature which we feel to represent the ominous trance of her own mind. 'The rooks stopped cawing in the golden sky, and the friendly evening hour lost for the unspeakable minute all its voice.' The horror of the story comes from the force with which it makes us realize the power that our minds possess for such excursions into the darkness. . .   (CE 295)

The epiphany, as Joyce might have called it, of James's governess-narrator is glossed by Woolf with fascination, with almost a kind of mystical participation. Something *shows itself* in the "unspeakable minute," in James's phrase that points to the emergence of something beyond the signifier, something hostile to the plausible discursive textures of reality. "An absolute hush and lapse of nature," Woolf writes, announces this uncanny abeyance of signifying reality: a moment, she goes on "which we *feel to represent*" (my emphasis) the entranced psychical condition of the governess. The off-kilter phrasing reveals Woolf's fragile sense that what happens here to signification—the "absolute hush" of a revelation barred from ordinary speech—corresponds to a kind of telepathic suspension of the interpretive eye, the showing-forth or immanence of something at odds with the very hermeneutics of reading.

Once again, a supernatural harmony inaudible in the everyday world suggests itself as an apt 'acousmatic' figure for this strange anamorphic point beyond hermeneutics. And we can hear in Woolf's "absolute hush and lapse of nature" a vivid rendition of *voice*, of non-discursive vocal apparition ("the voice says nothing; instead, it *shows* itself," writes Agamben).[7] The telepathic epiphany of James's writing, in other words, points Woolf away from mere considerations of literary style—where she would contrast Jamesian damp matches with Brontësque fire—and towards something much more disturbing: a meditation on the power of literature to reach beyond the legible scene of reality, to touch what Sinclair wrote as the "unappeasably crying thing" (US 210) made silent, kept secret by that specular reality.

"Woolf," concludes David Seed, "repeatedly draws on the psychic to suggest new dimensions to mental life and conversely uses the ghostly to question social forms previously thought immutable."[8] What we need to add to this assessment is that the complex psycho-political disturbance referred to here by Seed touches on the very essence of what literature, in Woolf's view, was concerned with and could achieve. Her intensely ambivalent response to James's ghosts—one minute finding them clichéd, the next terrifying—can be seen as an index of the importance ascribed to the ghostly for Woolf's whole modernist re-conceptualisation of literary experience. If we bear in mind how the idea of ghostly music allowed Woolf to articulate her complex reading of James, we will certainly read the following statement from her first novel, *The Voyage Out* (1915) in a new light:

> 'Novels,' she repeated. 'Why do you write novels? You ought to write music. Music, you see'—she shifted her eyes, and became less desirable as her brain began to work, inflicting a certain change upon her face— 'music goes straight for things. It says all there is to say at once. With writing it seems to me there's so much'—she paused for an expression, and rubbed her fingers in the earth—'scratching on the match-box.'[9]

The speaker is Rachel Vinrace, Woolf's portrait of the artist as a young musician, and she is addressing her self-appointed mentor, novelist Terence Hewet, who has been pressing her to start on his reading-list. The first thing to strike us about Rachel's very *fin de siècle* aesthetic, centred on Pater's idea of music being a more direct artistic medium than literature, is that it deploys a metaphor very similar to the one Woolf will use shortly afterwards in her ironic critique of James (his "laborious striking of damp matches"). What the obsolete form and the defunct master both therefore lack, according to this Woolfian rhetoric, is artistic *fire*; and it is consequently the promethean calling of the young modernist to re-ignite the aesthetic domain (and fire of course is an ancient, and oft-used, symbol of life and poetic inspiration: we recall, for instance, the "spark of life" in the scene highlighted by Deleuze from Dickens's *Our Mutual Friend*).

However, Rachel's sense of music as vital spark seems at first sight far removed from the realm of the ghostly—it is more a matter of vibrant chords than supernatural harmony. There is indeed a post-romantic directness in this youthful aesthetic, which by the time she wrote *Mrs Dalloway* (1925), Woolf had begun to complicate in terms of her developing feminist politics—a complication that returns her writing, as I see it, to the figure of ghostly music. In an early draft of the novel, Woolf describes hearing in a woman's voice

> a vibration in the core of the sound so that each word, or note, comes fluttering, alive, yet with some reluctance to inflict its vitality, some grief for the past which holds it back, some impulse nevertheless to glide into the recesses of the heart.[10]

This woman speaks in a ghost-voice, vibrating on the edge between life and death, caught between libidinal impulse and the bonds of memory. It is clear that a decade after writing *The Voyage Out*, Woolf's sense of what lies beyond the patriarchal enclosure of representation has undergone a crucial shift: now, the music of the voice does not simply present things in themselves or say all that can be said, as Rachel Vinrace had thought; it hosts instead an otherworldly scratching, a ghostly ontological vibration that marks something irreducible to a binary logic. We are indeed not far here from the "indescribably fine murmur" (*THJ* 352–353) of the spectral in Henry James, nor from Woolf's idea of a supernatural harmony in Jamesian writing that is irreducible to the opposition of presence and absence, the real and the imaginary.

A ghostly musical vibration, then, in Woolf gives voice to a life, a woman's life faintly discernable as pure ontological immanence yet constrained, mortified by the psychosocial bonds of patriarchal culture. To be liberated from those bonds, however, as Woolf sees in *Mrs Dalloway*, may be to become no more than a living ghost oneself:

> A sound interrupted [Peter Walsh]; a frail quivering sound, a voice bubbling up without direction, vigour, beginning or end, running weakly and shrilly and with an absence of all human meaning into
>
> ee um fah um so
> foo swee too eem oo—
>
> the voice of no age or sex, the voice of an ancient spring spouting from the earth; which issued, just opposite Regent's Park Tube Station, from a tall quivering shape, like a funnel, like a rusty pump, like a wind-beaten tree for ever barren of leaves which lets the wind run up and down its branches singing
>
> ee um fah um so
> foo swee too eem oo,
>
> and rocks and creaks and moans in the eternal breeze.[11]

If the "poor creature" (*MD* 91), as Peter Walsh casually labels her, no longer inhabits the plausible domain of human reality, having become an anonymous vessel for "the gust of life," to recall Woolf's comment on *Wuthering Heights*, she (or it) has become in one sense the perfect modernist artist: a pure aesthetic conduit for the impersonal, timeless manifestation of the "eternal breeze" of pure being. The obliteration of meaning in the amorphous phonemes of the song thus forms an ironic counterpoint to Woolf's scornful modernist dismissal, a decade earlier, of the orotund complexity of Jamesian style.

The otherworldly music of the ghost, then, which for Woolf once corresponded to a supreme over-subtlety of style in James, returns in the modernist city of *Mrs Dalloway* in a debased form as an acousmatic drone, a meaningless fragment of "frail quivering sound." The acousmatic quality of the old woman's broken love-song, however, also gives it a special distinction in Clarissa Dalloway's world: for such a voice serves not to represent but to *render* a woman's enjoyment, to figure it non-metaphorically and thus outside the discursive ontology of the dominant patriarchal culture. The woman's mouth has become "a mere hole in the ground" (*MD* 91), an inhuman orifice from which emanates a sound that "rocks and creaks and moans," no longer an utterance bound into the alienating chain of signifiers. This non-address to the symbolic Other opens the uncanny space of a private, self-absorbed oneness, identifiable only by the "damp stain" of an obscene enjoyment. The self-adequation of oral *jouissance* in the "old bubbling burbling song" points to an ontological plenitude in stark contrast to the constant self-dividedness of desire on show in Clarissa's anxious internal monologue:

> How much she wanted it—that people should look pleased when she came in, Clarissa thought and turned and walked back towards Bond Street, annoyed, because it was silly to have other reasons for doing things. Much rather would she have been one of those people like Richard who did things for themselves, whereas, she thought, waiting to cross, half the time she did things not simply, not for themselves; but to make people think this or that; perfect idiocy she knew (and now the policeman held up his hand) for no one was ever for a second taken in.
>
> [. . .] She had the oddest sense of being herself invisible; unseen; unknown; there being no more marrying, no more having children now, but only this astonishing and rather solemn progress with the rest of them, up Bond Street, this being Mrs. Dalloway; not even Clarissa any more; this being Mrs. Richard Dalloway.　　　　　(*MD* 12–13)

"Mrs Dalloway in Bond Street" was Woolf's original title for what she first envisaged as a short story and only later extended into *Mrs Dalloway*; and the name of the London street lingers on in the novel as a surreptitious pun naming the ontological alienation, the bond of patriarchal and societal identity, which Clarissa is contemplating. Her very thoughts, it seems, are subject to the authoritarian regime of the state: a policeman's hand cuts into them as if to freeze her utterance at a point—"perfect idiocy she knew"— which encapsulates, as it were, her subjection to an alienating masculine gaze and its governing discourse of gender identity.

This scene of a female protagonist in Bond Street, her very name and identity bonded to a patriarchal Other that wholly disregards her innermost being, is of course often read as a defiant statement of Woolf's feminist politics. There is no doubt that the alienating discourses of the culture she inhabits, discourses so often faithfully quoted by the men she knows, are a source of endless frustration to Clarissa: she can never forget once being scornfully dubbed "the perfect hostess" (*MD* 9) by Peter Walsh (and of course still more maddeningly his utterance turns out to be prophetic, since that very role awaits her at the party that evening, on 20 June 1923).[12]

If, however, for Clarissa Dalloway the role of hostess is a deadly spectre, a falsifying patriarchal fixation of her protean self, it is nonetheless preferable, the novel insists, to the *non*-alienated ontological manifestations that we are shown in the narrative. Of all the characters in Woolf's text, writes Gillian Beer, only Septimus Smith "haunts an absolute world:" only his psyche, that is, has suffered a radical implosion of the constitutive self-doubt which opens human subjectivity as such, and which makes people like Clarissa, Sally or Peter essentially non-identical with themselves, ontologically at odds with their 'own' discursive representations.[13] Unlike theirs, the psyche of Septimus has no interest in the vagaries of the signifier or the unfinishedness of identity, but—like music, according to Rachel Vinrace—it "goes straight for things:"

> The sparrows fluttering, rising and falling in jagged fountains were part of the pattern; the white and blue, barred with black branches. Sounds made harmonies with premeditation; the spaces between them were as significant as the sounds. A child cried. Rightly far away a horn sounded. All taken together meant the birth of a new religion—
>
> (*MD* 26)

What is revealed to Septimus recalls the hallucinatory epiphanies of May Sinclair's stories, whether Agatha's vision of the "stirring of the corruption that is Life" or Garvin's encounter with something lying "outside the order of his experience" (*US* 96, 200). Such ecstatic visions are impossible for a subject of rational discourse to *experience*: they occupy the ontological domain of *figure*, in Lyotard's sense, where what appears is "not reducible to the constraints of structure;" or that of mystical participation, to use Levinas's terms, where the whole diacritical basis of subjectivity is foreclosed by an "undifferentiated background" of amorphous, asemic *jouissance*.[14] Indeed, for Levinas this mystical state of *Einfühlung* ("in-feeling," usually translated as "sympathy") is directly linked to "the impersonality of the sacred in primitive religions:" what appears does so as absolute, innocent of pre-existing meanings, as if seen or felt for the first time. In Septimus, however, a ruined structure of subjectivity still survives, intermittently linking him to the existence of other people, to the signifying Other with its consensual fiction of 'reality,' thus to desire and to his wife Rezia. But that remnant of structure can no longer account for the events that happen to Septimus: there is no consistent multiple to include what is revealed in his hallucinations, so that all he can produce is a string of cryptic fragments, hermetic ciphers of private *jouissance* (very like the "epiphanies" scribbled down by the young James Joyce).

What Septimus writes, then—not unlike the "old bubbling burbling song" (*MD* 91) heard outside the tube station—is an effort to transmit something felt to be vital, world-changing, yet in itself irreducible to the constraints of discursive structure. This impossible aesthetic recalls Woolf's earlier sense of Emily Brontë's work as driven by a desire to radically dismantle the whole anthropocentric world, "as if she could tear up all that we know human beings by, and fill the unrecognizable transparences with such a gust of life that they transcend reality" (*CE* 190). This remark formulates exactly, in fact, the psychotic 'philosophical' project of Septimus: to abolish the whole ontological structure of human existence, to tear open the space of a new vision unconstrained by the trivial criteria of what has hitherto counted as 'reality.'

It is however of overwhelming importance in Woolf's writing that the "harmonies" revealed to Septimus—and those of *Wuthering Heights*, for that matter—are not presented as mere psychotic delusions to be comfortably dismissed as banally nonsensical. There is instead, Woolf's text insists, an essential dimension of *demand* in the act of writing or transmitting the 'mad' vision, which constitutes a fundamental link to the intersubjective structure of human existence and its creative *Gefühlsbindung* or aesthetic bond of feeling. What is crucial here is the response of the Other to the unsightly utterance of the possessed one—thus the coin given by Peter Walsh to the "poor creature" (*MD* 91), albeit no more than a half-conscious gesture on his part, nonetheless serves as an implicit act of symbolic recognition, an intersubjective response to the demand of the woman bound up in the "invincible thread of sound" (*MD* 92). By contrast, Rezia's reaction to seeing the old singer, like her response to her husband's prophetic writings, is hampered by her anxious consciousness of an ever-watchful patriarchal Other: "Suppose one's father, or somebody who had known one in better days had happened to pass, and saw one standing there in the gutter?" (92) This place of vigilant paternal knowledge is occupied, in the case of Rezia's relation to Septimus, by Dr Holmes or Dr Bradshaw; so that her emotional readiness to respond to her husband's nightmarish message, to identify with the place of his affective demand, is frozen—exactly as the policeman's hand telepathically freezes Clarissa's thoughts in their "perfect idiocy" (12)—under the specular regime of patriarchal authority.

Now, the ghostly encounter, we have argued, can be seen as a momentary suspension of that specular regime of knowledge, a figural gap opening in its discursive regulation, its reductive 'knowledge,' of the ontological. Woolf's writerly challenge to the epistemic gaze of patriarchal domination begins, as we have seen, under the influence of a Brontësque "gust of life" and of the ghostly music heard in Henry James, a music that estranges the very texture of reality. But if for Woolf Brontë's desire to dismantle the anthropocentric world is obviously of immense significance to the modernist poetic, it seems less clear that the ghost story as such, with its traditional conservatism of style, has influenced the modernist disruption and reinvention of literary form. Less clear, that is, until we read the following passage from *Mrs Dalloway*, where Peter is recalling a theory expounded by a youthful Clarissa on top of an omnibus (thus making it, the text hints with gentle irony, a theory *per omnibus*, for everyone):

It was to explain the feeling they had of dissatisfaction; not knowing people; not being known. For how could they know each other? [. . .] But she said, sitting on the bus going up Shaftesbury Avenue, she felt herself everywhere; not "here, here, here;" and she tapped the back of the seat; but everywhere. [. . .] It ended in a transcendental theory which, with her horror of death, allowed her to believe . . . that since our apparitions, the part of us which appears, are so momentary compared with the other, the unseen part of us, which spreads wide, the unseen might survive, be recovered somehow attached to this person or that, or even haunting certain places, after death.

(*MD* 167–168)

In what precise sense, then, does this passage link modernist writing back to the concerns of the ghost story? The scene Peter Walsh remembers is marked by a fundamental distinction between two registers of knowledge—that of communicable discourse (thus of public culture, of what is *per omnibus*); and that of 'life itself,' a private intensity or immanence of intuition or affect. In distinguishing between a telepathic surplus of self— never reducible, Clarissa insists, to a single site of interiority—and the mere "apparition" or ephemeral manifestation of the subject, this "transcendental theory" reformulates the essential topography of the ghost story. The ghostly encounter—whether we see it figured as enigmatic inscription in M. R. James, as the unbearable face of the other in Henry James, as the exposure of "an agony, made visible" in May Sinclair (*US* 188)—that encounter does not inhabit a consistent signifying multiple where a coherent intersubjective structure can be supposed; but rather emerges in the ontological domain of an unfeasible *jouissance*, where the hypnotic bond to the other has no regard for the logic or temporality of discursive rationality. The young Clarissa has unwittingly reversed the standard opposition of actual being and spectral double, so that "the unseen part of us" becomes the ontological essence of the self, not its haunting other; while the everyday subject is held to be a mere "apparition." But what is crucial is that the ephemeral, defective conscious reality of the empirical self is supplemented by another ontological figure subtracted from the multiple of that reality: an impossible, implausible spectre, a vision more real than reality itself.

This implausible other-self, in *Mrs Dalloway*, is of course the ghostly Septimus, whose very coherence as human subject has broken down in the face of the transfiguration of his world, as its discursive mesh is perforated by moments of absolute *jouissance* or revelation. What occurs to Septimus is unforgettable, in that it has no link to the rapidly moving circuits of signifying discourse that ensure the endless transference of affect away from the purview of consciousness; but it has its own inexpressibly rich music, as his cryptic scribblings vainly attempt to testify. Peter Walsh's reflection on memory offers a useful commentary on this notion of ontological otherness as psychical event:

There was a mystery about it. You were given a sharp, acute, uncom-
fortable grain—the actual meeting; horribly painful as often as not; yet
in absence, in the most unlikely places, it would flower out, open, shed
its scent, let you touch, taste, look about you, get the whole feel of it
and understanding, after years of lying lost. (*MD* 168–169)

What haunts is therefore something freed from logical time and space,
an otherness flowing from an eternal, unfathomable ontological event. If
modernist writing remembers the ghost story "after years of lying lost," it
does so in its search for a domain beyond the conscious surfaces of reflection or memory. Our next lesson in this ghostly mystery will be an exploration of "The Dead" by James Joyce.

THE JOYS OF VOICE

Early in *Mrs Dalloway*, Septimus makes a startling discovery about
the voice:

"K ... R ... " said the nursemaid, and Septimus heard her say "Kay
Arr" close to his ear, deeply, softly, like a mellow organ, but with a
roughness in her voice like a grasshopper's, which rasped his spine deli-
ciously and sent running up into his brain waves of sound which, con-
cussing, broke. A marvellous discovery indeed—that the human voice
in certain atmospheric conditions (for one must be scientific, above all
scientific) can quicken trees into life! (*MD* 25–26)

There is something *living* in this discovered voice, a musical vitality at
odds with the everyday agency of the letter (which Woolf mockingly portrays
in the not-quite-readable sky-writing of the aeroplane advertising toffee).

Nearly two decades before Woolf's novel, however, in a story first
drafted in 1907, Joyce shows that he is already alive to the figure of voice as
uncanny musical vitality. The story's title, "The Dead," as well as its setting
at a festive Dublin gathering of family and friends, at first suggests a ghost
story in the Dickens or Le Fanu tradition; but it is the medium of song that
gives Joyce his essential ontological figure for the ghostly element, the figure of a lost vitality haunting the constricted site of both Irish culture and
the individual psyche. The song *The Lass of Aughrim* is the key to Gretta
Conroy's haunting past, and its performance is marked in the text as a
fragile luminescence or phantasmal emanation: "the voice, made plaintive
by distance and by the singer's hoarseness, faintly illuminated the cadence
of the air" (*D* 165–166). The idea of the voice as barely visible phantasm
is also associated with another song, entitled *Arrayed for the Bridal* and
performed by Gabriel's Aunt Julia before the Christmas dinner; but what is
crucial here is the response of the audience to the "cadence of the air:"

> Her voice, strong and clear in tone, attacked with great spirit the runs
> which embellish the air and though she sang very rapidly, she did not
> miss even the smallest of the grace notes. To follow the voice, without
> looking at the singer's face, was to feel and share the excitement of
> swift and secure flight. Gabriel applauded loudly with all the others at
> the close of the song and loud applause was borne in from the invisible
> supper-table. It sounded so genuine that a little colour struggled into
> Aunt Julia's face. . . .   (D 151–152)

What is vital in the voice, its "great spirit," takes the listener up into the
air, on a "swift and secure flight" away from earth-bound reality; but this
transcendent mystical participation in the song all depends on one thing:
that is, on *not looking* at the singer's face. In other words, the specular
domain of social reality, its subjection to the gaze of the Other, is incommensurable with the phantasmatic ontology opened by the voice, anticipating the distinction to be staged on Clarissa Dalloway's omnibus between
communicable discourse and 'life itself.' Although in reality, that is, the
singer is an old woman whose world has shrunk to a cycle of empty social
rituals and repetitive gestures (she is not far indeed from being Clarissa's
dreaded "perfect hostess"), her song embodies a whole register of being
which is irreducible to that reality, something fired by vital—and indeed
fundamentally sexual—resistance to the mortifying syntax of a repressive
patriarchal culture.

Moreover Joyce's description of the response elicited by Aunt Julia's song
can itself be read as a subtle comment on that mortifying syntax. The conventional social form of the occasion, of course, demands a brief round of
applause; and Gabriel's response is duly governed by that formal demand:
he "applauded loudly *with all the others*" (my emphasis). Just as Mrs Dalloway went along Bond Street "with the rest of them" (MD 13), acutely
aware of her subjectivity being bound by and into forms of social existence
that take no account of her as singular, affective being, so Gabriel nurtures
a sharp consciousness that his identity as nephew and honorary host at
his aunts' annual party is a mere social fiction, a role determined by the
tedious rites of family tradition and with no bearing on the inner truth of
his life, which he imagines is safely located elsewhere (outside Ireland, in
fact). His applause for Aunt Julia is therefore a fully symbolic or alienated
act, a gesture dictated by the Other as pure demand for formal consistency;
as such it is an 'empty' gesture and is not remarked on by the text as a note-
worthy breach of the ostensibly realist narrative surface. (One thinks again
of Spencer Brydon's status as "a dim secondary social success" in Henry
James's "The Jolly Corner" [THJ 352]).

But it is here that the full subtlety of Joyce's writing in "The Dead"
begins to become visible. For alongside the symbolic event of applause
which absorbs Gabriel's act and empties it of any innerworldly significance, we are shown another, much more mysterious kind of response:

"loud applause was borne in from the invisible supper-table. It sounded so genuine that a little colour struggled into Aunt Julia's face. . ." (*D* 13). This applause, like Aunt Julia's song itself, has a specifically *ghostly* dimension: it emanates, with "great spirit," from an "invisible" other scene. As such, this moving air seems out of place, an element in excess of the occasion: it sounded "so genuine," speaking in a voice beyond the empty social signifier and thus rekindling the vitality of the old woman's face. This socially awkward, inappropriately "genuine" response is thus a matter of *jouissance*, of sexuality and the social symptom of embarrassment marked by Aunt Julia's unwilling blush. And while Gabriel has the good taste to avoid seeking to provoke such a reaction in the old lady, another member of the audience is altogether less tactful:

> Freddy Malins, who had listened with his head perched sideways to hear her better, was still applauding when everyone else had ceased . . . At last, when he could clap no more, he stood up suddenly and hurried across the room to Aunt Julia whose hand he seized and held in both his hands, shaking it when words failed him or the catch in his voice proved too much for him.
> —I was just telling my mother, he said, I never heard you sing so well, never. No, I never heard your voice so good as it is to-night. Now! Would you believe that now? That's the truth. Upon my word and honour that's the truth. I never heard your voice sound so fresh and so . . . so clear and fresh, never. (*D* 152)

Here words clearly *fail* Freddy Malins: the "catch in his voice" corresponds to something unutterable, a non-discursive object-voice coded by the text as maternal (the voice of Freddy's mother, we are told, "had a catch in it like her son's:" *D* 149). As I have argued elsewhere, the figural impropriety of voice in "The Dead" can be linked back to Stevenson's *The Strange Case of Dr Jekyll and Mr Hyde*.[15] Freddy Malins, I argue there, can be seen as an amiable intertextual avatar of the evil Mr Hyde, at once a strangely familiar guest whose untimely appearance makes Gabriel's aunts "dreadfully afraid" (*D* 139) and a ludicrous ghostly double of Gabriel himself. The Joycean text thus sets up an implicit distinction between an "imperfect and divided" subjectivity and one "more express and single," to quote Dr Jekyll's words as he gazes at his other-self in the mirror (*JH* 58)—between, that is, a 'normal' subject divided from full self-presence by the signifier and a "livelier image of the spirit" (as Jekyll sees Hyde; *ibid.*). Freddy's haplessly "genuine" response to Aunt Julia's song is thus an act less mortified by the symbolic law, thus closer to the unutterable ontological intensity of a telepathic *Gefühlsbindung*, than Gabriel's polite, insincere applause.

In both Joyce's story and Woolf's novel, then, a self-divided subjectivity belonging to a protagonist (Gabriel and Clarissa) is contrasted with a less 'normal' but "more express and single" being, the protagonist's ludicrous or uncanny double (Freddy and Septimus). The grammatical oddity of Stevenson's phrasing is crucial here: for the other-being, deprived of easy access to the social and innerworldly resources of the symbolic order, is *more single*—is excessively self-unified, as it were, and so at odds with the very syntax of identity. We saw how in May Sinclair's story "The Flaw in the Crystal" a reference to a character from Stevenson's *Strange Case*, Dr Lanyon, brought with it a whole problematic of the mimetic-affective bond, which Sinclair's text sought to present in its 'naked' form, outside the consistent multiple of social identities, as entailing an insufferable telepathic oneness. Both "The Dead" and *Mrs Dalloway* similarly explore the telepathic obliteration of psychical topography in ways that recall or rekindle the literary ghost as a figure of strange vitality and as *figure* in Lyotard's sense of a deictic element irreducible to an ontology defined by the space of discourse.

In Joyce, the haunting vitality of the ghost is above all figured through the music of the voice: in "The Dead" as a "distant music," a pure vibration that is barely audible, always vibrating on the point of becoming manifest or disappearing. In *Ulysses*, this musical dimension of the ghost-voice recurs, but now it is more explicitly coded as ontologically disruptive, at once mnemic and uncanny. In the book's first episode, Stephen Dedalus specifically associates the haunting memory of his mother's dying moments with a liminal voice, a song heard across a threshold: "Fergus' song: I sang it alone in the house, holding down the long dark chords. Her door was open: she wanted to hear my music" (U 1.249–251). Like *The Lass of Aughrim* or *Arrayed for the Bridal*, this Joycean moving air emanates from another space and time; and like the earlier songs too its evocation of "love's bitter mystery" is telepathic, an air traversing the proper borderlines of the psyche. But as Stephen's memories of his mother unfold, the music becomes more theatrical:

> She heard old Royce sing in the pantomime of *Turko the Terrible* and laughed with others when he sang:
>
> > *I am the boy*
> > *That can enjoy*
> > *Invisibility.*
>
> Phantasmal mirth, folded away: muskperfumed. (U 1.257–263)

The recollection of the recollection of music here takes another turn, if we attend carefully enough: for the pantomime *Turko the Terrible* recalls another Joycean pantomime, one mentioned by Freddy Malins over the Christmas dinner table in "The Dead;" and both pantomimes feature impersonations of exotic orientals, with the welcoming yuletide comedy playing host to an occult subtext which Joyce makes subtly relevant to Irish political reality. Freddy praises the singing voice of a "negro chieftain" (in fact only a "negro impersonator") who was performing in a 1903 Dublin pantomime, before rebuffing the predictable hum of racist disparagement with "and why couldn't he have a voice too? . . . Is it because he's only a black?" (*D* 156). Being without a voice of one's own, impossible to hear—an aural equivalent of old Royce's role as "the boy/That can enjoy/ Invisibility"—was indeed the precise condition of the Irish at the start of the twentieth century. Joyce's point was that only the Irish could enjoy their invisibility, overlook the disappearance of their language (a language which, Joyce had declared in Italian, "is oriental in origin").[16]

"And why couldn't he have a voice too?" We can hear the same question reverberating in *Mrs Dalloway*, as Septimus struggles in vain to take possession of the ghostly voices bubbling around and inside him, to convert the hallucinatory *jouissance* that constantly appears to him into a viable message for the world. The modernist demand for a transformation of the whole scope and significance of literary expression was bound up with an urgent sense of the need to give voice to a disruptive vitality that had been silenced or censored by public and aesthetic discourses in nineteenth-century culture. For Joyce in 1907 that repressed and distorted vitality corresponded primarily to a silenced Irish language, culture and history; while by the time Woolf was writing *Mrs Dalloway* in the 1920s it was clear that what official culture was energetically seeking—alongside the perennial exclusion of women's experience from public discourse—was to silence any hint of the inexpressible trauma that had occurred during the war. For both writers, as we have seen, the demand posed by these lost voices took on a force of such hallucinatory intensity that it could only be figured as a ghostly music or epiphany at odds with the ontologically consistent formal conventions imposed by the discourse of literary realism.

If modernist literature is often concerned, as Michael Bell writes, "with the question of how to live within a new context of thought," that question entails, in the work of Joyce, Sinclair and Woolf, a radical enquiry into literature itself as a means to open and sustain a thinking engagement with life.[17] But what is crucial to understand is that although this enquiry clearly has acute political significance and can be presented by criticism as a revolutionary political act—on behalf of an oppressed victim: Ireland, let's say, or traumatized soldiers or unrepresented women—it also exceeds that manifestly historical and as such easily interpretable significance. For these modernist writers, that is, the ego is primarily a reductive surface to be displaced and transformed by the vital ontological force potentially hosted by the literary text, and each in their different ways finds that force exemplified in the Victorian neo-gothic, where a "livelier image of the spirit" (*JH* 58) can be seen emerging beyond the everyday self: in the case of Woolf and Sinclair in the phantasmal figure of Emily Brontë, in Joyce's in the obscene vitality of Stevenson's Mr Hyde. For all three writers, reading and struggling to rewrite the traumatic vitality of these inspirational ghosts took literature beyond the domain of the signifier and into the 'quadrivial,' as Joyce liked to call it: the domain of algebra, geometry, astronomy and music (and of ontology, adds Badiou).[18] Thus, as we have seen, the importance in modernist writing of musical performance as an index of an aesthetic event—the luminous cadence of a voice as figure for the ontological singularity of a life—that exceeds the limited criteria of stylistic beauty, and as such becomes almost the signature event of modernism itself.

7 Double-Crossing
Elizabeth Bowen

BOWEN

Born a generation after Joyce and Woolf, Elizabeth Bowen (1899–1973) was, writes Neil Corcoran, "deeply impressed by the ambitions of High Modernism."[1] And like the modernists, as we will see, Bowen used the figure of the literary ghost in part as a way to re-inscribe and re-negotiate her own vexed position as heir to powerful literary traditions. On one side, there was the newly resurgent current of women's writing, which as we have seen both Sinclair and Woolf had at once affirmed as a tradition with its own creative genealogy reaching back to the Brontës, and in turn given new vitality through their own innovative fictions. On the other side, meanwhile, Bowen had to deal with what James Wurtz calls "the spectre of Anglo-Ireland:" a peculiarly ambivalent cultural history and 'modernity' that, Wurtz argues, produced in Bowen's work a literary 'modernism' that, while committed to stylistic experiment and new forms of thought, was at the same time fundamentally 'gothic.'[2]

If the literary ghost thus loomed large in Bowen's world, this was primarily an effect of a characteristically gothic (and Anglo-Irish) problem of personal and cultural identity. As we have seen, the modern ghost story often gravitated around the self as dubious centre—most strikingly, perhaps, in the work of Henry James. In Chapter 4 , we argued that the root of "The Jolly Corner," with its final uncanny encounter of self and other-self, was James's fatal moment in 1895 of theatrical rivalry with Oscar Wilde, a moment unthinkably refracted by a range of Jamesian and Wildean texts on split or double identity. Elsewhere in the modern ghost story, this uncanny gothic scenario of self and double often recurs, even if sometimes with a knowing ironic twist, as when M. R. James wearily asks his readers in an article of 1929 to take his word that he has read the most famous ghost story of all—written, of course, not by himself but by another man called James.[3]

If the modernism inherited and developed by Bowen can be seen as distinctively gothic, then, the question of identity and its duplicity was already a crucial stake in the ghost story, above all in the transition from its traditional form to its modern version. Even as a child, Bowen had begun encountering her literary double, her ghost-writing namesake: as Victoria Glendinning reports, young 'Bitha' Bowen, while still at school, was caught up in a craze "for witchcraft and the occult. Bitha and her companions learnt all they could about cursing and possession, and pored over Marjory Bowen's *Black Magic*."[4] The latter was not in fact a witches' handbook but a novel, *Black Magic: A Tale of the Rise and Fall of the Antichrist*, published in 1909 by 'Marjorie Bowen'—one of several pseudonyms used by an extraordinarily productive writer, Margaret Gabrielle Campbell. The novel enjoyed by young Bowen is a lurid neo-gothic affair, featuring a witch named Ursula who uses her diabolical powers to become not the antichrist but the pope (and, as 'Pope Joan,' ultimately a feminist legend). So we see young Bitha, a genuine Bowen, reading *Black Magic* by Margaret or Marjorie, a pseudo-Bowen, writing about a woman who changed her name and used black magic to seize control of patriarchal power, to misappropriate the name of the father.

The doubling of identity and misappropriation of names, moreover, did not stop haunting Bowen. As a middle-aged novelist of considerable repute, she made friends with Lady Ursula Vernon (although not a witch, this Ursula was, Glendinning writes with scare quotes, a 'haunted' person). Now, Lady Ursula was a racehorse-owner and through her, continues Glendinning, Bowen met "racing people who were totally ignorant, or confused, about her identity as a writer; one misinformed gentleman bore down upon her crying, 'Ah, *The Viper of Milan*! What a book!'"[5] It was in fact, of course, Marjorie Bowen (in other words, Margaret Campbell) who in 1906 had published *The Viper of Milan: A Romance of Lombardy*, another lurid historical romance, this time starring a black-hearted prince called Visconti (precisely how Bowen reacted to the horsey gentleman's misguided exclamation, Glendinning does not record).

The name Bowen, then, was already shadowed, marked by a certain 'gothic' non-authenticity or doubt for young Bitha: her proper name a sign not of genealogical certitude and self-recognition but of uncanny or ludicrous duplicity. And there were, in addition, other aspects of her familial and ethnic inheritance that involved her developing a sense of the self being a fundamentally double entity: the very term "Anglo-Irish," she famously remarked, evoked an unhomely self-division, since it named people who only really felt at home "in mid-crossing between Holyhead and Dun Laoghaire."[6] The "spectre of Anglo-Ireland," to recall Wurtz's phrase, has often been foregrounded in recent criticism of Bowen as the sign of a cultural unhomeliness that allows the "division and discontinuity" of her work to be re-read both in terms of the restless dynamic of modernist creativity and as a symptom of ghostly cultural non-self-identity.[7] Susan Osborn draws our attention to the odd decision by Lane and Clifford, the editors of a 1993 anthology of Irish writers, to disavow Bowen in a curiously literal manner by drawing a line of cancellation through her name—thus writing it as ~~Bowen~~—above her (fairly lengthy) entry.[8] Disturbed by "irregularities that complicated their desire to identify [Bowen] with one national identity or another," writes Osborn, the editors justified this strange act of typographical denegation as follows: "We include her in this anthology, in deleted form, in order to explain why she does not belong to it."[9]

To write ~~Bowen~~, however, for all its dubious political implications as a critical gesture, may nevertheless turn out to be curiously apt, since Bowen can be seen as an exemplary artist of non-belonging, her work bridging the gap between literary Ireland and the English novel (or, it might be added, between modernism and conservatism, or even perhaps between patriarchal tradition and women's writing); while her writing will always prove to be hybrid, irreducible to either term of the opposition. In this last chapter we will explore Bowen's literary non-belonging at a deeper level by looking at how her work, above all in the short story, draws her into the uncanny orbit of the neo-gothic genre of the modern ghost story, as we have seen it redirected in early modernism, in Henry James, May Sinclair and subsequently in Woolf and Joyce. What Bowen's ghostly writing ultimately reaches toward, we will argue, is an impossible event or encounter, a point of radical otherness lying beyond the legible surfaces of 'belonging,' be they those of nation, class, identity or heterosexual legitimacy.

DISJUNCTION

Writing a preface in the late 1950s for a new selection of her stories, Bowen makes some revealing comments on the genre of the short story:

> If I were a short-story writer only, I might well seem to be out of balance. But recall, more than half my life is under the steadying influence of the novel, with its calmer, stricter, more orthodox demands: into the novel goes such taste as I have for rational behaviour and social portraiture. The short story, as I see it, allows for what is crazy about humanity: obstinacies, inordinate heroisms, "immortal longings."[10]

While the novel should behave responsibly and "keep close to life," as Bowen had put it in *English Novelists* (1945), the short story has a kind of licence to be unbalanced: it should be governed not by rationality but by "compulsions," Bowen wrote elsewhere, and indeed as literary form it has a distinctly psychopathological bent, featuring "cases of oddness or deviation, of solitude, crisis, forlorn hope or, at least, eccentricity."[11] The short story, in brief, is for Bowen a deviant Mr Hyde to the novel's sober Dr Jekyll—a disturbing apparition of the implausible, the illegitimate, the asocial.

It is tempting to see the generic distinction Bowen makes here in terms of the "spectre of Anglo-Ireland," the 'gothic' self-dividedness or ethnocultural non-belonging we saw earlier as a characteristic trope of recent critical responses to her work. In this sense, we might imagine the short story, with its craziness or "inordinate heroisms," as an Irish alter-ego of the straight-laced English novel: like Mr Hyde, a twisted racial inferior of a "calmer, stricter, more orthodox" (more *white*) overlord. Or else we could see things in the light of Bowen's troublesome sexual self-division, with the short story now an impulsive, deviant, essentially extramarital, affair; in contrast to the husbandly composure, or dutiful wifeliness, of the novel (which classically, of course, often culminates in a marriage ceremony). But what is crucial not to miss here is how Bowen ascribes to the short story a special writerly privilege, involving what she calls "vision," which is to say a perception inherently *at odds with realism*:

> There is also the necessity to project, to make seen, and make seen with significance—the short story is for the eye (if the mind's eye). Also the short story, though it highlights what appears to be reality, is not— cannot wish or afford to be—realistic: it relies on devices, foreshortenings, "effects".[12]

The short-story writer thus resembles the painter who makes use of an optical device to give an anamorphic twist to the work's perspective: she cannot rely on the safe three-dimensional generic steadiness of the novel, but must bring her narrative to life with rapid dexterity, by means of some acrobatic textual trickery. Now, Bowen may not have known it, but this privileging of the short story as supreme technical challenge was a view shared by one of the most significant innovators of early modernism, namely Joseph Conrad. "C'est dans des courts recits (short story) que l'on voit la main du maitre," wrote Conrad in bad French to his cousin Marguerite Poradowska, a successful writer whom he sometimes liked to address as *chère Maître*.[13] The parenthetical phrase in English stands out, suggesting perhaps that Conrad had specific English-language examples of this narrative mastery in mind. As we will see, for Bowen the short story is of crucial significance for the literary impact of Anglophone modernism, above all because of what she saw as the genre's deviance from, its implicit rejection of, the supposedly 'rational' coherence of the Victorian novel. It was not for nothing that Bowen chose to name the eponymous figure in her story "The Dancing-Mistress" (1929), the "pretty but brittle" scourge of her clumsy pupils, Miss Joyce James: as if the spirit of the infamous author of *Dubliners* shadowed or bedeviled the Dublin-born Bowen's work, re-appeared like an anamorphic ghost on its surface.[14]

But what prepares the way for Bowen's short fiction, anticipating her obsessive concern with the dislocating impact of modernity on traditional forms of community and communication, was not in the first instance the bleak tales of Joyce's *Dubliners* but what seems at first sight a much more traditional kind of narrative: namely the Victorian and Edwardian ghost story. What is crucial here, though, is what we have glimpsed as the modernist subtext of the ghost story—in Dickens's "The Signalman," for instance, the spectral apparition takes place at the cutting edge of modernity, in the neo-gothic "dungeon" of a railway cutting (*SM* 175); while in Henry James's "The Jolly Corner" the haunted house is located in a New York ravaged by "the modern, the monstrous" (*THJ* 342). It is precisely this uncanny collision of ultra-modernity and traditional life-worlds that Bowen uses the short story to expose and examine.

The ghostly dimension of modern life is strikingly accentuated in Bowen's first collection of stories, *Encounters* (1923)—there is "something unearthly" (*CS* 53), she writes there, in the suburban environment suddenly emerging in the early twentieth century, as if its dislocation and dispersal of former communities were disturbing the whole ontological structure of the relation between human life and death. The opening of "The Shadowy Third" encapsulates this uncanny shift in psychical geography:

> He was a pale little man, with big teeth and prominent eyes; sitting opposite to him in a bus one would have found it incredible that there could be a woman to love him. As a matter of fact there were two, one dead, not counting a mother whose inarticulate devotion he resented, and a pale sister, also dead. (*CS* 75)

The imaginary encounter with this person takes place "in a bus"—in, that is, a truncated fragment of *omnibus* ('for everyone'), providing an apt figure for the fragmentary modern 'community' where the other is both obscenely close (one can almost smell his breath) and completely out of reach, unknowable.[15] The *Nebenmensch*, as Freud will put it in his 1930 essay *Civilization and its Discontents*, the man sat opposite me whom I am inexplicably commanded by Christianity to love, remains radically other to me, does not belong to 'my' world; in Bowen's text he is shown caught up in an enigmatic arithmetic of libido, an uncanny network of desire linking the living and the dead.[16] How can I count—account for—the desire of the other? Bowen's story, as its title already announces, hinges on just such a question. The "shadowy third" is an indiscernible anamorphic extra that intrudes on any relation between self and other, jeopardizing the very possibility of communication, throwing out of kilter the symbolic reciprocity of identification at the root of community.

The problem of community, of what allows or prevents the habitation and ownership of a shared cultural world—a 'gothic' problem that runs through all of Bowen's short fiction—is thus already strikingly visible in this early story. Although at the most obvious level Bowen dramatizes this as a question of sexual non-relation, it is also, and crucially, a matter of the non-authenticity, the ontological emptiness, of the hapless couple's suburban environment. This is how Bowen links these aspects of non-community:

> The fields were dotted here and there with clumps of elm; with here and there a farmhouse roof, the long roofs and gleaming windows of a factory.

'This open country stretches for such miles,' she said dreamily. 'Sometimes, on these quiet misty days, I begin to think the sea's over there, and
that if the clouds along the distance lifted I should see it suddenly, shining. And, with this wind, I could be sure I smell and hear it.'

'Yes, I know. One often gets that feeling.'

'Do *you*?'

'Well, no,' he said confusedly, 'but I'm sure one does. I can imagine
it.' Someone had said the same thing to him, just here, three or four
years ago.   (CS 76)

The suburban location, carefully tailored to give the illusion of proximity to rural innocence, parodies the romantic geography that still lingers in the woman's mind: in fact, although she doesn't know it, her
speech sounds more like estate agent's spiel than Wordsworthian vision.
What catches the eye in this landscape is not the shining sea but a fac-
tory window: the traditional organic pattern of dwelling and community
has disappeared, leaving behind an irrational jumble of incompatible elements, with shards of the old world jostling up against the stark geometry of modern industry. This modernist landscape cannot be properly
read or discursively owned (note the drifting of verb tenses: "I could be
sure I smell and hear it"); it is an ontological void, offering no comprehensible scene for the couple to share, no romantic idea through which
they can forge a bond. What is crucial is the last line quoted: the dead
wife "had said the same thing to him"—but said what, exactly? Had she
(as we no doubt think on a first reading) simply indulged in the same
pseudo-romantic rhetoric as the current wife—or did she rather admit
(as *he* has just had to) to only being able to "imagine" what the other
feels, to not really owning the signifying bond being offered? If the dead
wife is the "shadowy third" haunting the living couple, she is no more
than a cipher for a much more radical problem of mutual non-belonging
being staged in Bowen's text: the very possibility of living together, of
inhabiting a shared imaginary topography, is rendered doubtful in this
ontological lacuna, this fragmentary, inconsistent non-place.

In "The Storm," a story published three years after *Encounters* in
1926, Bowen chooses to transplant the sexual non-relation to another
non-place—not this time a vacuous suburban dwelling, but instead
one of the paradigmatic scenes of ersatz modern 'experience:' a tourist
attraction. We meet the couple perched dizzily on the terrace of a crum-
bling renaissance villa in the Italian mountains; and now their non-
relation is not just a matter of mutual misunderstanding but of direct,
bodily aversion:

'Don't come near me,' she said, turning sharply. 'I hate you! Why do
you keep on following me about?'   (CS 180)

There has clearly been a significant shift in Bowen's writing in the three years since *Encounters*. Everything that in "The Shadowy Third" was still caught up in the ambiguity of discursive signification returns in "The Storm" at the level of the fantasmatic real, as intransigent "compulsion" (to recall the term used by Bowen to define the short story as genre). Thus, while the self-experience of the woman in the earlier story is shadowed by the Other (personified as "Anybody," her spectral predecessor), and while the couple's relation to past tradition and 'their' place is emptied of share-able meaning by the deracinating impact of modernity, in "The Storm" both the self and its relation to history and others are traumatized by an encounter with what the collapsed pre-modern order has left behind: frag-ments of incomprehensible sensation, "a succession of uncertain impetuses" (181). We should pay special attention to what happens to *time* during the female protagonist's apparitional encounter:

> After the young woman in orange had passed her, she wondered dully where she had been going, whither she hurried so. Her urgency had cut like a knife through the opaque twilight, and her dress had been curiously brilliant in the drained-out colourlessness of the evening. The chief impression of her passing had been a rustling and a rushing sound, and though she had not passed in an imponderable moment there had been an effect of speed about her forehead and blown-back hair. She left a coolness of displaced air, like the single gesture of a fan. She had taken form out of the darkness of the stairway, simultaneously emerg-ing and descending. At its foot there had been a sort of hesitancy—a gesture of return; then she had rushed forwards with an impetus that made her almost luminous. (CS 182)

The apparition is initially enigmatic—is it real presence or mirage?—although it is quickly identified by the woman in terms of gothic melo-drama ("Oh Rupert, Rupert, I have seen a ghost!"). As figured by the text, however, with its strange 'expressionist' stylistic detail, what appears is a kind of ontological aberration, something essentially "imponderable". The viewing subject is essentially unprepared, unable to account, for this manifestation, which has all the force as well as the overwhelming other-ness of the erotic drive: she cannot *place* this apparition in empirical time (it simultaneously "had passed" and "had not passed in an imponderable moment," both emerging and descending, departing and returning, in a "single gesture"). The very geometry of realism cannot survive the displac-ing impetus of what manifests itself: "Then she felt the wall of the Villa tilt for a moment over toward her as she cried, 'Oh Rupert, Rupert, I have seen a ghost!'" (182).

What appears in "The Storm," then, does not conform to the ordinary grammar of everyday reality, either for the woman in the story or for her observer, the reader. Neither can finally tell what actually happened, although the woman later attempts to do just that:

> She also had it in her to project herself, to stamp on time her ineffaceable image. She had an urgency which made her timeless, like the woman on the terrace; which made her step clear of the dimensions. She had simply, as she now knew, beheld herself in a mirror as that other went past her; and stepped back, shaken, from her own reality. That was it: she was overcharged.   (CS 187)

We are offered a readymade theory to make sense of what has happened: she did not see a ghost but "beheld herself," a hallucinatory doppelganger, in an imaginary mirror; and the erotic force of the encounter was a mere excrescence of her own overcharged female libido. Bowen's satirical demolition of the intellectual narcissism on show here is altogether merciless: just as the woman's self-regard is phrased in cod-Shakespearean ("to stamp on time her ineffaceable image"), her self-diagnosis is lifted wholesale from the patriarchal lexicon of family medicine: "That was it: she was overcharged" is the wisdom of the doctor prescribing a rest-cure at the seaside.

Subjectivity, as a pathological skewing or distortion of reality, is thus everywhere in "The Storm," making it a defiantly anti-realist text that leaves the reader as bewildered—or else as invested in some comforting theoretical cliché or 'solution'—as the characters are themselves. The expressionist verve of the writing, corresponding to the symbolic vortex of the mediterranean wind, emphasizes this eclipse of objective reality:

> Pale gashes curled forward, slit and dissipated themselves like waves where the wind flung forward whole branches. Little eddies of sound sucked and whirled down in the shadows. Above it all, there was a high whistling.

> The pillar of a fountain, solid as marble, swerved, bent like a bow, and flung a cloud of fine spray into their faces.   (CS 186)

In this world where the habitual forms of reality are estranged, rendered almost abstract, subjects are left without a common language to communicate and identify what is happening: they are thrown back on no more than their own fantasmatic projections to lend support to their hypothetical interpretations. If the woman's wild exclamations about having seen a ghost are given no credibility whatsoever, neither is her husband's meek claim to have seen in the villa, of all things, some nuns:

> 'Nuns?' she said incredulously. She would not believe him, and when, feeling his way over to the corner of their exit, he drew back the

curtain, he found that there was nothing behind it but stone: it was a blocked-up archway.

'Well?' came her voice with a smile in it. It was beautiful to her that Rupert had been making himself nuns.

'They *seemed* to me to be nuns,' he faltered. . . .   (*CS* 188)

Each of the partners in the sexual non-relation, one might perhaps conclude, sees a different kind of ghost—one urgently sexual, one amusingly chaste. But as readers we cannot rest easy with this neat solution, for we too have to judge for ourselves (with no help from the narrator) the discrepant reality-claims presented. Both characters, it is clear, saw something; but there is no metalanguage in which to adjudicate their narratives of what precisely they did see, each of which is absurd in the eyes of the other. "The Storm" is therefore a peculiarly self-reflexive kind of ghost story, since it features apparitions that are genuinely shocking, experienced as fully 'real' by the characters, but at the same time offers an ironic critique of those apparitions as mere subjective delusions: we see Bowen's text poised dizzily on the edge between gothic and modernist writing, "simultaneously emerging and descending" (182).

DISCOUNTENANCE

Let us return to the imaginary scene on the bus at the start of "The Shadowy Third." We are sitting opposite the "pale little man" (*CS* 75), the Freudian *Nebenmensch* with his inscrutable desire, his "surplus enjoyment" (as Slavoj Žižek would call it). What is most disturbing about this scene is our sudden, over-close examination of the man's "big teeth and prominent eyes," as if we were seeing his face in cinematic close-up (Bowen was very attracted by early cinema and its new narrative possibilities). This excessive, voyeuristic inspection of the man's features heralds a pervasive feature of Bowen's short fiction: that is, its preoccupation with the human face as essential sign and site of subjectivity, as ethical basis for all communication and community.

"The proximity of the other is the face's meaning," declares Emmanuel Levinas, adding: "The Other becomes my neighbour precisely through the way the face summons me, calls for me . . . and calls me into question."[17] But when we are forced into a close-up encounter with the other's face in the meaningless, jostling anonymity of the modern bus, the ethical significance of the face is radically undermined: it is more likely to be the sheer ugliness of this over-close other that I experience, not its properly ethical challenge to my limited world. The stories by Bowen we have examined so far show this collapse of the symbolic matrix of identification, of a structure that once made it possible to encounter the Other face-to-face, through its impact on the modern couple. Stranded in their inauthentic, deracinated suburban privacy, the non-partners in "The Shadowy Third" have only each other to provide the ghost of a sense of community—but of course the spectral presence of another is always there to remind them that their relation is nothing but emptily iterative signifiers, only thinly veiled by fantasy. Similarly, in "The Storm," the relation to the other is mediated by a fantasy that can barely be sustained, so great is the pressure on it to provide a semblance of full, properly 'human' authenticity (thus its stereo-typical banality: "she had an urgency that made her timeless;" "God was with him, she was learning to cling to him:" 187; 189). In this non-relation, the other has to be disavowed as such, in its very otherness: it cannot be faced as ethical Other (to use the Levinasian distinction). This structure of disavowal is subtly inscribed in "The Shadowy Third" in another scene of close-up gazing:

> He had taken off his hat, and she watched the wind blowing through his fair hair, as soft and fine as a baby's. Little wrinkles were coming in the forehead that she thought so noble, and his face—well, one could not analyse it, but it was a lovely face.   (CS 76)

The woman thus looks at the face, and immediately looks away, substi-tuting a vapid cliché for any actual encounter with its disturbing otherness. This is the very structure of disavowal, where the subject refuses to recogn-ise the reality of something traumatic it nonetheless cannot help perceiving, producing an anxiety only seemingly at odds with the fetishistic surface-clichés (baby hair, noble forehead) that supposedly cover things up.[18]

Bowen's derisive critique of how fetishistic disavowal operates in the search for modern 'community' is taken further, beyond the domain of the sexual couple into that of larger social groups, in her short stories of the 1930s. The ironic tone of "The Cat Jumps" (1934) seems to herald a thor-oughly comic dissection of the modern family. We meet Harold and Jocelyn Wright as they are about to move into a suburban house formerly occupied by another Harold, namely convicted wife-murderer Harold Bentley:

> The Harold Wrights, however, were not deterred. They had light, bright, shadowless, thoroughly disinfected minds. They believed that they disbelieved in most things but were unprejudiced; they enjoyed frank discussions. They dreaded nothing but inhibitions; they had no inhibitions. They were pious agnostics, earnest for social reform; they explained everything to their children, and were annoyed to find their children could not sleep at nights because they thought there was a complex under the bed. . . . No family, in fact, could have been more unlike the mistaken Harold Bentleys. (CS 362)

The Harold Wrights take the place, as it were, of the Harold Wrongs: as the camp Wildean antitheses suggest, the ensuing story will be an arch black comedy, a wittily sharp exposure of these earnest, naively enlightened 'modernists.' The key word in the diagnostic vocabulary of the Wrights is *disinfect*, and they approach their new habitation as a kind of hygienic experiment, methodically stripping back the "disagreeably thick" décor of its grisly past, letting in rational light and air (but crucially failing to eliminate the "smell of unsavoury habitation:" 363). Indeed, what this naïve modernity amounts to, as Bowen's ironic narration heavily implies, is not merely a denial of Harold Bentley's specific murderous existence but the disavowal of human subjectivity as such, with all its peculiar proclivities and unsightly irregularities. It is this disavowal of the human subject that colours the enigmatic scene of the attempt by the Wrights and their guests to hold a rational conversation:

> In fact, on the intelligent sharp-featured faces all round the table something—perhaps simply clearness—seemed to be lacking, as though these were wax faces for one fatal instant exposed to a furnace. Voices came out from some dark interiority; in each conversational interchange a mutual vote of no confidence was implicit. You would have said that each personality had been attacked by some kind of decomposition.
>
> (CS 366)

The human face has lost its ethical significance as site of the encounter with the Other that founds community: just as the couple in "The Storm" can find no common fantasmatic ground, here every attempt at communication is marked by "a mutual vote of no confidence," with each speaker left stranded in the "dark interiority" of the individual psyche. The obsessive cleanliness of the "light, bright" Wrights corresponds to the fetishistic disavowal of the very thing that, if symbolically affirmed, might allow communities a degree of coherence: namely the fundamental singularity, the otherness to rational calculation, of the human subject. Modernity thus functions in Bowen's story according to a veritable 'dialectic of enlightenment' in Adorno and Horkheimer's sense: that is, as its own reversal into barbaric fanaticism, its "decomposition" into blind domination.[19] It is this dialectic that turns a rationalist project like a modern suburb into what Bowen, in another story, calls "a sort of nightmare of whim" (547): instead of a space of neutral, 'disinfected' collective living, what the modern suburb embodies is an uncanny return of the disavowed oddity, the unsavoury smell, of subjective libido. Thus, in "The Cat Jumps," the libidinal real disavowed by the rationalist Wrights insidiously returns in their new suburban location: both in what they knowingly theorize as the "sex-antagonism" (365) of their servants and in the whiff of the pungently named "Trèfle Incarnat" (364) caught by the nostrils of a guest (with the French phrase suggesting at once the 'foreign' intensity and the 'incarnadine' fleshy-goriness of the lingering aroma).

It is not until the conclusion of "The Cat Jumps," however, that Bowen's ironic critique of her characters' 'modernist' worldview comes under any pressure from the structure of the narrative: at the very end of the story, that is, it seems she has either to allow the Wrights to persist in their absurdly rationalist theory of life or to introduce some irrational event that will shatter it (and so distinctly darken the story's black comedy). The key question for the reader is: do the 'gothic' tropes throughout the story that shadow the Wrights's complacent 'enlightenment,' finally testify to something real (the continuing presence, somehow, of the murderous Harold Bentley); or is it, as the Wrights themselves think, nothing more than imaginary shadow-play? Bowen's solution is a characteristic bit of writerly double-crossing:

> The door opened on Harold, looking more dreadfully at her than she had imagined. With a quick, vague movement he roused himself from his meditation. Therein he had assumed the entire burden of Harold Bentley. Forces he did not know of assembling darkly, he had faced for untold ages the imperturbable door to his wife's room. She would be there, densely, smotheringly there. She lay like a great cat, always, over the mouth of his life.
>
> The Harolds, superimposed on each other, stood searching the bedroom strangely.   (CS 369)

Here it is again a question of the face: not this time, though, as the site of an ethical encounter but of an *imaginary* identity. The ego's imaginary relation with the mirror-other is tarnished, invaded by an uncanny "shadowy third," so that Harold's face can no longer communicate (and receive back as a message from his wife) an enlightened, rational self. The 'dialectic of enlightenment'—the Möbius strip reversal-twist of pure reason and absolute barbarism—is embodied in the figure of the two superimposed Harolds, for one of whom the wife is a rational partner, while for the other she is a smothering animal that must be done away with. As a rational ego, we might say, Harold has thus been thoroughly *discountenanced*—his familiar self-image shattered by the return of the "entire burden" embodied by his murderous double: everything—the suffocating proximity of the other in the libidinal real—disavowed by his hygienic modernity.

As we have seen, then, Bowen returns to the human face as a figure in her writing to disclose something of the strange relation, the ambiguous bond, of self and other. This figurative preoccupation with the face runs throughout her work, but becomes especially prominent at those 'gothic' moments when subjectivity itself, as an ontologically coherent structure, seems to unravel. Thus, in Bowen's wartime story "The Demon Lover" (1941), Kathleen's memory of her dead soldier fiancé comes to her in an uncannily disfigured mnemic image: "She remembered—but with one white burning blank as where acid has dropped on a photograph: *under no conditions* could she remember his face" (665). The blank, unreadable face becomes for Bowen the index of an uncanny otherness, something incommensurable with the dimensions of everyday, rational reality. The hapless Louie Lewis in the novel *The Heat of the Day* (1949) is haunted by her absent husband's gaze according to the same figurative economy:

> It had been Louie who—chair tilted back, tongue exploring her palate, mind blank of anything in particular—had hour-long passively gazed at Tom. Why now, therefore, should it be his chair that gazed at her? It directed something at her whichever way she pushed, pulled or turned it, in whatever direction she turned herself. The discountenancing of the chair by filling it had been her object in bringing strangers she met in the park back here.[20]

Louie's psychical "object" thus involves the "discountenancing" of her husband's absent-present face, the gaze that fixes her being precisely by withholding itself from discursive communication with her.

But if we return to Bowen's earlier short stories, we can see her already using the figure of the blanked-out face to inscribe a withdrawal from the rational space of intersubjectivity. While in "The Cat Jumps" the uncannily absent face is still caught up in the story's black comedy (with the absurdly paranoid Muriel seeing "a kind of insane glitter" in harmless Edward Cartaret's face), in "The Disinherited" (1934) there is nothing comic about the enigmatic face of the chauffeur Prothero: "his face was always shadowless, abstract, null; a face remembered as being unmemorable" (CS 380). It is this unreadable face that seals the human subject into its "dark interiority" (366), that makes it ultimately incompatible with any rational topography projected by 'modern' enlightenment.

Thus, however we choose to read the conclusion of "The Cat Jumps" (is Harold now bent on murdering Jocelyn or is it a nightmare from which he will awaken as his same old reasonable self?), we could see the final image of the story—each guest locked into the dark interiority of a room and barred from the communal space of dialogue and rationality once so dear to their modernist hosts—as a good summary of Bowen's political vision. Despite the arch, quasi-Wildean playfulness of her style in this story, it is clear that Bowen's view of modern life is radically pessimistic. Whether glimpsed in the secretly incompatible life-worlds of men and women, or manifested as an occult fantasmatic violence at odds with the smug reasonableness of modern liberalism, there is something badly wrong, in Bowen's eyes, with the world as currently lived: there is, as Freud had put it, an underlying *unbehagen in der Kultur*.[21] It is this acerbic vision of her contemporary reality that Bowen will push to an extreme in her key short story of the 1930s, entitled "The Disinherited".

DISPOSSESSION

If we begin by recalling those aspects of Bowen's work we have touched on in the argument so far—self-dividedness, cultural non-belonging, sexual non-relation, the dislocating impact of modernity on the space of community, the monstrous proximity of the nameless other or faceless 'man next door'—we will see how each one returns, and is given a new degree of traumatic intensity, in "The Disinherited." Indeed, Bowen's story recalls the great modernist ghost stories of Henry James and May Sinclair in the way it approaches the encounter with terror through a complex meditation on the dislocated, fragmentary selves of its characters and on itself as fragmentary text.

The story begins with a kind of autumnal overture, playfully suggesting ideas of change, decay and living-on: "eternity seemed to have set in at late autumn" (375). It is the reaction of the story's two female protagonists to this undying world outside that gives an immediate indication of their antithetical positions with regard to the key opposition in Bowen's text between modernity and tradition:

> Marianne Harvey was not aware of the autumn to which her friend was becoming a prey. Since August, Marianne had been cheerfully busy, without a moment for any kind of reflection; the Harveys were nesting over again, after twelve years of marriage, making a new home. But all those weeks Davina Archworth had been idle with a melancholy and hollow idleness, with all day to kick the wet leaf-drifts and watch the birds go.   (CS 375)

The two women come from different eras, different genres almost: on the one hand Marianne is a sprightly Jamesian heroine busily immersed in a modernist life-world defined by its split from the timeless cycle of the organic environment; whilst on the other Davina is an idle relic from an obsolete culture, caught, like some reincarnation of Lady Dedlock from Dickens's *Bleak House*, in a melancholy state of identification with natural decay. Just as Marianne's "nesting" is diametrically at odds with the autumnal departure of the birds, so her new location is defined by the alienating technological cut of modernity into the natural order of things:

> Few houses had gone up so far; those there were stood apart, like Englishmen not yet acquainted, washed by clear upland air and each in its acre of wiry grass that had lost its nature, being no longer meadow and not yet lawn. Half-made roads, like the first knowing cuts of a scalpel, mapped the flank of the hill out, up to the concrete water-tower upon its crest.   (CS 376)

This "exclusive" housing estate is precisely not a historical community, but rather the arbitrary product of a scientific rationality (its cuts are "knowing") with no time for the ragged, motley inclusivity of traditional habitation and whatever organic, non-conceptual kinds of knowledge it once fostered. In line with the opening set of contrasts between the two women, just as modernist-arriviste Marianne lives on the prefabricated "genteel hill," so decayed-aristocrat Davina lives down in the valley of olden times:

> At the foot of this genteel hill, at the river level, the old village frowsted inside its ring of elm trees, mouldy and snug. Its lichened barn-roofs were yellow, and from the church spire the weathercock now and then shot out one sharp gold ray; from the tower there came up, climbing the hill on Sundays, ponderous chimes. A clot of thin smoke hung melting in watery river light over the roofs of the village; after sunset a few dark lights outlined the three-cornered green. (CS 376)

"Frowsted:" the very word Bowen chooses to describe the village—meaning roughly 'inhabited a stuffy enclosure'—is already half-obsolete when she writes her story (the OED locates "frowst" as late nineteenth century). The village is thus a place of both literal and figurative obsolescence, its buildings metaphorically blending into the rotting vegetation of autumn, its atmosphere suffused with a hazy, amnesic suspension of clear demarcations. If Marianne's house on the hilltop is a blank page, painted white and "freshly-built" (376), the house where Davina is staying, owned by the regulation gothic aunt, "had a high, narrow face, with dark inanimate windows, and looked like the frontispiece to a ghost-story" (377). The description is deliberately, self-consciously mannered: pure literary neo-gothic, à la M. R. James or Sheridan LeFanu.

The antithetical structure we thus see at the opening of "The Disinherited," with the two women and their locations linked in turn to disruptive modernity and gothic obsolescence, is in fact a characteristic device of the modernist ghost story. In Henry James's "The Jolly Corner," we recall, the protagonist Spencer Brydon owns two properties in New York whose diametrical contrast fits with exactly the same structure: a modern apartment in a "tall mass of flats" and an old gothic family home with its haunting "great grey rooms." [22] It is the latter location, the eponymous house on the jolly corner, which in James's story still harbours a precious ghostly remnant of the life that has been erased from the technocratic modern city with its empty re-iterations and over-rational multiplications. Bowen's text, it is clear from the outset, shares something of this gothic conservatism, this privileging of the past as the scene of a vital presence under threat from a soulless 'enlightened' modernity. When Davina visits Marianne's new house, she is struck by its impeccably tasteful lifelessness:

> The hearth was bare, but steam heating drew out sweat from the plaster while, to Davina's senses, devitalizing and parching the air. Ranged round the cold brick hearth, three low chairs with sailcloth cushions

invited a confidence everything else forbade. A clock ticked, but the
room had no pulse.   (CS 379)

If the modern dwelling is hygienically removed from the putrescent vitality of the old village, however, "The Disinherited" is far from simply idealizing the past as a site of authentic human dwelling. Rather than offering
some lost hospitable alternative to the barren rationality of modernity, traditional architecture looms over the women in the story like some gigantic,
grimly hostile spectre:

> The immense façade of the house rushed glaring on to their headlamps:
> between high white-shuttered windows pilasters soared out of sight
> above an unlit fanlight like patterns of black ice.   (CS 385)

This arrival of guests at the spectral ancestral mansion, indeed, recalls
a more famous Anglo-Irish neo-gothic scene of arrival: the moment when
Jonathan Harker reaches "a vast ruined castle, from whose windows came
no ray of light:" namely Castle Dracula.[23] And Bowen's phrase "fanlight
like" in fact carries an unconscious echo of 'fang-like:' this house, like that
of Stoker's monstrous Count, threatens to consume and entomb its visitors.
The life that has been drained away from the cold surfaces of the modern
interior thus returns in the tomb-like chill of this "masterless" house as an
undead pulsation. Marianne's position is again diametrically opposed to
Davina's—while for the latter the suburban villa had too little life, for the
former the ancestral manor has far too much:

> Marianne trembled and stood up, eyeing her empty glass. She thought:
> 'Where am I?' put down her glass, and began to finger her way along the
> mantelpiece's swags and medallions. She thought the marble throbbed.
>   (CS 390)

The modern woman's encounter with what remains of the obsolete aristocratic colonial order is fully incomprehensible, an empirical fragment
split off from the symbolic structure that once made sense of it (and that
missing structure is figured by the absent landlord or "unconscious host,"
whom the narrator, along with the characters, mocks by giving the derisive name "Lord Thingummy" [389]). It is therefore 'life itself,' as sensory
pulsation stripped of any identifiable symbolic features, that now surges
up in the absence of the paternal law-bearer: and this uncanny persistence
of nameless or faceless life is what gives the episode at the dysfunctional
manor house its eerie, dream-like atmosphere.

Just as James had in "The Jolly Corner," then, in "The Disinherited"
Bowen makes subtle use of the contrast between the modern world and
a decayed traditional order to amplify the ghostly significance of her narrative. For frustrated ex-aristocrat Davina, the modern suburban environment induces nothing but "a dry weariness" (384); and when the two

women arrive at an all-night road-side café (with its "glittering Neon sign like wolves' eyes:" another echo of *Dracula*) they find a morbid scene of departed life:

> But inside there was no one. A long row of swinging lanterns bobbed in their own horrid light as they pushed open the door. The lounge was empty and bald as the inside of a band-box, glazed with synthetic panelling. The chairs were askew, empty, with flattened cushions; ashtrays sent up a cold fume; the place wore an air of sudden, sheepish vacuity, as though a large party had just got up and gone out.   (CS 384)

Suburban modernity, with its synthetic surfaces and the "fictitious glow" (384) of its technology, has generated a non-world, a state of ontological dispossession; the human subject and its erstwhile community cannot inhabit such a place. But if the life of a community or "large party" has vanished from the scene of modern experience, its return shortly afterwards at the 'party' in the ghostly manor house is no less unhomely:

> Smoke and human stuffiness thickened the air of this room with its dead undertone of chill on which a snapping wood fire had little effect. It was a high, shabby, gilt-and-white octagonal ante-room, the naked shutters of three windows fortified by iron bars. Bottles crowded a top-heavy ornate table under the chandelier; panels of tarnished mirror kept multiplying the company, and on a red marble column a Psyche balanced with one hand over a breast.   (CS 386)

The obsolete grandeur of colonial domination, with its hostile barred windows, now plays host to a meaningless assembly of unrelated people and objects, figured as both a delirious excess of empty signification (the images multiplying in the "tarnished mirror") and a Psyche precariously balanced, like some allegorical pole-dancer, on a kinky phallic column. What is involved here, as Bowen's writing makes clear with a degree of dark comical relish, is a radical unbalancing of the ontological structure that allowed for the very possibility of social and individual coherence: all that remains, after the withdrawal of the defunct paternal regime, is an insane collision of atomized subjectivities and fragmented body-parts ("one hand over a breast").

What is left behind, then, by the absent lord or "unconscious host" is life; but life exposed in a scene of perversion, with libido uncoupled from legitimate social relations, unbalancing the psyche and skewing the rational geometry of reality. "The Disinherited" makes clear Bowen's radical pessimism with regard to what she saw as the consequences of patriarchal decline ("We have everything to fear from the dispossessed," she would write later in *Bowen's Court* [1942]).[24] Above all, the story shows this through its representation of masculinity, which like that of femininity Bowen structures in starkly binary, mock-allegorical terms. If the distinction between the old regime and the modern age was linked, as we saw, to frustrated Davina and bewildered Marianne, Bowen's equivalent opposition between old and new masculinities is much more disturbing.

On the one hand, there are the frauds: Oliver, with his stammer and his boozy tears, along with his embarrassing friends gathered in the empty 'parental' home like "a party of bandit children" (388), represents the decayed aristocrat, a sad remnant of the ruling class (and in this he resembles a long string of fraudulent defunct aristocrats in Bowen's fiction). But at least, we might say, Oliver is still vaguely connected to a social group (and seems to have some past shared with another subject, Davina); whereas the other kind of man produced by the new age in Bowen's text is a radical version of Marianne's 'exclusive' modern social disconnectedness, a man with absolutely no investment in the social bond: the monstrous psychotic Prothero.

What is initially disturbing about this character, as we have already seen, is encapsulated in his blank, unreadable face: "His life at the edge of this household of women remained inscrutable" (381). 'Prothero'—since that is not, we discover, his real name, the mark of his link to a symbolic community—is a characteristically modernist figure, a 'man without qualities' or 'unnamable' subject. Bowen pushes the idea of the man's disconnectedness from social reality to an extreme, giving his character, like his nocturnal candlelight soliloquy, the circular self-adequation of psychotic experience: "I always was what I am, now I am what I always was, what you said that time. Flunkey. I like what I am, a free man" (393). This is the voice of Beckett's *L'innomable*, as written by Bowen in 1934 (when Beckett himself, moving like Bowen between Ireland and London, had not yet begun to write *Murphy*).

As a radically "free" man, a kind of self-enclosed libidinal pulsation, Prothero is clearly a symptom of the modern transformation of social and psychical geography mapped by Bowen in "The Disinherited:" he is a man from nowhere, with no history but a single occult narrative which he ceaselessly rewrites each night before, in "an automatic and mindless movement" (398), burning the text. This self-consuming narrative self is an avatar of modernity itself, its disruption of the sense of what defines a self—an ethical bond to the Other, to a specific community and its history—as briskly destructive of tradition as were the modernist architects who planned Marianne's exclusive new home.

Bowen's critics have tended to regard "The Disinherited" rather as Pussy regards her husband's face in "The Shadowy Third:" by not looking at it too closely. For Glendinning, although the story "encapsulates the confusion of social change," it includes "a piece of flagrant self-indulgence on Elizabeth's part:" the fragment of Prothero's monologue (which for Glendinning is not so much proto-Beckettian as "sub-Lawrentian").[25] Bowen is chided for an uncharacteristic—perhaps an unfeminine—lack of subtlety ("it's vulgar but it's vivid" adds Glendinning, not over-subtly): there is something in this text that exceeds the rational account of Bowen, a kind of writerly misbehaviour.

In my view "The Disinherited" marks a radical, innovatory point in Bowen's writing, where it reaches forward, as it were, to late modernism—beyond the complex human voices of James, Sinclair, Joyce, Woolf and indeed Bowen's own novels, to the 'nameless' utterance, the fundamental traumatic self-disclosure of a human subject split off from the legible structures of tradition and community (an utterance to be famously [re]written a decade later by another Anglo-Irish author: Beckett).[26] But it also reaches back to the earlier moment of the ghost story, where the writing of 'life itself' began to perforate the conventional surface of neo-gothic style, pushing the text to the edges of signification through figures of music or epiphany, voice or gaze. It was her sense of "the horror beneath the surface," as Bowen once put it, that made her short stories actively disrupt the palliative conventions of realism to give voice to the strange enjoyment underlying human utterance, "like someone hugging a thought" (*CS* 383).[27]

Conclusion
The Ghostly Path

The question of the ghost as a problem of representation was posed by writers from the very beginning of the genre. Although there was clearly a metaphysical aspect lurking somewhere in that question, it was most often addressed as primarily a matter of literary technique. How, after all, could a supposedly *super*natural element be made to inhabit a literary form, that of consistent realist (or 'naturalist') narrative, without which the very essence of the ghost—that is, its capacity to intrude on *our* world, to haunt the actual space of everyday reality—would disappear? In 1827, Walter Scott sets out this technical problem with exemplary lucidity:

> . . . the supernatural in fictitious composition requires to be man-
> aged with considerable delicacy, as criticism begins to be more on the
> alert. The interest which it excites is indeed a powerful spring; but it
> is one which is peculiarly subject to be exhausted by coarse handling
> and repeated pressure. It is also of a character which it is extremely
> difficult to sustain, and of which only a very small proportion may
> be said to be better than the whole. The marvellous, more than any
> other attribute of fictitious narrative, loses its effect by being brought
> much into view. The imagination of the reader is to be excited if pos-
> sible, without being gratified.[1]

The aesthetic presented here by Scott will repay some further consider-
ation. The power of the "withheld glimpse," as Henry James will put it in
a 1908 preface to *The Turn of the Screw*, is already apparent to Scott as
an essential and extremely precarious constituent of the "marvellous" in
literature. But the figurative economy through which Scott thinks about
that power, with its arc from the "powerful spring" of excitement to the
exhausted reserves of gratification, bears a striking resemblance to the
metaphorical economy of libido to be developed by Freud almost a century
later. The sexual drive, wrote Freud in 1915, has its "source" in bodily excitation, while its aim "is in every instance satisfaction, which can only be
obtained by removing the state of stimulation at the source of the drive."[2]
If our excited interest in the supernatural is linked to the *Schautrieb* or

"scopophilic" drive, which according to Freud rapidly mutates in young children into the *Wissentrieb* or drive for knowledge, then the literary problem of exploiting that interest certainly needs to be "managed with considerable delicacy"—and it is almost as if Scott's language, with its talk of "handling" and "pressure," already implies this sexual dimension.[3] The drive to see and to know, which is stimulated by the appearance of something radically strange within the diegetic space of a realist narrative, needs, in other words, to be maintained in a state of constant dissatisfaction in the ghost story, never fully "gratified" (as it might be, for instance, by a detective story with its ultimately resolved puzzles).

How can we link this libidinal economy of the ghost, the need to stimulate and yet frustrate the reader's scopophilic desire for the full representation of the apparition, to the trajectory of our argument? If we recall our opening scene—where Deleuze sees the vacillating life-or-death of Rogue Riderhood in *Our Mutual Friend* as a Dickensian rendering of a "spark of life" (*OMF* 503) as pure immanence—we can take that scene as the manifestation of the hypnotic, fascinating bond that links the subject to the singular apparition of life as absolute, appearing at the very threshold of consistent legible reality. The severe excitation, as Freud might have called it, caused by this apparition between life and death, this emergence of something neither properly subject to the logic of the signifier nor simply unreal, makes it an overwhelmingly libidinal event, the unleashing of drive energy in a sensory paroxysm that eclipses the signifying subject as such. It is this libidinal eclipse of the subject as rational agent that we saw vividly staged in the scene of Riderhood's resuscitation, as the various witnesses (including, if the magic of Dickensian style has worked, the reader) are confronted by a specular "indubitable token of life" (*OMF* 504), an entrancingly *singular* apparition, beyond the equivocal, negotiable domain of the signifier.

Moreover, as we saw, a careful reading of Dickens's novel picks up a crucial clue to how to interpret this scene from an earlier episode when Riderhood, on his first appearance, is explicitly identified by a witness as a ghost: in other words, the resuscitation scene, with its strange 'scopophilic' breach of the novel's style, needs to be understood as a moment of pure ghostly apparition. Here we have one side of what could be called a Dickensian antinomy—the ghost as "spark of life" (*OMF* 503) or phantom ontological remainder beyond the signifier. The other side of the antinomy, by contrast, can be clearly seen in earlier texts by Dickens, notably the festive monologue of 1850 entitled "A Christmas Tree," where he writes of how the fictional ghost has become nothing more than a Yuletide cliché: "reducible to a very few general types and classes. . . ghosts have little originality and 'walk' in a beaten track."[4] On the one hand, that is, the Dickensian ghost emerges as a singular epiphany, utterly unknown, indeed beyond the very scope of narrative signification; while on the other, it is seen as a routine product of the beaten track of formulaic generic conventions, so well-known as to be oddly comforting but devoid of any literary interest or originality.

What is crucial, however, to grasp about this Dickensian antinomy, which still resonates through many of the texts explored in our earlier argument, is that it is not a simple symmetrical difference of perspective, but in fact harbours an *ontological* discrepancy. That is, the question of being is posed differently, in entirely different registers, when we move from the 'haunting interval' of the apparition in the fictional text—whether Riderhood's reawakening or the signalman's "steep cutting" (*SM* 174)—to the playfully metafictional discourse of "A Christmas Tree," with its self-consciously authorial narrative persona.

One way of putting this would be to start from the deceptively 'self-evident' distinction between showing and telling. The ghost as pure immanent life-energy, that is, can only be shown, 'rendered' in a language of the eye, as we have put it, or presented as *figure* in Lyotard's sense: thus as something incompatible with narrative discourse, an anamorphic phantom skewed away from the representational scope of a realist diegesis. In this sense the ghost constitutes a phenomenon at odds with narrative as such, an element inconsistent with the domain of story-telling and its "beaten track" of traditional forms or conventional rhetorical tropes. Now, it is clearly from a position situated well within that domain of endlessly recycled literary signification that the Dickensian persona of "A Christmas Tree" speaks in order to ironize fictional ghosts for having "little originality"—for being, in other words, with their over-familiar 'ghostly' characteristics, *not properly ghostly.*

The authentic ghost is therefore implicitly identified by Dickens as a figure never fully at home within a narrative discourse, never more than a guest, an unhomely intruder, within the hospitable domain of story-telling. There are of course many literary consequences of this ghostly ontological difference, this antinomy between the absolute *punctum* of immanent 'life itself' and the fictional discursive mesh of everyday subjective experience. One of the most striking of these has to do with the fictional representation of *time*, always a crucial stylistic question in the ghost story. The moment of the apparition—as figured vividly in "The Signalman," "Oh Whistle And I'll Come to You My Lad," "The Jolly Corner" or "The Storm"—occurs, as we have seen, *out of time*, as a graphic suspension of ordinary diachronic experience. The moment of the ghost is thus presented in these texts as quintessentially non-empirical, a haunting interval excluded by definition from the ordinary temporal, representable ontology of worldly facts. Thus the signalman himself distinguishes with scholarly exactitude between the *factual* event of his bell ringing and the "strange vibration" of its telepathic ghost-voice: he has, as he puts it, "never confused the spectre's ring with the man's" (*SM* 183). Likewise when Professor Parkins foolishly blows on the ghostly whistle "[h]e saw quite clearly for a moment a vision of a wide, dark expanse at night, with a fresh wind blowing, and in the midst a lonely figure" (*CG* 83): the hallucinatory epiphany is given a mobile, anamorphic quality that skews it away from the realist ontological register of discrete, narratable elements. But the clearest versions of this ghostly scene divorced from the temporal fabric of subjective experience come in the epiphanies seen by the traumatized or hypnotically entranced characters of Sinclair, Woolf and Bowen: the sublime visions of Agatha Verall, Septimus Smith or the female protagonist of "The Storm," like that of Garvin in "The Intercessor," lie "outside the order of [the subject's] experience" (*US* 200).

What shows itself in the apparition, then, is something that *does not count*: something inconsistent with the fictional discursive tissue and narrative temporality of meaningful everyday existence. What is most terrifying about the ghost is therefore its sheer *originality*, its radical status as a cleft in the network of signifiers that organize and make knowable empirical reality; and this unspeakable or indiscernible quality means that any fictional representation of ghosts, being necessarily already bound into the habitual structures of literary form, is immediately vulnerable to the Dickensian irony of "A Christmas Tree:" that is, to seeming derivative or clichéd, having "little originality." Because the ontological temporality of the subject is wholly determined by repetition, by the always-already, the non-original, any truly original manifestation can only emerge as an anamorphic breach of signifying geometry, something forbidden, a transgression of the veridical law of reality.

We can begin to see, then, how and why modernist writing recalls and reanimates (whether consciously or not) the enigmatic figure of the literary ghost. For the essential early modernist protagonist—and this is consistently true from Spencer Brydon or Agatha Verrall to Gabriel Conroy and Clarissa Dalloway—there is a definitive restless dissatisfaction with the everyday self, a sense of that self as non-original or alienated, ontologically trivial or superficial. For Spencer or Agatha, though, the meaninglessness of the everyday self is compensated for by "the other, the real, the waiting life" (*THJ* 352) offered either by the haunted house with its mnemic archive or the mystical trance, another scene where a non-alienated, 'original' self can take shape; while for Gabriel and Clarissa, both profoundly ill at ease with their respective identities as husband-host and wife-hostess, there is a confrontation in store with 'living ghosts' or uncanny doubles of themselves in the shape of Freddy Malins and Septimus Smith, respectively.

In its evocation of this other scene of selfhood, as we saw, modernist writing draws on something that often features in the ghost story: namely the figure of music, and especially of song, seen as the index of an ontological plenitude foreclosed from the sphere of merely linguistic signification and subjectivity. Music has indeed a special status in "The Dead" for Freddy Malins, whose response to the "great spirit" of Aunt Julia's song goes beyond the trivial social surface of signification; as it has in *Mrs Dalloway* for Septimus, who hears harmonies in birdsong that herald, he imagines, "the birth of a new religion" (*MD* 26).

The ghost story, then, plays host to a "rich music" (*THJ* 352) that offers modernist writers a mystical imaginary alternative to the alienated discursive matrix of modern identity. In the work of Sinclair, Woolf and Bowen, that music could give voice to what had been silenced and suppressed by official patriarchal culture, whether as a Brontësque "language of a joy too deep for articulate expression" (*TB* 60) or in the entrancing harmonies of the Jamesian supernatural. And for Henry James himself, as we saw in Chapter 4, the ghost story offered a way to escape from the idea of the self as social masquerade, an idea James confronted at a moment of artistic crisis provoked by his unfortunate rivalry with the great celebrant of modern identity as self-conscious simulation, Oscar Wilde. In "The Jolly Corner" this turn from the social surfaces of identity to its original essence is figured as a *return*: going back to a remembered childhood and to a musical inwardness or *Einfühlung* prior to the empty reflectivity of the alienated adult linguistic subject. When the haunting interval takes place in narrative, arresting the flow of signification in endless figures or unfeasible singularities, it reveals for a moment what readable fictional discourse always holds in abeyance: the "unnameable secret of pity and fear" (*US* 209), as May Sinclair puts it, that constitutes our vital bond to literary experience.

"It struck chill to me," comments the Dickensian narrator of *The Signalman* as he reaches the bottom of a dark and precipitate railway cutting, "as if I had left the natural world" (*SM* 175). This narrative departure from reality, and indeed from the stylistic dictates of realism, must have seemed to the readers of *All the Year Round* gathered around the Christmas hearth in 1866 no more than a familiar, and thus an oddly comforting, gothic conceit. As we have seen, however, what the subsequent decades would increasingly make clear was that the ghost story, for all its generic melodrama and occasional gimmickry, in fact played host to an insistent, fundamental ontological question. We have explored this ghostly departure from the natural world by tracing its interlinked literary scenes—from a hotel room with an uncanny extra guest to the mysterious house on the jolly corner, from the telepathic loop of Haworth to the singular rapture of the singing voice to the dizzying "nakedness of the heights."[5] These apparitional scenes all raise a fundamental question of arithmetic: what counts as truth in the ontological relation between selves? If modernist literature strove to pursue that question beyond the hermeneutic consolations of established knowledge, it did so in pursuit of the "rough zigzag descending path" (*SM* 175) of the literary ghost.

Notes

NOTES TO THE PROLOGUE

1. H. James, *Letters Volume III, 1883–1895*, ed. L. Edel, London: Macmillan, 1980, 277.
2. H. James, *Letters Volume IV, 1895–1916* ed. L. Edel, Cambridge, Mass: Bellknap, 1984, 86.
3. Anonymous review in *Knight's Quarterly*, Aug.–Nov. 1824, quoted in M. Shelley, *Frankenstein: A Critical Edition*, ed. J. P. Hunter, New York: Norton, 1996, 197.
4. E. Nesbit, "Man-Size in Marble" (1893) in *The Oxford Book of English Ghost Stories*, eds. M. Cox and R. A. Gilbert, Oxford: Oxford University Press, 1986, 125.
5. H. James, *The Turn of the Screw* (1898), ed. P. Beidler, New York: Bedford/St. Martin's, 1995, 38–39.
6. H. James, Preface to 1908 Edition, in *Ibid*, 118.
7. C. Dickens, *Our Mutual Friend* (1865), ed. S. Gill, London: Penguin, 1971, 504 (Hereafter *OMF*).
8. J. Joyce, *Ulysses* (1922), ed. W. Gabler, London: Bodley Head, 1986, 9.147–149 (Hereafter *U*).
9. H. James, "The Jolly Corner" (1908) in *The Tales of Henry James*, ed. C. Wegelin & H. Wonham, New York: Norton, 2003, 356 (Hereafter *THJ*).
10. A. Badiou, *Being and Event*, trans. O. Feltham, London: Continuum, 2005, 183 (Hereafter *BE*).
11. For a cogent discussion of the problem of time in psychoanalytic interpretation, see Jean Laplanche, "Notes on Afterwardsness" in *Jean Laplanche: Seduction, Translation, Drives*, eds. J. Fletcher and M. Stanton, London: Institute of Contemporary Arts, 1992, 217–223.
12. J. Joyce, *Ulysses* 9.841–2. For a painstakingly lucid account of Badiou's mathematical ontology, see A. Gibson, *Beckett & Badiou: the Pathos of Intermittency*, Oxford: Oxford University Press, 2006, esp. 41–75.
13. J. Laplanche, "Psychoanalysis as Anti-hermeneutics," trans. L. Thurston, *Radical Philosophy*, No.79, Sept.–Oct. 1996, 7–12.
14. *Ibid*, 12.

NOTE TO CHAPTER 1

Epigraph: C. Maturin, *Melmoth the Wanderer* (1820), ed. Douglas Grant, Oxford University Press, 1986, 118 (Hereafter *MW*).

1. S. Critchley, *The Book of Dead Philosophers*, London: Granta, 2008, 270.
2. G. Deleuze, *Essays Critical and Clinical*, trans. D. W. Smith and A. A. Greco, Minneapolis: University of Minnesota Press, 1997, 66.
3. G. Agamben, "Absolute Immanence" in *Potentialities: Collected Essays in Philosophy*, ed. and trans. D. Heller-Roazen, Stanford: Stanford University Press, 1999, 228 (Hereafter *P*).
4. G. Deleuze, "Immanence: Une vie. . .," *Philosophie*, 47 (1995), 5.
5. Agamben, "Absolute Immanence," *P*, 229.
6. W. Benjamin, "The Storyteller" in *Illuminations*, trans. H. Zohn, New York: Harcourt, Brace & World, 1968, 93.
7. *Ibid*, 94.
8. G. Deleuze, "Immanence: Une vie. . .," *op. cit.*, 5.
9. G. K. Chesterton, *Charles Dickens* (1906), London: Methuen, 1911, 264.
10. Cf. E. K. Sedgwick, *Between Men: English Literature and Male Homosocial Desire*, New York: Columbia Press, 1985; and esp. on *Our Mutual Friend*, 163–179.
11. See Stephen Gill's note referring to Henry Mayhew's *London Labour and the London Poor* (1851) as a source: *OMF*, 895–896.
12. Agamben, "The Idea of Language," *P*, 43.
13. J.-L. Nancy, "Vox Clamans in Deserto," *The Birth to Presence*, trans. B. Holmes et al., Stanford: Stanford University Press, 1993, 247.
14. But note also the subtlety of Dickensian naming, as the names Eugene Wrayburn and Mortimer Lightwood also encode an intertextual web of Luciferan signifiers: well-born, light-bearer, death-dealer, etc.
15. W. Shakespeare, *Macbeth*, 3.4. 106–108, Cambridge: Cambridge University Press, 1997, 182.
16. J.-L. Nancy, "Noli Me Frangere," *The Birth to Presence, op. cit.*, 269.
17. F. Schlegel, quoted in R. Immerwahr, "The Subjectivity or Objectivity of Friedrich Schlegel's Poetic Irony," *The Germanic Review* 26 (1951), 177.
18. See Agamben's discussion of Plato's Seventh Letter in "The Thing Itself," *P*, 27–38.
19. J. Lacan, *The Seminar, Book II: The Ego in Freud's Theory and in the Technique of Psychoanalysis, 1954–1955*, ed. J-A. Miller, trans. S. Tomaselli, Cambridge: Cambridge University Press, 1988, 231–232.
20. R. Barthes, "Textual Analysis of Poe's 'Valdemar'," trans. G. Bennington, in *Untying the Text*, ed. R. Young, London: Routledge, 1981, 154.
21. E. A. Poe, "The Facts in the Case of M. Valdemar" (1845), *Complete Stories and Poems*, London: Chancellor Press, 1988, 206–207.
22. E. A. Poe, *Complete Stories and Poems, op. cit.*, 207–208.
23. See *MW*, Explanatory Notes, 549. Maturin's text has μεΐργουσι for με εΐργουσι, thus, as it were, writing a non-existent Greek verb and 'deleting' the personal pronoun με. Since the 'subjectivity' or psyche of Patroklos is what is in question in the Homeric text—is he alive or dead, a reality or a memory?—the error seems peculiarly apt.
24. Homer, *The Iliad*, trans. R. Fitzgerald, Oxford: Oxford University Press, 1984, 398.
25. S. Žižek, *The Ticklish Subject: The Absent Centre of Political Ontology*, London: Verso, 1999, 155.
26. H. James, "The Beast in the Jungle," *THJ*, 339.
27. J. L. Matus, "Trauma, Memory and Railway Disaster: The Dickensian Connection," *Victorian Studies*, Vol. 43, No. 3, Spring 2001, 413.
28. *The Letters of Charles Dickens*, ed. G. Story, Vol. XI, Oxford: Clarendon Press, 1999, 55.
29. *Ibid*, 50.
30. *Ibid*, 56–57.

NOTES TO CHAPTER 2

Epigraph: G. K. Chesterton, *Charles Dickens, op. cit.*, 169.
1. R. Luckhurst, *The Invention of Telepathy 1870–1901*, Oxford: Oxford University Press, 2002, 78.
2. C. Dickens, *No. 1 Branch Line: The Signalman*, first published in the "Mugby Junction" Christmas Edition of *All the Year Round* (1866); reprinted in *The Ghost Stories of Charles Dickens*, ed. P. Haining, London: Coronet, 1982, 174 (Hereafter *SM*).
3. J. Derrida, "Ulysses Gramophone: Hear Say Yes in Joyce," *Acts of Literature*, ed. D. Attridge, New York: Routledge, 1992, 271.
4. For an account of the special relation between the Dickensian short story and Christmas in terms of how Dickens set about "establishing rapport with the public," see Harold Orel, *The Victorian Short Story*, Cambridge: Cambridge University Press, 1986, 61–64.
5. G. Bennington, *Lyotard: Writing the Event*, Manchester University Press, 1988, 63.
6. *Ibid*, 57.
7. J.-F. Lyotard, *Discours, figure*, Paris: Klincksieck, 1971, 61 (my translation).
8. M. Merleau-Ponty, "Eye and Mind," trans. C. Dallery, *The Primacy of Perception*, Northwestern University Press, 1964, 163.
9. A. Gibson, *Beckett & Badiou, op. cit.*, 54.
10. B. Readings, *Introducing Lyotard: Art and Politics*, London: Routledge, 1991, 84.
11. J. A. Hammerton, Preface to Dickens's *Complete Works*, 1910; quoted in P. Haining, *Ghost Stories of Charles Dickens, op. cit.*, 8.
12. Chesterton, *Charles Dickens, op. cit.*, 170.
13. *Ibid*, quoted in Haining, 7.
14. C. Waters, "Gender, family and domestic ideology" in *The Cambridge Companion to Charles Dickens*, ed. J. O. Jordan, Cambridge: Cambridge University Press, 2001, 121.
15. Quoted in *Ibid*.
16. C. Dickens, "A Christmas Tree," *Household Words* 1850; reprinted in *Christmas Stories*, London: Hazell, Watson & Viney, 1905, 15 (Hereafter *DCS*).
17. "The Haunted House," *All the Year Round*, 1859; reprinted in *DCS*, 168.
18. *DCS*, 179.
19. Chesterton, *Charles Dickens, op. cit.*, 85.
20. G. Orwell, 'Charles Dickens,' *Inside the Whale* (1940); reprinted in *The Collected Essays, Journalism and Letters of George Orwell, Volume 1: An Age Like This, 1920–1940*, eds. S. Orwell & I. Angus, London: Penguin, 1968, 496.
21. Orel sees *The Signalman* as an essential factor in Dickens's decision to discontinue the production of a 'unified' Christmas issue of the periodical *All the Year Round*: there was too radical a discrepancy between the hospitable world of the loquacious "Mugby Boy" and the inhospitable ontological cutting of the Signalman. See H. Orel, *The Victorian Short Story, op. cit.*, 77–78.

NOTES TO CHAPTER 3

1. M. R. James, *Collected Ghost Stories*, ed. D. Jones, Oxford: Oxford University Press, 2011, 407 (Hereafter *CG*).
2. There is some doubt as to exactly when (and indeed for whom) James started writing the stories: see M. Cox, *M. R. James: An Informal Portrait*, Oxford: Oxford University Press, 1983, 135.

3. C. Dickens, *Great Expectations* (1861), ed. J. Carlisle, New York: Bedford/ St. Martin's, 1996, 24.
4. *Ibid.*
5. P. Brooks, "Repetition, Repression and Return: The Plotting of *Great Expectations,*" *Reading for the Plot*, Cambridge: Harvard University Press, 1992, 117–118.
6. S. Freud, *Die Traumdeutung, GW* 2/3, 284; *The Interpretation of Dreams, SE* 4–5, 277–278.
7. S. Freud, *The Interpretation of Dreams, SE* 4–5, 317–318.
8. T. Hardy, *Tess of the d'Urbervilles* (1891), ed. J. P. Riquelme, New York: Bedford/St. Martin's, 362.
9. Thomas Hardy, "Places", *The Complete Poems*, ed. James Gibson, New York: Palgrave, 2001, 353.

NOTES TO CHAPTER TO CHAPTER 4

Epigraph: W. Pater, *The Renaissance: Studies in Art and Poetry* (1873), New York: Dover, 2005, 90.
1. J. Lacan, "The Mirror Stage as Formative of the *I* Function," *Écrits*, trans. B. Fink, New York: Norton, 2006, 79.
2. In his double review of the plays for *The Saturday Review* on 12 January 1895, George Bernard Shaw sets out to defend James against the "handful of rowdies who brawled at him," but he does criticise the play's structure, noting that the second act "made fuss instead of drama;" while he goes on to praise *An Ideal Husband* as an "unapproachably playful" drama. G. B. Shaw, 'Two New Plays,' *The Saturday Review*, 12 January 1895; reprinted in *Our Theatres in the Nineties*, London: Constable, 1932, 6–12.
3. L. Edel, *Henry James: A Life*, New York: Harper and Row, 1977, 419.
4. J. Tambling, *Henry James: Critical Issues*, London: Macmillan, 2000, 208.
5. For a discussion of the Hitchcockian trope of the MacGuffin, see Thomas Elaesser, "The Dandy in Hitchcock" in *Alfred Hitchcock: Centenary Essays*, ed. R. Allen and S. I. Gonzales, London: BFI, 1999.
6. S. Žižek, *Looking Awry: An Introduction to Jacques Lacan through Popular Culture*, Cambridge, Mass: MIT Press, 1991, 41.
7. S. Žižek, 'In His Bold Gaze My Ruin Is Writ Large,' in *Everything You Always Wanted to Know About Lacan But Were Afraid to Ask Hitchcock*, ed. S. Žižek, London: Verso, 1992, 231–232.
8. *The Letters of Charles Dickens*, ed. G. Story, Vol. XI, Oxford: Clarendon Press, 1999, 50.
9. See Esther Rashkin's ingenious effort to read, among other things, Brydon's "monocle" as a sign of avuncular misbehaviour; *Family Secrets and the Psychoanalysis of Narrative*, Princeton University Press, 1992, 93–122.
10. J. Tambling, *Henry James: Critical Issues, op. cit.*, 208.
11. For an analysis of these liminal sounds in modern cinema, see Michel Chion, "Revolution douce" in *La toile trouée*, Paris: Editions de l'Etoile, 1988.
12. S. Žižek, *Looking Awry: An Introduction to Jacques Lacan through Popular Culture, op. cit.*
13. W. Pater, *The Renaissance, op. cit.*, 90.

NOTES TO CHAPTER 5

Epigraph: E. Levinas, "There is: existence without existents," *The Levinas Reader*, ed. S. Hand, Oxford: Blackwell, 1989, 33 (translation modified).

1. S. Connor, 'The Machine in the Ghost: Spiritualism, Technology and the 'Direct Voice" in *Ghosts: Deconstruction, Psychoanalysis, History*, eds. P. Buse and A. Stott, London: Macmillan, 1999, 211.

2. W. T. Stead, 'Telepathy: A Passing Note Reporting Progress in Telepathic Automatism' (1894) in *The Fin de Siècle: A Reader in Cultural History, c. 1880–1900*, eds. S. Ledger and R. Luckhurst, Oxford: Oxford University Press, 2000, 286.

3. *Ibid*, 285.

4. *William James on Psychical Research*, eds. G. Murphy and R. Ballon, London: Chatto & Windus, 1961, 27; quoted in David Seed, '"Psychical' Cases: Transformations of the Supernatural in Virginia Woolf and May Sinclair'" in *Gothic Modernisms*, eds. A. Smith and J. Wallace, New York: Palgrave, 2001, 55.

5. See R. Luckhurst, *The Invention of Telepathy*, Oxford: Oxford University Press, 2002, 56–57; Steven Connor 'The Machine in the Ghost,' *op. cit.*, 203.

6. M. Sinclair, *Uncanny Stories*, ed. P. March-Russell, London: Wordsworth Editions, 2006, 74 (Hereafter *US*). Quotations from this work are reproduced with permission of Curtis Brown Group Ltd, London, on behalf of the Estate of May Sinclair (Copyright © May Sinclair, 1923).

7. S. Freud, 'The Dynamics of Transference' (1912), *SE* XII, 105–106.

8. S. Connor, 'The Machine in the Ghost,' *op. cit.*, 212.

9. M. Henry, *The Genealogy of Psychoanalysis*, trans. D. Brick, Stanford University Press, 1993, 22.

10. Cf. M. Chion, "Revolution douce" in *La toile trouée, op. cit.*

11. See Mikkel Borch-Jakobsen's trenchant analysis of this term in *The Freudian Subject*, trans. C. Porter, Stanford: Stanford University Press, 1988, 164–182.

12. R. L. Stevenson, *The Strange Case of Dr Jekyll and Mr Hyde* (1886), ed. R. Mighall, London: Penguin, 2002, 2 (Hereafter *JH*).

13. May Sinclair, letter of 26 February 1911, quoted in Suzanne Raitt, *May Sinclair: A Modern Victorian*, Oxford: Oxford University Press, 2000, 132 fn82 (Hereafter *MS*).

14. M. Sinclair, *The Three Brontës*, London: Hutchinson, 1912, 81 (Hereafter *TB*).

15. *MS*, 115.

16. G. Bataille, *Literature and Evil* (1957), trans. A. Hamilton, New York: Marion Boyars, 1973, 15.

17. C. Brontë, *Jane Eyre* (1847), London: Collins, 1954, 175.

18. E. Brontë, *Wuthering Heights* (1847), London: Collins, 1953, 34.

19. G. Bataille, *Literature and Evil, op. cit.*, 30.

20. J. Lacan, *The Seminar, Book II: The Ego in Freud's Theory and in the Technique of Psychoanalysis, 1954–1955, op. cit.*, 232.

21. For the classic account, see Harold Bloom, *The Anxiety of Influence*, New York: Oxford University Press, 1973.

22. See Paul H. Fry, *A Defense of Poetry: Reflections on the Occasion of Writing*, Stanford: Stanford University Press, 1995, 50–69.

23. See *MS* 137, and J. Laplanche and J-B Pontalis, *The Language of Psychoanalysis*, trans. D. Nicholson-Smith, London: Karnac, 1973, 335–336, 455–462.

24. E. Levinas, "There is: existence without existents," *op. cit.*, 32.

25. Cf. J. Lacan, *Le Séminaire, Livre XVII, L'envers de la psychanalyse* (1969–1970), texte établi par J.-A. Miller, Paris; Seuil, 1991, 18.

26. J. Derrida, "*Fors*: The Anglish Words of Nicolas Abraham and Maria Torok," in N. Abraham and M. Torok, *The Wolf Man's Magic Word*, trans. N. Rand, Minneapolis: University of Minnesota Press, 1986, xliii–xliv.
27. J. Lacan, *The Seminar, Book VII: The Ethics of Psychoanalysis, 1959–1960*, trans D. Porter, London: Routledge, 1992, 69.
28. See S. Ferenczi, "Confusion of tongues between adults and the child" (1932) in *Final Contributions to the Problems and Methods of Psychoanalysis*, London: Hogarth Press, 1955, 156–167.
29. *BE*, 524–525.

NOTES TO CHAPTER 6

1. *U* 9.147.
2. E. Pound, 'Canto LIII,' *Selected Cantos of Ezra Pound*, London: Faber, 1967, 75.
3. Cf. A. J. Kunka and M. K. Troy, *May Sinclair: Moving Towards the Modern*, Aldershot: Ashgate, 2006.
4. M. Sinclair, *The Judgment of Eve and Other Stories*, London: Hutchison, 1914, xii; quoted in *MS*, 244.
5. V. Woolf, 'Jane Eyre and Wuthering Heights,' *Collected Essays*, Vol. 1, ed. L. Woolf, London: Chatto & Windus, 1966, 188–189 (Hereafter *CE*).
6. *The Question of Things Happening, The Letters of Virginia Woolf, 1912–1922*, ed. N. Nicolson, London: Hogarth Press, 1976, 181.
7. G. Agamben, "The Idea of Language," *P*, 43.
8. D. Seed, "'Psychical' Cases: Transformations of the Supernatural in Virginia Woolf and May Sinclair" in *Gothic Modernisms*, eds. A. Smith and J. Wallace, New York: Palgrave, 2001, 51.
9. V. Woolf, *The Voyage Out* (1915), London: Penguin, 1992, 195–196.
10. Quoted in Suzanne Raitt, 'Virginia Woolf's early novels,' *The Cambridge Companion to Virginia Woolf*, ed. S. Roe and S. Sellers, Cambridge University Press, 2000, 32.
11. V. Woolf, *Mrs Dalloway* (1925), London: Hogarth Press, 1963, 90 (Hereafter *MD*).
12. For the date of the action in *Mrs Dalloway*, see Susan Dick, "Literary realism in *Mrs Dalloway, To the Lighthouse, Orlando* and *The Waves*" in *The Cambridge Companion to Virginia Woolf, op. cit.*, 52.
13. G. Beer, "The Body of the People in Virginia Woolf," *Women Reading Women's Writing*, ed. S. Roe, Brighton: Harvester Press, 1987, 91.
14. J. F. Lyotard, *Discours, figure, op. cit.*, 61; E. Levinas, "There is: existence without existents," *op. cit.*, 32.
15. L. Thurston, "Mr Joyce and Dr Hydes: Irish Selves and Doubles in 'The Dead'," *Textual Practice* 22.3, Sept. 2008, 453–468.
16. See L. Thurston, 'Mr Joyce and Dr Hydes,' *op. cit.*, 460–461.
17. M. Bell, "The metaphysics of Modernism" in *The Cambridge Companion to Modernism*, ed. Michael Levenson, Cambridge: Cambridge University Press, 1999, 10.
18. For a discussion of the Joycean quadrivial, see my *James Joyce and the Problem of Psychoanalysis*, Cambridge: Cambridge University Press, 2004, 146–147.

NOTES TO CHAPTER 7

1. N. Corcoran, *Elizabeth Bowen: The Enforced Return*, Oxford: Oxford University Press, 2004, 4.

2. J. F. Wurtz, "Elizabeth Bowen, Modernism, and the Spectre of Anglo-Ireland," *Estudios Irlandeses*, No. 5, 2010, 119.
3. M. R. James, "Some Remarks on Ghost Stories," *The Bookman*, December 1929; reprinted in *CG*, 416.
4. V. Glendinning, *Elizabeth Bowen: Portrait of a Writer*, London: Weidenfeld and Nicolson, 1977, 29.
5. *Ibid*, 196.
6. *Ibid*, 11.
7. N. Corcoran, *Elizabeth Bowen: the Enforced Return*, op. cit., 29–30.
8. S. Osborn, 'Introduction: Elizabeth Bowen: New Directions for Critical Thinking,' *Modern Fiction Studies* 53.2, Summer 2007, 225.
9. J. Lane and B. Clifford, eds. *A North Cork Anthology*, Millstreet: Aubane Historical Society, 1993, 9; quoted in Osborn, 225.
10. E. Bowen, Preface, *Stories by Elizabeth Bowen*, New York: Alfred A. Knopf, 1959; quoted in A. E. Austin, *Elizabeth Bowen*, New York: Twayne, 1971, 94.
11. E. Bowen, *People, Places, Things*, ed. Allan Hepburn, Edinburgh: Edinburgh University Press, 2008, 313; 319.
12. *Ibid*, 258.
13. *The Collected Letters of Joseph Conrad*, Vol. I, eds. F. R. Karl and L. Davies, Cambridge: Cambridge University Press, 1983, Letter of 3 February 1893; 123–124 ("It takes a small-scale narrative (short story) to show the master's hand"). Conrad's French is not wholly correct, with some missing accents. For a discussion of Conrad, Poradowska and the short story, see Gail Fraser's article "The short fiction" in *The Cambridge Companion to Joseph Conrad*, ed. J. H. Stape, Cambridge: Cambridge University Press, 1996, 25–44.
14. *The Collected Stories of Elizabeth Bowen*, London: Jonathan Cape, 1980, 254 (Hereafter *CS*). Quotations from this work are reproduced with permission of Curtis Brown Group Ltd, London, on behalf of the Estate of Elizabeth Bowen (Copyright © Elizabeth Bowen, 1980).
15. For Maud Ellmann, however, the "pale little man" is a serial killer who has murdered his first wife and is duly planning to do away with the current one. Here we see an astute critic responding to the uncanny dimension of Bowen's text, but perhaps also seeking a solution to the problem of knowledge posed by the *Nebenmensch*: to see him as a Hitchcockian villain is to place him within a legible, epistemologically consistent genre. See M. Ellmann, *Elizabeth Bowen: The Shadow Across the Page*, Edinburgh: Edinburgh University Press, 2003, 84.
16. S. Freud, *Civilization and its Discontents* (1930), *SE XXI*.
17. E. Levinas, "From existence to ethics" in *The Levinas Reader*, ed. Sean Hand, Oxford: Blackwell, 1989, 82–83.
18. See 'Disavowal' in Jean Laplanche and Jean-Bertrand Pontalis, *The Language of Psychoanalysis*, op. cit, 1988, 118–120.
19. See T. Adorno and M. Horkheimer, *Dialectic of Enlightenment*, trans. J. Cumming, New York: Verso, 1979, 5–27.
20. E. Bowen, *The Heat of the Day*, London: Jonathan Cape, 1949, 140.
21. The title of Freud's 1930 work could be translated as 'Misery in Society,' not, as in Strachey's much tamer version, *Civilization and its Discontents*.
22. H. James, "The Jolly Corner," *THJ*, 342; 346.
23. B. Stoker, *Dracula* (1897), New York: Bedford/St. Martin's, 2002, 39.
24. E. Bowen, *Bowen's Court and Seven Winters: Memories of a Dublin Childhood*, London: Virago, 1984, 338.
25. Glendinning, *Elizabeth Bowen: Portrait of a Writer*, op. cit., 93–94.

26. Had Beckett read Bowen's work before he wrote the *Trilogy*? There is no mention at all of Bowen in Knowlson's biography of Beckett.
27. Elizabeth Bowen interviewed by Jocelyn Brooke, BBC, 1950; quoted in R. F. Foster, "The Irishness of Elizabeth Bowen" in *Paddy and Mr Punch: Connections in Irish and English History*, London: Penguin, 1993, 103.

NOTES TO THE CONCLUSION

1. W. Scott, "On the Supernatural in Fictitious Composition; and particularly on the Works of Ernest Theodore William Hoffmann," *Foreign Quarterly Review* I, 1827.
2. S. Freud, "Instincts and Their Vicissitudes" (1915), *SE* XIV, 115 (translation modified). The well-known confusion in Strachey's translation of *Trieb* and *Instinkt*, crucially distinct terms in Freud, is clear in this title; I avoid it in the quotation by altering 'instinct' to 'drive.'
3. S. Freud, *Three Essays on the Theory of Sexuality* (1905), *SE* VII, 190.
4. C. Dickens, "A Christmas Tree" (1850), *CSD*, 15.
5. S. Žižek, *Looking Awry: An Introduction to Jacques Lacan through Popular Culture*, op. cit.

Bibliography

Abraham, Nicolas and Torok, Maria. *The Wolf Man's Magic Word*, trans. N. Rand, Minneapolis: University of Minnesota Press, 1986.

Adorno, Theodor and Horkheimer, Max. *Dialectic of Enlightenment*, trans. J. Cumming, London: Allen Lane, 1973.

Agamben, Giorgio. *Potentialities: Collected Essays in Philosophy*, ed. and trans. D. Heller-Roazen, Stanford: Stanford University Press, 1999.

Austin, A. E. *Elizabeth Bowen*, New York: Twayne, 1971.

Badiou, Alain. *Being and Event*, trans. O. Feltham, London: Continuum, 2005.

Barthes, Roland. "Textual Analysis of Poe's 'Valdemar'," trans. G. Bennington, in *Untying the Text*, ed. R. Young, London: Routledge, 1981.

Bataille, Georges. *Literature and Evil* (1957), trans. A. Hamilton, New York: Marion Boyars, 1973.

Beer, Gillian. "The Body of the People in Virginia Woolf," in *Women Reading Women's Writing*, ed. S. Roe, Brighton: Harvester Press, 1987.

Bell, Michael. "The Metaphysics of Modernism" in *The Cambridge Companion to Modernism*, ed. M. Levenson, Cambridge: Cambridge University Press, 1999.

Benjamin, Walter. *Illuminations*, trans. H. Zohn, New York: Harcourt, Brace & World, 1968.

Bennington, Geoffrey. *Lyotard: Writing the Event*, Manchester: Manchester University Press, 1988.

Bloom, Harold. *The Anxiety of Influence*, New York: Oxford University Press, 1973.

Borch-Jakobsen, Mikkel. *The Freudian Subject*, trans. C. Porter, Stanford: Stanford University Press, 1988.

Bowen, Elizabeth. *Collected Stories of Elizabeth Bowen*, London: Jonathan Cape, 1980.

———. *The Heat of the Day*, London: Jonathan Cape, 1949.

———. *Bowen's Court and Seven Winters: Memories of a Dublin Childhood*, London: Virago, 1984.

———. *People, Places, Things*, ed. A. Hepburn, Edinburgh: Edinburgh University Press, 2008.

Brontë, Emily. *Wuthering Heights* (1847), London: Collins, 1953.

Brontë, Charlotte. *Jane Eyre* (1847), London: Collins, 1954.

Brooks, Peter. *Reading for the Plot: Design and Intention in Narrative*, Cambridge, Mass.: Harvard University Press, 1992.

Chesterton, G. K. *Charles Dickens* , London: Methuen, 1906 .

Chion, Michel. *La toile trouée*, Paris: Editions de l'Etoile, 1988.

Connor, Steven. "The Machine in the Ghost: Spiritualism, Technology and the 'Direct Voice'" in *Ghosts: Deconstruction, Psychoanalysis, History*, eds. P. Buse and A. Stott, London: Macmillan, 1999.

Conrad, Joseph. *Collected Letters*, Vol. 1, eds. F. R. Karl and L. Davies, Cambridge: Cambridge University Press, 1983.

Corcoran, Neil. *Elizabeth Bowen: The Enforced Return*, Oxford: Oxford University Press, 2004.

Critchley, Simon. *The Book of Dead Philosophers*, London: Granta, 2008.

Deleuze, Gilles. *Essays Critical and Clinical*, trans. D. W. Smith and A. A. Greco, Minneapolis: University of Minnesota Press, 1997.

———. "Immanence: Une vie . . . ," *Philosophie* 47 (1995).

Derrida, Jacques. "*Fors*: The Anglish Words of Nicolas Abraham and Maria Torok," in N. Abraham and M. Torok, *The Wolf Man's Magic Word*, trans. N. Rand, Minneapolis: University of Minnesota Press, 1986.

———. *Acts of Literature*, ed. D. Attridge, New York: Routledge, 1992.

Dick, Susan. "Literary realism in *Mrs Dalloway, To the Lighthouse, Orlando* and *The Waves*" in *The Cambridge Companion to Virginia Woolf*, ed. S. Roe and S. Sellers, Cambridge: Cambridge University Press, 2000.

Dickens, Charles. *Great Expectations* (1861), ed. J. Carlisle, Boston: Bedford/St. Martin's, 1996.

———. *Our Mutual Friend* (1865), ed. S. Gill, London: Penguin, 1971.

———. "A Christmas Tree" (1850) in *Christmas Stories*, London: Hazell, Watson & Viney, 1905.

———. "The Haunted House" (1859) in *Christmas Stories*, London: Hazell, Watson & Viney, 1905.

———. *No. 1 Branch Line: The Signalman* (1866) in *The Ghost Stories of Charles Dickens*, ed. P. Haining, London: Coronet, 1982.

———. *The Letters of Charles Dickens*, ed. G. Story, Vol. XI, Oxford: Clarendon Press, 1999.

Edel, Leon. *Henry James: A Life*, New York: Harper and Row, 1977.

Elaesser, Thomas. "The Dandy in Hitchcock" in *Alfred Hitchcock: Centenary Essays*, ed. R. Allen and S. I. Gonzales, London: BFI, 1999.

Ellmann, Maud. *Elizabeth Bowen: The Shadow Across the Page*, Edinburgh: Edinburgh University Press, 2003.

Ferenczi, Sandor. "Confusion of tongues between adults and the child" (1932) in *Final Contributions to the Problems and Methods of Psychoanalysis*, London: Hogarth Press, 1955.

Foster, R. F. *Paddy and Mr Punch: Connections in Irish and English History*, London: Penguin, 1993.

Fraser, Gail. "The short fiction" in *The Cambridge Companion to Joseph Conrad*, ed. J. H. Stape, Cambridge: Cambridge University Press, 1996.

Freud, Sigmund. *The Standard Edition of the Complete Psychological Works*, trans. J. Strachey, London: Hogarth Press, 1953–1974 [abbreviated as *SE*].

———. *Die Traumdeutung, Gesammelte Werke*, Vol. 2/3, London: Imago, 1942.

———. *The Interpretation of Dreams* (1900), *SE* IV–V.

———. *Three Essays on the Theory of Sexuality* (1905), *SE* VII.

———. "The Dynamics of Transference" (1912), *SE* XII.

———. "Instincts and Their Vicissitudes" (1915), *SE* XIV.

———. *Civilization and its Discontents* (1930), *SE* XXI.

Fry, Paul H. *A Defense of Poetry: Reflections on the Occasion of Writing*, Stanford: Stanford University Press, 1995.

Gibson, Andrew. *Beckett & Badiou: the Pathos of Intermittency*, Oxford: Oxford University Press, 2006.

Glendinning, Victoria. *Elizabeth Bowen: Portrait of a Writer*, London: Weidenfeld & Nicolson, 1977.

Henry, Michel. *The Genealogy of Psychoanalysis*, trans. D. Brick, Stanford: Stanford University Press, 1993.

Homer. *The Iliad*, trans. R. Fitzgerald, Oxford: Oxford University Press, 1984.

Immerwahr, R. "The Subjectivity or Objectivity of Friedrich Schlegel's Poetic Irony," *The Germanic Review* 26 (1951).

James, Henry. *The Turn of the Screw* (1898), ed. P. Beidler, New York: Bedford/ St. Martin's, 1995.

———. "The Beast in the Jungle" (1903) in *Tales of Henry James*, ed. C. Wegelin and H. Wonham, New York: Norton, 2003.

———. "The Jolly Corner" (1908) in *Tales of Henry James*, ed. C. Wegelin and H. Wonham, New York: Norton, 2003.

———. *Letters* Volume III, 1883–1895, ed. L. Edel, London: Macmillan, 1980.

———. *Letters* Volume IV, 1895–1916, ed. L. Edel, Cambridge, Mass.: Bellknap, 1984.

James, M. R. *Collected Ghost Stories*, ed. D. Jones, Oxford: Oxford University Press, 2011.

James, William. *William James on Psychical Research*, eds. G. Murphy and R. Ballon, London: Chatto & Windus, 1961.

Joyce, James. *Dubliners* (1914), ed. J. Johnson, Oxford: Oxford University Press, 2000.

———. *Ulysses* (1922), ed. W. Gabler, London: Bodley Head, 1986.

Kunka, A. J. and Troy, M. K., eds. *May Sinclair: Moving Towards the Modern*, Aldershot: Ashgate, 2006.

Lacan, Jacques. *The Seminar Book II The Ego in Freud's Theory and in the Technique of Psychoanalysis, 1954–1955*, ed. J.-A. Miller, trans. S. Tomaselli, Cambridge: Cambridge University Press, 1988.

———. *The Seminar Book VII: The Ethics of Psychoanalysis, 1959–1960*, ed. J.-A. Miller, trans. D. Porter, London: Routledge, 1992.

———. *Le Séminaire, Livre XVII, L'envers de la psychanalyse* (1969–1970), texte établi par J.-A. Miller, Paris: Seuil, 1991.

———. *Écrits*, trans. B. Fink, New York: Norton, 2006.

Lane, J. and Clifford, B. *A North Cork Anthology*, Millstreet: Aubane Historical Society, 1993.

Laplanche, Jean. "Notes on Afterwardsness" in *Jean Laplanche: Seduction, Translation, Drives*, ed. J. Fletcher and M. Stanton, London: Institute of Contemporary Arts, 1992.

———. "Psychoanalysis as Anti-Hermeneutic," trans. L. Thurston, *Radical Philosophy*, No. 79, Sept.–Oct. 1996, 7–12.

Laplanche, Jean and Pontalis, Jean-Bertrand. *The Language of Psychoanalysis*, trans. D. Nicholson-Smith, London: Karnac, 1973.

Ledger, Sally and Luckhurst, Roger. *The Fin de Siècle: A Reader in Cultural History, c. 1880–1900*, Oxford: Oxford University Press, 2000.

Levinas, Emmanuel. "There is: existence without existents" in *The Levinas Reader*, ed. S. Hand, Oxford: Blackwell, 1989.

Luckhurst, Roger. *The Invention of Telepathy, 1870–1901*, Oxford: Oxford University Press, 2002.

Lyotard, Jean-François. *Discours, figure*, Paris: Klincksieck, 1971.

Maturin, Charles. *Melmoth the Wanderer* (1820), ed. D. Grant, Oxford: Oxford University Press, 1986.

Matus, J. L. "Trauma, Memory and Railway Disaster: The Dickensian Connection," *Victorian Studies*, Vol. 43, No. 3, Spring 2001.

Merleau-Ponty, Maurice. *The Primacy of Perception*, trans. C. Dallery, Evanston: Northwestern University Press, 1964.

Nancy, Jean-Luc. *The Birth to Presence*, trans. B. Holmes et al., Stanford: Stanford University Press, 1993.

Nesbit, Edith. "Man-Size in Marble" (1893) in *The Oxford Book of English Ghost Stories*, eds. M. Cox and R. A. Gilbert, Oxford: Oxford University Press, 1986.

Orel, Harold. *The Victorian Short Story*, Cambridge: Cambridge University Press, 1986.

Orwell, George. "Charles Dickens" in *The Collected Essays, Journalism and Letters of George Orwell, Volume 1: An Age Like This, 1920–1940*, eds. S. Orwell and I. Angus, London: Penguin, 1968.

Osborn, Susan. "Introduction: Elizabeth Bowen: New Directions for Critical Thinking," *Modern Fiction Studies* 53.2, Summer 2007.

Pater, Walter. *The Renaissance: Studies in Art and Poetry* (1873), New York: Dover, 2005.

Poe, E. A. *Complete Stories and Poems*, London: Chancellor Press, 1988.

Pound, Ezra. *Selected Cantos*, London: Faber, 1967.

Raitt, Suzanne. "Virginia Woolf's early novels" in *The Cambridge Companion to Virginia Woolf*, eds. S. Roe and S. Sellers, Cambridge: Cambridge University Press, 2000.

———. *May Sinclair: A Modern Victorian*, Oxford: Oxford University Press, 2000.

Rashkin, E. *Family Secrets and the Psychoanalysis of Narrative*, Princeton: Princeton University Press, 1992.

Readings, Bill. *Introducing Lyotard: Art and Politics*, London: Routledge, 1991.

Scott, Walter. "On the Supernatural in Fictitious Composition; and particularly on the Works of Ernest Theodore William Hoffmann," *Foreign Quarterly Review* I, 1827.

Sedgwick, E. K. *Between Men: English Literature and Male Homosocial Desire*, New York: Columbia Press, 1985.

Seed, David. "'Psychical' Cases: Transformations of the Supernatural in Virginia Woolf and May Sinclair" in *Gothic Modernisms*, eds. A. Smith and J. Wallace, New York: Palgrave, 2001.

Shakespeare, W. *Macbeth*, Cambridge: Cambridge University Press, 1997.

Shaw, George Bernard. *Our Theatres in the Nineties*, London: Constable, 1932.

Shelley, Mary. *Frankenstein: A Critical Edition*, ed. J. P. Hunter, New York: Norton, 1996.

Sinclair, May. *Uncanny Stories*, ed. P. March-Russell, London: Wordsworth Editions, 2006.

———. *The Three Brontës*, London: Hutchinson, 1912.

———. *The Judgement of Eve and Other Stories*, London: Hutchison, 1914.

Smith, A. and Wallace, J. *Gothic Modernisms*, New York: Palgrave, 2001.

Stevenson, Robert-Louis. *The Strange Case of Dr Jekyll and Mr Hyde* (1886), ed. R. Mighall, London: Penguin, 2002.

Stoker, Bram. *Dracula* (1897), New York: Bedford/St. Martin's, 2002.

Tambling, Jeremy. *Henry James: Critical Issues*, London: Macmillan, 2000.

Thurston, Luke. "Mr Joyce and Dr Hydes: Irish Selves and Doubles in 'The Dead'," *Textual Practice* 22.3, Sept. 2008.

———. *James Joyce and the Problem of Psychoanalysis*, Cambridge: Cambridge University Press, 2004.

Waters, C. "Gender, family and domestic ideology" in *The Cambridge Companion to Charles Dickens*, ed. J. O. Jordan, Cambridge: Cambridge University Press, 2001.

Woolf, Virginia. *The Voyage Out* (1915), London: Penguin, 1992.

———. *Mrs Dalloway* (1925), London: Hogarth Press, 1963.

————. "Jane Eyre and Wuthering Heights," *Collected Essays*, Vol. 1, ed. L. Woolf, London: Chatto & Windus, 1966.

————. *The Question of Things Happening: The Letters of Virginia Woolf, 1912–1922*, ed. N. Nicholson, London: Hogarth Press, 1976.

Wurtz, J. F. "Elizabeth Bowen, Modernism and the Spectre of Anglo-Ireland," *Estudios Irlandeses*, No. 5, 2010.

Žižek, Slavoj. *Looking Awry: An Introduction to Jacques Lacan through Popular Culture*, Cambridge, Mass.: MIT Press, 1991.

————. "In His Bold Gaze My Ruin Is Writ Large" in *Everything You Always Wanted to Know About Lacan But Were Afraid To Ask Hitchcock*, ed. S. Žižek, London: Verso, 1992.

Index